PUBLISHING

EXCITING EXTRA ONLINE RESOURCES INCLUDED

THIS COMPLETE TEXT COMES WITH
FREE ONLINE ACCESS
SO THAT YOU CAN STUDY ANYTIME, ANYWHERE

IN ADDITION TO THE CONTENTS OF THE TEXT, EN-gage ALSO ENABLES YOU TO BENEFIT FROM EXTRA ONLINE TESTING AND OTHER USEFUL STUDY MATERIALS:

- An online version of the Text which allows you to click in and out of the expandable content and view the answers to the Test Your Understanding exercises
- Fixed Online Tests with instant answers
- Test History and Reports to allow you to track and compare your results
- Interim and Final Assessment Questions and Answers

And you can access all of these extra resources anytime, anywhere using your EN-gage account.

How to access your online resources

If you are a Kaplan Financial student

You will already have an EN-gage account and these extra resources will be available to you online. You do not need to register again, as this process was completed when you enrolled. If you are having problems accessing online materials, please ask your course administrator.

If you purchased through Kaplan Flexible Learning or via the Kaplan Publishing website

You will automatically receive an e-mail invitation to EN-gage online. Please register your details using this e-mail to gain access to your content. If you do not receive the e-mail or book content, please contact Kaplan Flexible Learning.

If you are already a registered EN-gage user

Go to www.EN-gage.co.uk and log in. Select the 'add a book' feature and enter the ISBN number of this book and the unique pass key at the bottom of this card. Then click 'finished' or 'add another book'. You may add as many books as you have purchased from this screen.

If you are a new EN-gage user

Register at www.EN-gage.co.uk and click on the link contained in the e-mail we sent you to activate your account. Then select the 'add a book' feature, enter the ISBN number of this book and the unique pass key at the bottom of this card. Then click 'finished' or 'add another book'.

Your Code and Information

This code can only be ....ration of one book online. This registration will e∨ .... xaminations covered by this book h .... ır from the time you submitted yo .... request.

Leeds Metropolitan University

17 0548103 7

D1438366

HhET-vHCa-FcEq-XiZ0

For technical support, please visit www.EN-gage.co.uk

ACCA

Paper F8 INT

Audit and assurance

Complete text

British library cataloguing-in-publication data

A catalogue record for this book is available from the British Library.

Published by:
Kaplan Publishing UK
Unit 2 The Business Centre
Molly Millars Lane
Wokingham
Berkshire
RG41 2QZ

ISBN 978-1-84710-950-7

© Kaplan Financial Limited, 2010

Printed in the UK by CPI William Clowes Beccles NR34 7TL.

Acknowledgements

We are grateful to the Association of Chartered Certified Accountants and the Chartered Institute of Management Accountants for permission to reproduce past examination questions. The answers have been prepared by Kaplan Publishing.

Contents

Paper Introduction

How to Use the Materials

These Kaplan Publishing learning materials have been carefully designed to make your learning experience as easy as possible and to give you the best chances of success in your examinations.

The product range contains a number of features to help you in the study process. They include:

(1) Detailed study guide and syllabus objectives

(2) Description of the examination

(3) Study skills and revision guidance

(4) Complete text or essential text

(5) Question practice

The sections on the study guide, the syllabus objectives, the examination and study skills should all be read before you commence your studies. They are designed to familiarise you with the nature and content of the examination and give you tips on how to best to approach your learning.

The **complete text or essential text** comprises the main learning materials and gives guidance as to the importance of topics and where other related resources can be found. Each chapter includes:

- The **learning objectives** contained in each chapter, which have been carefully mapped to the examining body's own syllabus learning objectives or outcomes. You should use these to check you have a clear understanding of all the topics on which you might be assessed in the examination.

- The **chapter diagram** provides a visual reference for the content in the chapter, giving an overview of the topics and how they link together.

- The **content** for each topic area commences with a brief explanation or definition to put the topic into context before covering the topic in detail. You should follow your studying of the content with a review of the illustration/s. These are worked examples which will help you to understand better how to apply the content for the topic.

- **Test your understanding** sections provide an opportunity to assess your understanding of the key topics by applying what you have learned to short questions. Answers can be found at the back of each chapter.

- **Summary diagrams** complete each chapter to show the important links between topics and the overall content of the paper. These diagrams should be used to check that you have covered and understood the core topics before moving on.

- **Question practice** is provided at the back of each text.

On-line subscribers

Our on-line resources are designed to increase the flexibility of your learning materials and provide you with immediate feedback on how your studies are progressing.

If you are subscribed to our on-line resources you will find:

(1) On-line referenceware: reproduces your Complete or Essential Text on-line, giving you anytime, anywhere access.

(2) On-line testing: provides you with additional on-line objective testing so you can practice what you have learned further.

(3) On-line performance management: immediate access to your on-line testing results. Review your performance by key topics and chart your achievement through the course relative to your peer group.

Ask your local customer services staff if you are not already a subscriber and wish to join.

Syllabus

Paper background

The aim of ACCA Paper F8 (INT), Audit and Assurance, is to develop knowledge and understanding of the process of carrying out the assurance engagement and its application in the context of the professional regulatory framework.

Objectives of the syllabus

- Explain the nature, purpose and scope of assurance engagements including the role of the external audit and its regulatory and ethical framework.

- Explain the nature of internal audit and describe its role as part of overall performance management and its relationship with the external audit.

- Demonstrate how the auditor obtains an understanding of the entity and its environment, assesses the risk of material misstatement, whether arising from fraud or other irregularities, and plans an audit of financial statements.

- Describe and evaluate information systems and internal controls to identify and communicate control risks and their potential consequences, making appropriate recommendations.

- Identify and describe the work and evidence required to meet the objectives of audit engagements and the application of the International Standards on Auditing.

- Evaluate findings and modify the audit plan as necessary.

- Explain how the conclusions from audit work are reflected in different types of audit report, explain the elements of each type of report.

Core areas of the syllabus

- Audit framework and regulation.

- Internal audit.

- Planning and risk assessment.

- Internal control.

- Audit evidence.

- Review.

- Reporting.

Syllabus objectives and chapter references

We have reproduced the ACCA's syllabus below, showing where the objectives are explored within this book. Within the chapters, we have broken down the extensive information found in the syllabus into easily digestible and relevant sections, called Content Objectives. These correspond to the objectives at the beginning of each chapter.

Syllabus learning objective

A AUDIT FRAMEWORK AND REGULATION

1 The concept of audit and other assurance engagements

(a) Identify and describe the objective and general principles of external audit engagements.[2] **Ch. 1**

(b) Explain the nature and development of audit and other assurance engagements.[1] **Ch. 1**

(c) Discuss the concepts of accountability, stewardship and agency.[2] **Ch. 1**

(d) Discuss the concepts of materiality, true and fair presentation and reasonable assurance.[2] **Ch. 1**

(e) Explain reporting as a means of communication to different stakeholders.[1] **Ch. 1**

(f)   Explain the level of assurance provided by audit and other review assignments.[1] **Ch. 1**

2 Statutory audits

(a)   Describe the regulatory environment within which statutory audits take place.[1] **Ch. 2**

(b)   Discuss the reasons and mechanisms for the regulation of auditors. [2] **Ch. 2**

(c)   Explain the statutory regulations governing the appointment, removal and resignation of auditors.[1] **Ch. 2**

(d)   Discuss the types of opinion provided in statutory audits.[2] **Ch. 12**

(e)   State the objectives and principal activities of statutory audit and assess its value (e.g. in assisting management to reduce risk and improve performance).[1] **Ch. 1**

(f)   Describe the limitations of statutory audits.[1] **Ch. 1**

3 The regulatory environment and corporate governance

(a) Explain the development and status of International Standards on Auditing.[1] **Ch. 2**

(b) Explain the relationship between International Standards on Auditing and national standards.[1] **Ch. 2**

(c) Discuss the objective, relevance and importance of corporate governance.[2] **Ch. 3**

(d) Discuss the need for auditors to communicate with those charged with governance.[2] **Ch. 4**

(e) Discuss the provisions of international codes of corporate governance (such as OECD) that are most relevant to auditors.[2] **Ch. 3**

(f) Describe good corporate governance requirements relating to directors' responsibilities (e.g. for risk management and internal control) and the reporting responsibilities of auditors.[1] **Ch. 3**

(g) Analyse the structure and roles of audit committees and discuss their drawbacks and limitations.[2] **Ch. 3**

(h) Explain the importance of internal control and risk management.[1] **Ch. 4**

(i) Compare the responsibilities of management and auditors for the design and operation of systems and controls.[2] **Ch. 3**

4 Professional ethics and ACCA's Code of Ethics and Conduct

(a) Define and apply the fundamental principles of professional ethics of integrity, objectivity, professional competence and due care, confidentiality and professional behaviour.[2] **Ch. 5**

(b) Define and apply the conceptual framework.[2] **Ch. 5**

(c) Discuss the sources of, and enforcement mechanisms associated with, ACCA's Code of Ethics and Conduct.[2] **Ch. 5**

(d) Discuss the requirements of professional ethics and other requirements in relation to the acceptance of new audit engagements.[2] **Ch. 5**

(e) Discuss the process by which an auditor obtains an audit engagement. [2] **Ch. 5**

(f) Explain the importance of engagement letters and state their contents. [1] **Ch. 5**

B INTERNAL AUDIT

1 Internal audit and corporate governance

(a) Discuss the factors to be taken into account when assessing the need for internal audit.[2] **Ch. 3**

(b) Discuss the elements of best practice in the structure and operations of internal audit with reference to appropriate international codes of corporate governance.[2] **Ch. 3**

2 Differences between external and internal audit

(a) Compare and contrast the role of external and internal audit regarding audit planning and the collection of audit evidence.[2] **Ch. 4**

(b) Compare and contrast the types of report provided by internal and external audit.[2] **Ch. 4**

3 The scope of the internal audit function

(a) Discuss the scope of internal audit and the limitations of the internal audit function.[2] **Ch. 3**

(b) Explain the types of audit report provided in internal audit assignments. [1] **Ch. 3**

(c) Discuss the responsibilities of internal and external auditors for the prevention and detection of fraud and error.[2] **Ch. 4**

4 Outsourcing the internal audit department

(a) Explain the advantages and disadvantages of outsourcing internal audit.[1] **Ch. 3**

5 Internal audit assignments

(a) Discuss the nature and purpose of internal audit assignments including value for money, IT, best value and financial.[2] **Ch. 3**

(b) Discuss the nature and purpose of operational internal audit assignments including procurement, marketing, treasury and human resources management.[2] **Ch. 3**

C PLANNING AND RISK ASSESSMENT

1 Objective and general principles

(a) Identify and describe the need to plan and perform audits with an attitude of professional scepticism.[2] **Ch. 7**

(b) Identify and describe engagement risks affecting the audit of an entity. [1] **Ch. 7**

(c) Explain the components of audit risk.[1] **Ch. 7**

(d) Compare and contrast risk based, procedural and other approaches to audit work.[2] **Ch. 7**

(e) Discuss the importance of risk analysis.[2] **Ch. 7**

(f) Describe the use of information technology in risk analysis.[1] **Ch. 7**

2 Understanding the entity and knowledge of the business

(a) Explain how auditors obtain an initial understanding of the entity and knowledge of its business environment.[2] **Ch. 6**

3 Assessing the risks of material misstatement and fraud

(a) Define and explain the concepts of materiality and tolerable error. [2] **Ch. 6**

(b) Compute indicative materiality levels from financial information.[2] **Ch. 6**

(c) Discuss the effect of fraud and misstatements on the audit strategy and extent of audit work.[2] **Ch. 6**

4 Analytical procedures

(a) Describe and explain the nature and purpose of analytical procedures in planning.[2] **Ch. 6**

(b) Compute and interpret key ratios used in analytical procedures.[2] **Ch. 10**

5 Planning an audit

(a) Identify and explain the need for planning an audit.[2] **Ch. 6**

(b) Identify and describe the contents of the overall audit strategy and audit plan.[2] **Ch. 6**

(c) Explain and describe the relationship between the overall audit strategy and the audit plan.[2] **Ch. 6**

(d) Develop and document an audit plan.[2] **Ch. 6**

(e) Explain the difference between interim and final audit.[1] **Ch. 6**

6 Audit documentation

(a) Explain the need for and the importance of audit documentation.[1] **Ch. 9**

(b) Describe and prepare working papers and supporting documentation. [2] **Ch. 9**

(c) Explain the procedures to ensure safe custody and retention of working papers.[1] **Ch. 9**

7 The work of others

(a) Discuss the extent to which auditors are able to rely on the work of experts.[2] **Ch. 10**

(b) Discuss the extent to which external auditors are able to rely on the work of internal audit.[2] **Ch. 10**

(c) Discuss the audit considerations relating to entities using service organisations.[2] **Ch. 10**

(d) Discuss why auditors rely on the work of others.[2] **Ch. 10**

(e) Explain the extent to which reference to the work of others can be made in audit reports.[1] **Ch. 10**

D INTERNAL CONTROL

The following transaction cycles and account balances are relevant to this capability:

- revenue
- purchases
- inventory
- revenue and capital expenditure
- payroll
- bank and cash.

1 Internal control systems

(a) Explain why an auditor needs to obtain an understanding of internal control activities relevant to the audit.[1] **Ch. 8**

(b) Describe and explain the key components of an internal control system. [1] **Ch. 8**

(c) Identify and describe the important elements of internal control, including the control environment and management control activities. [1] **Ch. 8**

(d) Discuss the difference between tests of control and substantive procedures.[2] **Ch. 8**

2 The use of internal control systems by auditors

(a) Explain the importance of internal control to auditors.[1] **Ch. 8**

(b) Explain how auditors identify weaknesses in internal control systems and how those weaknesses limit the extent of auditors' reliance on those systems.[2] **Ch. 8**

3 Transaction cycles

(a) Explain, analyse and provide examples of internal control procedures and control activities.[2] **Ch. 8**

(b) Provide examples of computer system controls.[2] **Ch. 8**

4 Tests of control

(i) Explain and tabulate tests of control in the transaction cycles and account balances relevant to this sub-capability, suitable for inclusion in audit working papers.[2] **Ch. 8**

(ii) List examples of application controls and general IT controls.[2] **Ch. 8**

5 The evaluation of internal control components

(a) Analyse the limitations of internal control components in the context of fraud and error.[2] **Ch. 8**

(b) Explain the need to modify the audit strategy and audit plan following the results of tests of control.[1] **Ch. 8**

(c) Identify and explain management's risk assessment process with reference to internal control components.[1] **Ch. 8**

6 Communication on internal control

(a) Discuss and provide examples of how the reporting of internal control weaknesses and recommendations to overcome those weaknesses are provided to management.[2] **Ch. 8**

E AUDIT EVIDENCE

1 The use of assertions by auditors

(a) Explain the assertions contained in the financial statements.[2] **Ch. 9**

(b) Explain the principles and objectives of transaction testing, account balance testing and disclosure testing.[1] **Ch. 9**

(c) Explain the use of assertions in obtaining audit evidence.[2] **Ch. 9**

2 Audit procedures

(a) Discuss the sources and relative merits of the different types of evidence available.[2] **Ch. 9**

(b) Discuss and provide examples of how analytical procedures are used as substantive procedures.[2] **Ch. 10**

(c) Discuss the problems associated with the audit and review of accounting estimates.[2] **Ch. 10**

(d) Describe why smaller entities may have different control environments and describe the types of evidence likely to be available in smaller entities.[1] **Ch. 9**

(e) Discuss the quality of evidence obtained.[2] **Ch. 9**

3 The audit of specific items

For each of the account balances stated in this sub-capability:

- explain the purpose of substantive procedures in relation to financial statement assertions
- explain the substantive procedures used in auditing each balance, and
- tabulate those substantive procedures in a work program.

(a) Receivables:[2] **Ch. 10**

    (i) direct confirmation of accounts receivable

    (ii) other evidence in relation to receivables and prepayments, and

    (iii) the related income statement entries.

(b) Inventory:[2] **Ch. 10**

    (i) inventory counting procedures in relation to year-end and continuous inventory systems

    (ii) cut-off

    (iii) auditor's attendance at inventory counting

    (iv) direct confirmation of inventory held by third parties,

    (v) other evidence in relation to inventory.

(c) Payables and accruals:[2] **Ch. 10**

    (i) supplier statement reconciliations and direct confirmation of accounts payable

    (ii) obtain evidence in relation to payables and accruals, and

    (iii) the related income statement entries.

(d) Bank and cash:[2] **Ch. 10**

    (i) bank confirmation reports used in obtaining evidence in relation to bank and cash

    (ii) other evidence in relation to bank and cash, and

    (iii) the related income statement entries.

(e) Tangible non-current assets and long-term liabilities:[2] **Ch. 10**

   (i) evidence in relation to non-current assets and

   (ii) non-current liabilities and

   (iii) the related income statement entries.

4 Audit sampling and other means of testing

(a) Define audit sampling and explain the need for sampling.[1] **Ch. 9**

(b) Identify and discuss the differences between statistical and non-statistical sampling.[2] **Ch. 9**

(c) Discuss and provide relevant examples of, the application of the basic principles of statistical sampling and other selective testing procedures. [2] **Ch. 9**

(d) Discuss the results of statistical sampling, including consideration of whether additional testing is required.[2] **Ch. 9**

5 Computer-assisted audit techniques

(a) Explain the use of computer-assisted audit techniques in the context of an audit.[1] **Ch. 10**

(b) Discuss and provide relevant examples of the use of test data and audit software for the transaction cycles and balances mentioned in sub-capability 3.[2] **Ch. 10**

(c) Discuss the use of computers in relation to the administration of the audit.[2] **Ch. 10**

6 Not-for-profit organisations

(a) Apply audit techniques to small not-for-profit organisations.[2] **Ch. 10**

(b) Explain how the audit of small not-for-profit organisations differs from the audit of for-profit organisations.[1] **Ch. 10**

F REVIEW

1 Subsequent events

(a) Explain the purpose of a subsequent events review.[1] **Ch. 11**

(b) Discuss the procedures to be undertaken in performing a subsequent events review.[2] **Ch. 11**

2 Going concern

(a) Define and discuss the significance of the concept of going concern. [2] **Ch. 11**

(b) Explain the importance of and the need for going concern reviews. [2] **Ch. 11**

(c) Explain the respective responsibilities of auditors and management regarding going concern.[1] **Ch. 11**

(d) Discuss the procedures to be applied in performing going concern reviews.[2] **Ch. 11**

(e) Discuss the disclosure requirements in relation to going concern issues.[2] **Ch. 11**

(f) Discuss the reporting implications of the findings of going concern reviews.[2] **Ch. 11**

3 Management representations

(a) Explain the purpose of and procedure for obtaining management representations.[2] **Ch. 11**

(b) Discuss the quality and reliability of management representations as audit evidence.[2] **Ch. 11**

(c) Discuss the circumstances where management representations are necessary and the matters on which representations are commonly obtained.[2] **Ch. 11**

4 Audit finalisation and the final review

(a) Discuss the importance of the overall review of evidence obtained. [2] **Ch. 11**

(b) Explain the significance of unadjusted differences.[1] **Ch. 11**

G REPORTING

1 Audit reports

(a) Describe and analyse the format and content of unmodified audit reports.[2] **Ch. 12**

(b) Describe and analyse the format and content of modified audit reports. [2] **Ch. 12**

2 Reports to management

(a) Identify and analyse internal control and system weaknesses and their potential effects and make appropriate recommendations to management.[2] **Ch. 8**

3 Internal audit reports

(a) Describe and explain the format and content of internal audit review reports and other reports dealing with the enhancement of performance. [1] **Ch. 3**

(b) Explain the process for producing an internal audit report.[1] **Ch. 3**

The superscript numbers in square brackets indicate the intellectual depth at which the subject area could be assessed within the examination. Level 1 (knowledge and comprehension) broadly equates with the Knowledge module, Level 2 (application and analysis) with the Skills module and Level 3 (synthesis and evaluation) to the Professional level. However, lower level skills can continue to be assessed as you progress through each module and level.

For a list of examinable documents, see the ACCA web site (www. accaglobal/pubs/students).

The Examination

Examination format

The examination is a three-hour paper covering five compulsory questions. The bulk of the questions will be discursive but some questions involving computational elements will be set from time to time.

The questions will cover all areas of the syllabus:

	Number of marks
Question 1 (scenario based)	30
Question 2 (knowledge based)	10
Questions 3-5 (each question will be worth 20 marks each)	60
	100

Total time allowed: reading and planning 15 minutes; writing 3 hours.

Paper-based examination tips

Spend the first few minutes of the examination reading the paper.

Divide the time you spend on questions in proportion to the marks on offer. One suggestion **for this examination** is to allocate 1.8 minutes to each mark available, so a 10-mark question should be completed in approximately 18 minutes.

Unless you know exactly how to answer the question, spend some time planning your answer. Stick to the question and tailor your answer to what you are asked. Pay particular attention to the verbs in the question.

Spend the last five minutes reading through your answers and making any additions or corrections.

If you **get completely stuck** with a question, leave space in your answer book and return to it later.

If you do not understand what a question is asking, state your assumptions. Even if you do not answer in precisely the way the examiner hoped, you should be given some credit, if your assumptions are reasonable.

You should do everything you can to make things easy for the marker. The marker will find it easier to identify the points you have made if your answers are legible.

Written questions: Your essay should have a clear structure. It should contain a brief introduction, a main section and a conclusion. Be concise. It is better to write a little about a lot of different points than a great deal about one or two points.

Reports, memos and other documents: some questions ask you to present your answer in the form of a report or a memo or other document. So use the correct format - there are easy marks to gain here.

Study skills and revision guidance

This section aims to give guidance on how to study for your ACCA exams and to give ideas on how to improve your existing study techniques.

Preparing to study

Set your objectives

Before starting to study decide what you want to achieve - the type of pass you wish to obtain. This will decide the level of commitment and time you need to dedicate to your studies.

Devise a study plan

Determine which times of the week you will study.

Split these times into sessions of at least one hour for study of new material. Any shorter periods could be used for revision or practice.

Put the times you plan to study onto a study plan for the weeks from now until the exam and set yourself targets for each period of study – in your sessions make sure you cover the course, course assignments and revision.

If you are studying for more than one paper at a time, try to vary your subjects as this can help you to keep interested and see subjects as part of wider knowledge.

When working through your course, compare your progress with your plan and, if necessary, re-plan your work (perhaps including extra sessions) or, if you are ahead, do some extra revision/practice questions.

Effective studying

Active reading

You are not expected to learn the text by rote, rather, you must understand what you are reading and be able to use it to pass the exam and develop good practice. A good technique to use is SQ3Rs – Survey, Question, Read, Recall, Review:

(1) **Survey the chapter** – look at the headings and read the introduction, summary and objectives, so as to get an overview of what the chapter deals with.

(2) **Question** – whilst undertaking the survey, ask yourself the questions that you hope the chapter will answer for you.

(3) **Read** through the chapter thoroughly, answering the questions and making sure you can meet the objectives. Attempt the exercises and activities in the text, and work through all the examples.

(4) **Recall** – at the end of each section and at the end of the chapter, try to recall the main ideas of the section/chapter without referring to the text. This is best done after a short break of a couple of minutes after the reading stage.

(5) **Review** – check that your recall notes are correct.

You may also find it helpful to re-read the chapter to try to see the topic(s) it deals with as a whole.

Note-taking

Taking notes is a useful way of learning, but do not simply copy out the text. The notes must:

- be in your own words
- be concise
- cover the key points
- be well-organised
- be modified as you study further chapters in this text or in related ones.

Trying to summarise a chapter without referring to the text can be a useful way of determining which areas you know and which you don't.

Three ways of taking notes:

Summarise the key points of a chapter.

Make linear notes – a list of headings, divided up with subheadings listing the key points. If you use linear notes, you can use different colours to highlight key points and keep topic areas together. Use plenty of space to make your notes easy to use.

Try a diagrammatic form – the most common of which is a mind-map. To make a mind-map, put the main heading in the centre of the paper and put a circle around it. Then draw short lines radiating from this to the main sub-headings, which again have circles around them. Then continue the process from the sub-headings to sub-sub-headings, advantages, disadvantages, etc.

Highlighting and underlining

You may find it useful to underline or highlight key points in your study text – but do be selective. You may also wish to make notes in the margins.

Revision

The best approach to revision is to revise the course as you work through it. Also try to leave four to six weeks before the exam for final revision. Make sure you cover the whole syllabus and pay special attention to those areas where your knowledge is weak. Here are some recommendations:

Read through the text and your notes again and condense your notes into key phrases. It may help to put key revision points onto index cards to look at when you have a few minutes to spare.

Review any assignments you have completed and look at where you lost marks – put more work into those areas where you were weak.

Practise exam standard questions under timed conditions. If you are short of time, list the points that you would cover in your answer and then read the model answer, but do try to complete at least a few questions under exam conditions.

Also practise producing answer plans and comparing them to the model answer.

If you are stuck on a topic find somebody (a tutor) to explain it to you.

Read good newspapers and professional journals, especially ACCA's Student Accountant – this can give you an advantage in the exam.

Ensure you know the structure of the exam – how many questions and of what type you will be expected to answer. During your revision attempt all the different styles of questions you may be asked.

Further reading

You can find further reading and technical articles under the student section of ACCA's website.

Icon Explanations

 Definition – these sections explain important areas of Knowledge which must be understood and reproduced in an exam environment.

 Key Point – identifies topics which are key to success and are often examined.

 New – identifies topics that are brand new in papers that build on, and therefore also contain, learning covered in earlier papers.

 Expandable Text – within the online version of the work book is a more detailed explanation of key terms, these sections will help to provide a deeper understanding of core areas. Reference to this text is vital when self studying.

 Test Your Understanding – following key points and definitions are exercises which give the opportunity to assess the understanding of these core areas. Within the work book the answers to these sections are left blank, explanations to the questions can be found within the online version which can be hidden or shown on screen to enable repetition of activities.

 Illustration – to help develop an understanding of topics and the test your understanding exercises the illustrative examples can be used.

 Exclamation Mark – this symbol signifies a topic which can be more difficult to understand, when reviewing these areas care should be taken.

1

What is assurance?

Chapter learning objectives

Upon completion of this chapter you will be able to:

- Identify and describe the objectives, general principles and principal activities of statutory audit;

- Explain the nature of audit and other assurance engagements;

- Discuss the concepts of accountability, stewardship and agency;

- Discuss the concepts of materiality; true and fair presentation and reasonable assurance;

- Explain reporting as a means of communication to different stakeholders;

- Explain the level of assurance provided by audit and other review assignments; and

- Describe the limitations of statutory audit.

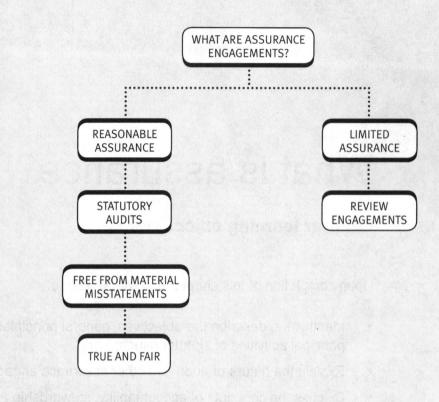

1 Why we need assurance

The purpose of an assurance service is to increase the confidence of the user of that service and to help them reduce the risk associated with their decision making.

2 How does assurance work?

Consider almost any purchase you have made of anything significant to you. You will probably ask someone else's **opinion** before you buy:

- Do I look okay in these clothes?
- Have you heard whether this make of car is reliable?
- Is this software easy to use for a novice?

You may even do some research prior to purchasing.

If the purchase was a new house, you would almost certainly get a surveyor to look at it to give you some confidence that it was structurally sound before you committed yourself to buy it.

All of these transactions have similar elements. The most obvious ones are:

- you – the potential **user** of the thing you want to buy
- the thing you want to buy – the **subject matter** of the transaction
- your friend, the magazine or the surveyor who tells you what they think – in a formal assurance context known as the **practitioner.**

However, there are at least two other elements to the transaction:

- the person supplying the goods or services – the **responsible party**
- your expectations – the **criteria** against which you will decide whether your purchase is worthwhile.

There **may** be one more thing:

- it is possible that the subject matter cannot be examined directly – with a house or a car you can normally go and look, but to judge a property in an overseas country or the performance of a company over a year, you will be dependent on information about the subject matter – the real estate agent's details of the property or some financial statements – known as **subject matter information.**

Note that there are three parties involved – the **tripartite engagement:**

- the user
- the responsible party
- the practitioner.

Note also that because the practitioner is offering a professional service (there is rather more to it than the "is this OK?" question above for which he or she expects to be paid a number of other issues arise:

- the need for competence
- the need for objectivity and independence
- the need for work to be carried out to expected standards.

All of these issues will be considered in the chapters which follow.

3 Assurance engagements

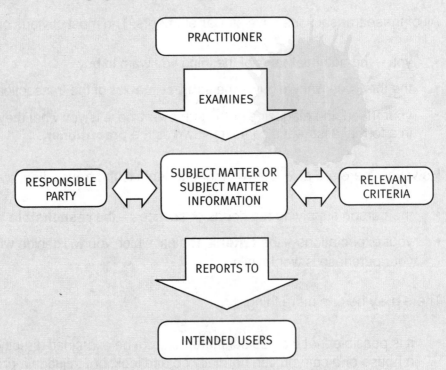

The engagement process usually involves:

- agreeing the terms of the engagement in an engagement letter
- deciding on a methodology for evidence gathering, and evaluation and measurement to support a conclusion
- agreeing the type of report to be produced at the end of the engagement.

Illustration 1 – Assurance engagements

Types of assurance services

- an audit of financial statements
- a review of financial statements
- risk assessment reports
- systems reliability reports
- reports on social and environmental issues (e.g. to validate an employer's claims about being an equal opportunities employer or a company's claims about sustainable sourcing of materials)
- reviews of internal controls
- value for money audit in public sector organisations.

4 Types of assurance engagement

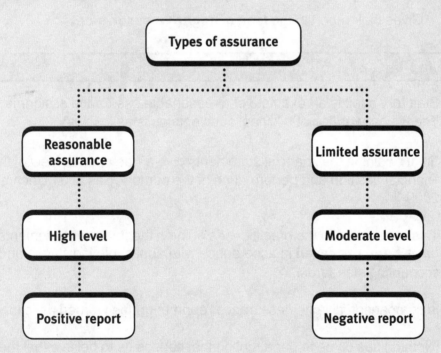

The Framework permits two types of assurance engagement to be performed:

- a reasonable assurance engagement
- a limited assurance engagement.

Reasonable assurance engagements

In a reasonable assurance engagement, the practitioner:

- Gathers **sufficient appropriate evidence** to be able to draw rational conclusions;
- Concludes that the subject matter conforms in **all material respects** with identified suitable criteria; and
- Gives their report in the form of **positive assurance.**

Limited assurance engagement

In a limited assurance assignment the practitioner:

- Gathers **sufficient appropriate evidence** to be able to draw rational conclusions;
- Concludes that the subject matter, with respect to identified suitable criteria, is plausible in the circumstances; and
- Gives their report in the form of **negative assurance.**

Illustration 2 – Wording of Different Assurance Reports

Statutory audit is an example of a reasonable assurance assignment. The typical wording of a 'clean' audit opinion is as follows:

"In our opinion the financial statements give a true and fair view of the financial position and performance of the company as at 31 December 2009."

This means that in the practitioner's opinion the financial statements **have been prepared** in accordance with applicable legislation and accounting standards.

In comparison a limited assurance report might be worded as follows:

"Nothing has come to our attention that causes us to believe that the financial statements as of 31 December 2009 are not prepared, in all material respects, in accordance with an applicable financial reporting framework."

The level of assurance in the last opinion is much weaker and a user of such a report would place less reliance on this than on a reasonable assurance opinion.

The level of assurance

The framework states that the level of assurance given by a reasonable assurance engagement is **high**, whereas a limited assurance engagement gives a **moderate** level of assurance.

There is no precise definition of what is meant by high or moderate in this context.

What is clear is that the confidence inspired in the user by the report produced after a reasonable assurance engagement is designed to be greater than the outcome of a limited assurance engagement.

It follows therefore that

- the procedures carried out will be more intensive
- the evidence gathered needs to be of higher quality

[handwritten: reasonable ass.]

for a reasonable assurance engagement and this is reflected in the nature of the opinion given.

Not absolute assurance

It is not possible to give an absolute level of assurance due to:

- the lack of precision often associated with the subject matter – e.g. financial statements are often subject to estimation and judgement
- the nature, timing and extent of procedures
- the fact that evidence is usually persuasive rather than conclusive
- the fact that evidence is gathered on a test basis.

[handwritten: NO ABSOLUTE]

Even if everything reported on was examined and found to be satisfactory, there may be other items which should have been included – the **completeness** problem.

The 'Expectation Gap'

The objective of an audit is to provide a reasonable level of assurance when forming an opinion. For the reasons identified above it is impossible to give a higher level of assurance.

However, the public often believe that the role of the auditor is to discover all errors and frauds. This phenomenon is known as the **'expectation gap'**.

Statutory audit – a reasonable assurance engagement

The most common example of a reasonable assurance engagement is statutory, external audit. Using the terminology of the earlier paragraphs in this section, we can identify the elements of an audit engagement and the elements of an audit report.

The elements of an audit engagement are:

- a three party relationship between
    - a professional accountant (the auditor)
    - a responsible party (the board of directors of the company being audited)
    - intended users (the readers of the financial statements)
- a subject matter (the performance of the company)
- subject matter information (the annual financial statements)
- suitable criteria (the applicable financial reporting framework, e.g. national or international accounting standards and relevant law)
- sufficient appropriate evidence (the results of the tests that the auditor carries out to reach his conclusion)
- a written report (the audit report that is contained within the published financial statements).

Review engagements – limited assurance engagements

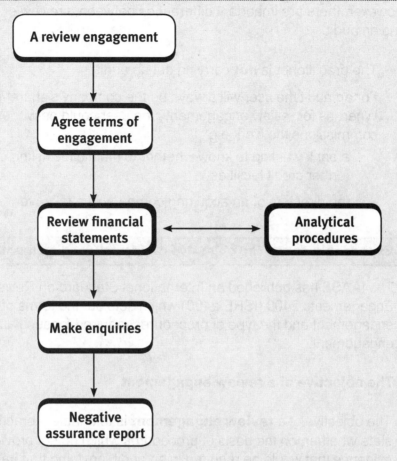

Characteristics of a review engagement

A review engagement has all the attributes of any assurance engagement:

- A **practitioner** who conducts the work;
- An end **user** who commissioned the work:
- A **responsible party**;
- The **subject matter** under review;
- The **subject matter information**;
- The engagement **criteria**;
- **Sufficient appropriate evidence** which needs to be **documented;** and
- A **report.**

However, there are important differences between a review engagement and an audit.

- The practitioner is **not** carrying out an audit;
- For an audit the user will always be the company's shareholders. Whereas for review engagements the user could be whoever commissions the work e.g.:
  - a bank wanting to know whether to maintain existing or extend further credit facilities
  - the directors of an acquiring company in a takeover.

Expandable Text - The objective of a review engagement

The IAASB has published an International Standard on Review Engagements 2400 (ISRE 2400) which sets out the terms of engagement and the type of procedures required for such an engagement.

The objective of a review engagement

The objective of a **review engagement** is to enable a practitioner to state whether, on the basis of procedures which do not provide all the evidence that would be required in an audit, anything that has come to the practitioner's attention that causes the practitioner to believe that the financial statements are not prepared, in all material respects, in accordance with an applicable financial reporting framework.

ISRE 2400

In a review engagement, therefore, the auditor gives **negative assurance**, reporting that he is not aware that anything is materially wrong.

Expandable Text - Subject matter

- The subject matter depends entirely upon the requirements of the end user. However, it is likely to involve some element of company performance and/or position. In contrast to an audit:
    - the period reviewed could be any period determined in the terms of engagement; and
    - the information under review could include: management accounts; forecasts and projections; and ad hoc reports.

- The criteria for audited financial statements are applicable laws and accounting standards. For a review engagement the criteria will be whatever is agreed in the terms of engagement.

- The concept of sufficient appropriate evidence for an audit will be reviewed in chapters 9 and 10. However, statutory audits do require a significant amount and broad range of procedures to be performed. The requirement is usually less for a review engagement and normally includes:
    - analytical procedures, i.e. examining the relationships and trends between sets of data and information;
    - enquiries of management and other relevant parties;
    - follow up procedures where analytical procedures and enquiries indicate that material misstatements might have occurred;

- Finally, an audit report gives positive assurance whereas the report after a review engagement gives negative assurance.

Test your understanding 1

What is the difference between a review and an audit?

Review gives a negative assurance
Audit gives a positive assurance.

(10 marks)

5 Reporting the outcome of assurance engagements

Who are the stakeholders of a company?

The **stakeholders** of a company are all those who are influenced by, or can influence, the company's decisions and actions. Examples of stakeholder groups are:

- shareholders

- management, i.e. the directors or other senior officials with an executive role

- other employees

- those charged with governance, i.e. those whose role is to supervise management to ensure that they operate the business in the interests of the shareholders and other stakeholders and not, purely in their own, personal interests. This will be dealt with in more depth in chapter 3.

- customers

- suppliers

- the government

- lenders of funds

- community organisations, especially in the local neighbourhood.

The financial statements give an account of the performance of the company over the relevant period and of management's stewardship of the company. As such they contain a great deal of information which is useful to many stakeholder groups other than the shareholders for whom they are intended.

Expandable Text - Usefulness of Financial Statements

- Employees may be able to judge whether they think their levels of pay are adequate compared to the directors and results of the company.

- Those charged with governance can see whether they think management have struck the right balance between their own need for reward (remuneration, share options etc) and the needs of other stakeholders.

- Customers' suppliers and lenders can make judgements about whether the company has sufficient financial strengths for business relationships with it to be worthwhile.

- The government can decide whether the right amounts of tax have been paid etc.

6 The development of audit and other assurance engagements

Incorporation and the relationship between the owners and managers of a business

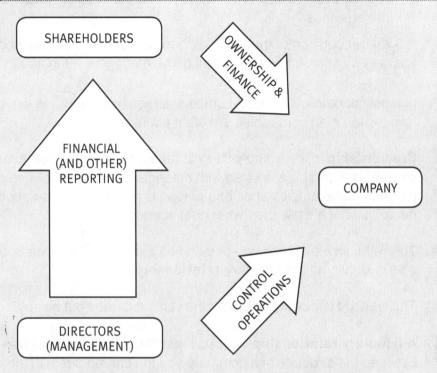

In most countries it is possible for businesses to be operated through companies – a process known as **incorporation.**

Incorporation has two implications:

- the creation of a distinction between the owners of the business and the business itself, which may in turn lead to the business being run by managers who are distinct from its owners

- the granting of limited liability status so that, if the business fails, the owners only stand to lose a specific amount of money – hence the term **'limited'.** It is possible to have companies without limited liability status, but they are uncommon.

A legal framework was therefore needed for how companies should be operated

- to protect business owners from unscrupulous managers

- to protect the business world and the public at large from owners taking unfair advantage of limited liability status.

This in turn had two results:

- the legal requirement for accounts to be produced by management on a regular basis to account to the shareholders for their **stewardship** of the business
- the recognition of the need for these accounts to be checked in some way by someone independent of the managers – the auditor.

In most countries, therefore, companies require an audit. However, small or owner-managed companies are often exempt.

 Stewardship is the responsibility to take good care of resources. A steward is a person entrusted with management of another person's property, for example, when one person is paid to look after another person's house while the owner goes abroad on holiday.

This relationship, where one person has a duty of care towards someone else is known as a **'Fiduciary relationship'.**

The steward is **accountable** for the way he carries out his role.

 A fiduciary relationship is a relationship of 'good faith' such as that between the directors of a company and the shareholders of the company. There is a 'separation of ownership and control' in the sense that the shareholders own the company, while the directors take the decisions. The directors must take their decisions in the interests of the shareholders rather than in their own selfish personal interests.

 Accountability means that people in positions of power can be held to account for their actions, i.e. they can be compelled to explain their decisions and can be criticised or punished if they have abused their position.

In a company this works as follows:

- It is the **shareholders** of the company who own the shares in the company and thus indirectly own the assets of the company.
- The **directors** are accountable to the shareholders and to society at large for:
  - making decisions on behalf of the company's owners (the shareholders)
  - using the assets of the company efficiently and effectively.
- The shareholders in turn have the right to remove the directors by voting in a general meeting and are likely to do this if they are dissatisfied with the decisions taken.

- Additionally, if the directors have acted illegally while running the company, they can be fined or even sent to jail.

Accountability is thus central to the concept of good **corporate governance** – the process of ensuring that companies are well run – which we will look at in more detail in chapter 3.

The concept of agency

Agency relationships occur when one party, the **principal**, employs another party, the **agent**, to perform a task on their behalf.

Modern organisational theory views an organisation as comprising various interest groups often called **stakeholders** (see above). The relationships between the various stakeholders in a company are often described in terms of **agency theory**. For example, directors can be seen as the agents of shareholders, employees as the agents of directors and external auditors as agents of shareholders.

Each principal needs to recognise that, although he is employing the agent, the agent will have interests of his own to protect and thus may not fully carry out the requirements of the principal – a conflict of interests may arise.

Illustration 3 – Agency theory considerations

For example, the directors have a duty of stewardship of the company's assets. However, they are also interested in their level of remuneration and, if this increases, the assets of the company go down. The decision to award directors pay increases may be in the hands of the directors themselves.

The role of the auditor

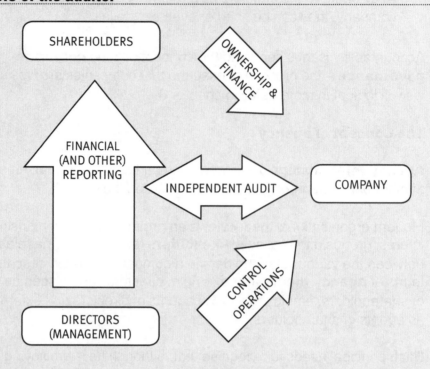

The requirement for a company's management to produce financial statements giving an account of their stewardship of the company at regular intervals, certainly helps with the accountability concept. But what if the financial statements contain errors or are fraudulently prepared?

Clearly there is a need for some kind of independent validation of the financial statements – there is a need for **independent audit.**

Over time the role of the auditor has been established as forming an independent opinion about the truth and fairness of financial statements and their compliance with legal and regulatory requirements.

The statutory audit is going through a period of criticism and change. Part of this is due to the perceived failure of auditors to identify companies about to collapse, often due to massive frauds and accounting irregularities. The obvious examples include: Barings Bank; Enron; WorldCom; and Parmalat.

Linked to this, is the growing belief that many firms of auditors are unable to make objective judgements, because they are too familiar with the companies they audit. As objectivity is vitally important to any opinion, this is extremely important and will be looked at in depth in chapter 5.

Test your understanding 2

What is the purpose of an audit?

To give an independent opinions about the truth & fairness of financial statement and in compliance to legal & reg framework. **(2 marks)**

7 Audit engagements

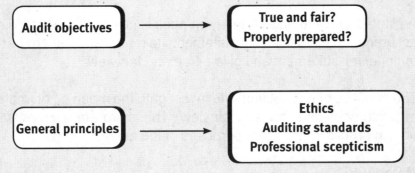

External audit

In most developed countries, publicly quoted companies and large companies are required by law to produce annual financial statements and have them audited by an external auditor. The majority of the syllabus is designed around this process.

Other organisations (e.g. small private companies, partnerships, etc.) may choose to be audited even if there is no legal requirement.

Objective of an external audit

The objective of an external audit engagement is to enable the auditor to express an opinion on whether the financial statements

- give a true and fair view (or present fairly in all material respects)
- are prepared, in all material respects, in accordance with an applicable financial reporting framework.

The financial reporting framework to be applied will vary from country to country.

General principles to be followed

The auditor should follow certain general principles in the conduct of an external audit.

- Compliance with applicable ethical principles, i.e. the IFAC Code of Ethics for Professional Accountants and the ethical pronouncements of the auditor's professional body (e.g. the ACCA's Rules of Professional Conduct) (See chapter 5).

- Compliance with applicable auditing standards, i.e. the International Auditing and Assurance Standards Board's (IAASB's) International Standards on Auditing (ISAs).

- Planning and performing the audit with an attitude of **professional scepticism** that recognises that the financial statements being audited may be materially misstated.

8 Key concepts in the process of auditing

As stated earlier in this chapter, an audit is designed to provide reasonable assurance that the financial statements taken as a whole are free from material misstatement and give a true and fair view.

The purpose of this section is to investigate the meaning of 'material misstatement' and 'true and fair view'. These are vitally important concepts, both in practice and for the purposes of the exam.

Materiality

Misstatements, including omissions, are considered to be **material** if they, individually or in aggregate, could reasonably be expected to influence the economic decisions of users.

You have already seen that it is impossible for anyone to state that financial statements are precisely and absolutely correct. By stating that the accounts are free from material misstatement the auditor is saying that there are no alterations required that could alter the decisions that users, as a group, might make having read the accounts (in other words, they are close enough to the truth!).

Expandable Text - Key concepts in the process of auditing

Illustration – Key concepts in the process of auditing

Material misstatement

Suppose that the correct income statement for Company X for the year just ended is as follows:

	$
Revenue	1,000,000
Cost of sales	(600,000)
Gross profit	400,000
Expenses	(300,000)
Net profit	100,000

If the accountant had added up the sales figure incorrectly for the year by $1,000, he would submit the following income statement to the auditors to be audited:

	$
Revenue	1,001,000
Cost of sales	(600,000)
Gross profit	401,000
Expenses	(300,000)
Net profit	101,000

When the auditors discover the error, they must decide whether this is a material misstatement.

- Will it influence the economic decisions of users?
- Will new investors be attracted to buy shares in the company because they are deceived by the over-statement of profits?

A **judgement** must be made by the auditor that considers the unique position of the business and information requirements of the users.

As a rule of thumb misstatements are considered material if they exceed 10% of profit before tax. Here we have a misstatement of 1% of profit before tax, so it is unlikely to be material in size.

True and fair

In most countries the directors have a statutory duty to produce financial statements that give a true and fair view. The auditors are required by law to report whether, in their opinion, the financial statements give a true and fair view. However, there is no official definition in the IAASB Glossary of Terms, or in any individual ISA, of the meaning of 'true and fair'.

'Truth' in accounting terms can be taken to mean not factually incorrect. In the context of an audit this generally embodies the concept that the financial statements under review are free from material misstatement and prepared in accordance with applicable laws and regulations.

The word **fair** can have the following meanings:

- Clear, distinct and plain; and
- Impartial/unbiased, just and equitable.

Both can be considered relevant when fair is used in an accounting context.

Limitations and benefits of statutory audits

Benefits

- High quality, reliable information circulates the market (gives investors faith and improves reputation of the market).

- Independent verification (management value having their business scrutinised).

- Reduces the risk of management bias, fraud and error (by acting as a deterrent).

- Enhances the creditability of the information (especially for raising finance and for the tax authorities).

- Deficiencies may be highlighted in the management letter.

Limitations

- Financial information includes subjective and judgemental matters.

- Inherent limitations of controls used as audit evidence.

- Representations from management may have to be relied upon as the only source of evidence in some areas.

- Evidence is persuasive not conclusive.

- Do not review 100% of the transactions.

9 Chapter summary

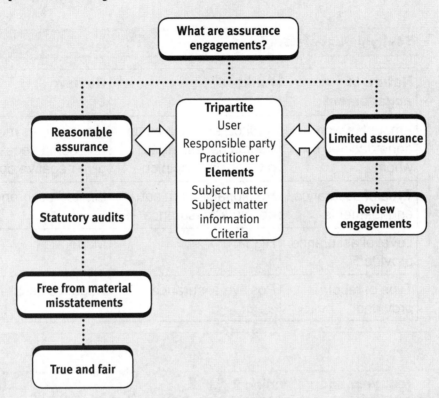

Test your understanding answers

Test your understanding 1

Nature of engagement	Audit	Review
Amount of work done decided by whom	Auditor, as much as he deems necessary to give positive opinion	Reviewer, as much as he deems necessary to give negative opinion
Type of assurance engagements	Reasonable, (but not absolute) assurance	Limited assurance
Level of assurance provided	High	Moderate
Type of report provided	Positive assurance	Negative assurance

Test your understanding 2

What is the purpose of an audit?	To provide confidence for the shareholders that the financial statements are true and fair. To reduce the risk of misstatement, as someone independent, qualified reviews and gives an opinion on the truth and fairness of the financial statements.

The rules and who sets them

Chapter learning objectives

Upon completion of this chapter you will be able to:

*   Describe the regulatory environment within which statutory audits take place

*   Explain the development and status of International Standards on Auditing

*   Explain the relationship between International Standards on Auditing and national auditing standards

*   Discuss the reasons and mechanisms for the regulation of auditors

*   Explain the statutory regulations governing the appointment, removal and resignation of auditors

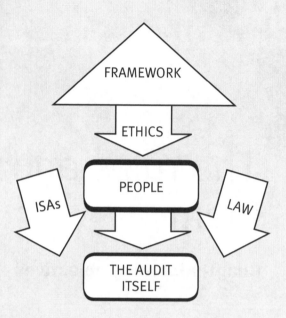

1 Conduct of audit

The conduct of an audit is governed by three sets of rules:

*   The Code of Ethics
*   Auditing Standards (ISAs)
*   Company law.

In addition, Governments have increasingly tried to ensure that audits are conducted by people who are suitably qualified and whose work is of satisfactory quality – a process known as Audit Regulation.

2 Setting auditing standards

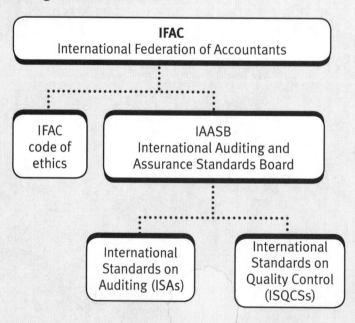

KAPLAN PUBLISHING

IFAC

The International Federation of Accountants (IFAC) is the global organisation for the accountancy profession. It was formed in 1977 and is based in New York. IFAC has more than 160 member bodies of accountants (including the ACCA), representing 2.5 million accountants from 120 separate countries.

IFAC's overall mission is to serve the public interest, strengthen the worldwide accountancy profession, and contribute to the development of strong international economies by establishing and promoting adherence to high-quality professional standards.

International standards on auditing (ISAs)

- Set by: **International Auditing and Assurance Standards Board (IAASB)**.

- IAASB is a subsidiary of the **International Federation of Accountants (IFAC)**.

- There are more than 30 ISAs.

All audits carried out under the laws of member states of the EU have had to be conducted under ISAs for all accounting periods beginning on or after 1 January 2005.

Expandable Text - The standard setting process

The standard setting process

- IAASB identifies new projects based on a review of auditing developments and suggestions from interested parties.

- IAASB then appoints a project task force to work up the detail of the standard.

- There may be consultation through a round table meeting or the issue of a consultation paper for comment.

- A draft standard is then produced for public exposure, usually for a period of 120 days, during which interested parties may submit their comments. Comments are a matter of public record and posted on the IAASB's website.

- The project task force considers the comments and amends the draft standard as appropriate.

- If there are significant changes there may be another exposure period.
- When the standard is finalised it is formally approved by a meeting of the IAASB at which there must be a quorum (minimum) of 12 members.

Other IFAC and IAASB activities

- IFAC publishes a code of ethics governing all assurance engagements carried out under IAASB standards.
- IAASB publishes International Standard on Quality Control 1 (ISQC1) setting out quality control principles for all assurance engagements (including audits) conducted under its standards.
- IAASB sets standards for other types of assurance engagements in addition to audits.

The relationship between international and national standards and regulation

Because IFAC is simply a grouping of accountancy bodies, it has no legal standing in individual countries. Countries therefore need to have arrangements in place for:

- regulating the audit profession
- implementing auditing standards.

National Regulatory bodies:

- enforce the implementation of auditing standards
- have disciplinary powers to enforce quality of audit work
- have rights to inspect audit files to monitor audit quality.

There are two possible schemes for regulation at the national level:

- self regulation by the audit/accountancy profession
- regulation by government or by some independent body set up by government for the purpose.

National standard setters

- may set their own auditing standards
- may adopt and implement ISAs, possibly after modifying them to suit national needs.

Following the decision by the EU to implement ISAs in all member states for all accounting periods beginning on or after 1 January 2005, countries with their own standard setting bodies such as the UK had to decide whether to:

- modify their own standards to bring them into line with ISAs
- adopt ISAs and modify them to suit national requirements.

In the UK the national standard setter – The Auditing Practices Board – decided to adopt and modify ISAs.

Test your understanding 1

(1) Describe the role of the IFAC?

(3 marks)

(2) Describe how ISAs and national auditing standards influence each other.

(2 marks)

3 The Law

Who needs an audit and why?

In most countries it is possible for businesses to operate through companies – a process known as **incorporation**. This concept was discussed in more detail in chapter 1.

In most countries companies are generally required to carry out an audit, as it is a legal requirement. However, small or owner managed companies are often exempt (e.g. in UK, companies with annual turnover < £6.5 million).

Audit exemption

The main reasons for exempting small companies are:

- for owner-managed companies, those receiving the audit report are those running the company (and hence preparing the accounts!)
- the advice/value which accountants can add to a small company is more likely to concern other services, such as accounting and tax, rather than audit and which may also give rise to a conflict of interest under the ethics rules
- the impact of misstatements in the accounts of small companies is unlikely to be material to the wider economy
- given the above points, the audit fee and related disruption are seen as too great a cost for any benefits the audit might bring.

The auditor's duties

Fundamental duties are to:

- form an opinion on whether the financial statements give a true and fair view and are prepared in accordance with applicable reporting framework

- issue an audit report.

In addition to this national law may also impose duties upon the auditor. For example; in the UK auditors are required to incorporate the following implicit matters into their consideration of the audit opinion:

- Proper returns received from branches not visited by the auditor.

- The company's financial statements agree with the underlying accounting records.

- Proper accounting records have been kept.

- All necessary information and explanations have been obtained.

- Information issued with the financial statements is consistent with the financial statements.

- Other information required by law, if not included in the financial statements, is included in the auditors' report. For example, information about directors' pay and benefits.

The above are only reported by **exception**, i.e. they are not referred to in the audit report unless there is a problem.

Expandable Text - Other work required by Law

Other work required by law

Some countries require the auditors to carry out and report on other matters, e.g.:

- in Ireland – to check that the company's capital has not been eroded beyond certain limits

- in the UK, for listed companies, to report on compliance with the rules for the disclosure of Directors' Remuneration.

4 Who may act as auditor?

To be eligible to act as auditor, a person must be:

- A member of a Recognised Supervisory Body (RSB), e.g. ACCA and allowed by the rules of that body to be an auditor; **or**

- Someone directly authorised by the state.

Individuals who are authorised to conduct audit work may be:

- sole practitioners

- partners in a partnership

- members of an LLP

- directors of an audit company.

To be eligible to act as auditor, a firm must be:

- controlled by members of a suitably authorised supervisory body; **or**

- a firm directly authorised by the state.

NB. In some countries only individuals can be authorised to act as auditor and need to be directly authorised by the state.

5 Who may not act as auditor?

Excluded by law

The law in most countries excludes those involved with managing the company and those who have business or personal connections with them.

For example, in the UK the following are excluded by company law:

- an officer (Director or secretary) of the company

- an employee of the company

- a business partner or employee of the above.

Excluded by the Code of Ethics (See chapter 5 for more detail)

The IFAC and ACCA Code of Ethics and the APB's Ethics Standards require Auditors to consider whether their objectivity and independence might be questioned by external parties because of:

- business relationships
- personal relationships
- long association with the client
- fee dependency
- non audit services provided.

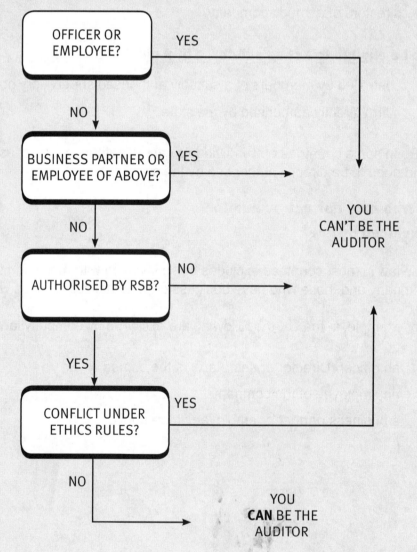

6 How are auditors appointed and removed?

Who appoints the auditor?

In most jurisdictions the members (shareholders) of the company appoint the auditor. However, directors can appoint the first auditor to fill a 'casual vacancy' this requires the members' approval at next Annual General Meeting (AGM).

However, in some countries the auditors may be appointed by the directors as a matter of course.

How long for?

Auditor are appointed runs from one AGM until the end of the next one.

Private companies no longer have to hold an annual general meeting if an elective resolution is made. In these circumstances the auditor is automatically reappointed unless a shareholder objects (small companies can elect to dispense with the requirement for an AGM).

Removing the auditor

Arrangements for removing the auditor have to be structured in such a way that:

- the auditor has sufficiently secure tenure of office, to maintain independence of management

- incumbent auditors can be removed if there are doubts about their continuing abilities to carry out their duties effectively.

To enable this balance to be maintained, the removal of auditors can usually be achieved by a simple majority at a general meeting of the company, but with some safeguards such as a specified notice period, to prevent the resolution to remove the auditors being 'sprung' on the meeting.

In practice, if the auditors and management find it difficult to work together, the auditors will usually resign.

To prevent the circumstances of the resignation being hidden from the company's members, the auditors have to submit a statement of the circumstances surrounding their resignation.

The details which follow about the appointment and removal of the auditors are taken from UK law and practice, but give an example of the way these things are usually handled.

The auditor's responsibilities on appointment and removal

On appointment

- Obtain clearance from the client to write to the existing auditor (if denied, appointment should be declined).
- Write to the existing auditor asking if there are any reasons why the appointment should not be accepted

On removal/resignation

- Deposit at the company's registered office a statement of the circumstances connected with the removal/resignation or
- A statement that there are no such circumstances
- Deal promptly with requests for clearance from new auditors.

7 The auditor's rights

During the audit/continued appointment

- Access to the company's books and records.
- To receive information and explanations necessary for the audit.
- To receive notice of and attend any general meeting of members of the company.
- To be heard at such meetings on matters of concern to the auditor.

On resignation

- To request an Extraordinary General Meeting (EGM) of the company to explain the circumstances of the resignation.
- To require the company to circulate the notice of circumstances relating to the resignation.

Test your understanding 2

(1) List the statutory duties of the auditor?

(3 marks)

(2) Who may act as auditor of a company?

(2 marks)

(3) Who may not act as the auditor of a company?

(3 marks)

(4) Who may appoint the first auditors of a company?

(1 mark)

(5) What action should a company take if the auditor resigns prior to completion of his term of office?

(1 mark)
(10 marks)

8 Chapter summary

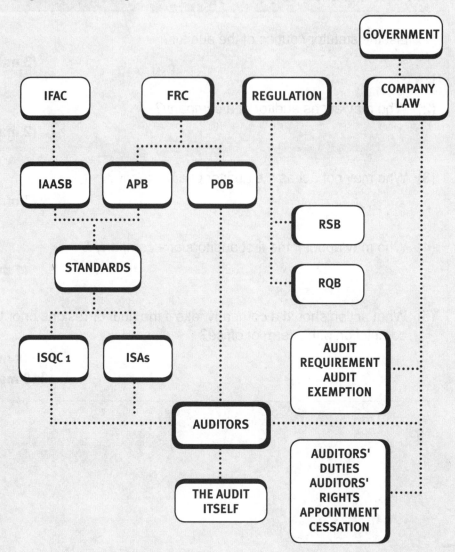

Test your understanding answers

Test your understanding 1

(1) Describe the role of the IFAC?	IFAC is a federation of accountancy bodies throughout the world.	1 mark
	Through its boards and committees it aims to encourage best practice by the members of its constituent bodies.	1 mark
	It has developed a code of ethics for its members and through the IAASB it sets standards for audit and other assurance engagements.	1 mark
(2) Describe how ISAs and national auditing standards influence each other?	National standard-setters may adopt ISAs if they choose to do so, except that all audits in the EU must be conducted under ISAs.	1 mark
	National standard-setters may choose to modify ISAs in order to make them more stringent or to suit national requirements.	1 mark

Test your understanding 2		
(1) List the statutory duties of the auditor?	To form an opinion on the financial statements of the company To issue an audit report Other duties imposed by law, e.g. to report if: • returns from branches have not been received • accounting records are inconsistent with the financial statements • information or explanations have not been received • proper accounting records have not been kept • disclosures regarding directors' pay and balances with the company have not been made • other information issued with the financial statements conflicts with those statements.	½ mark per point
(2) Who may act as auditor of a company?	An individual authorised by the state to be an auditor or the members of a professional body authorised by the state.	1 mark 1 mark

(3) Who may not act as the auditor of a company?	Those who are unable to comply with ethics rules with respect to independence, objectivity and competence to act as auditor for any particular client.	1 mark
	Those who are prohibited by law from acting as auditor for particular clients:	1 mark
	e.g. officers and employees of the company being audited and those closely associated with them – business partners, close relatives, etc.	1 mark
(4) Who may appoint the first auditors of a company?	The directors or the members.	1 mark
(5) What action should a company take if the auditor resigns prior to completion of his term of office?	Hold an EGM if so requested by the auditor	½ mark
	Circulate the auditors' notice of the circumstances surrounding the resignation.	½ mark

3

Corporate governance and internal audit

Chapter learning objectives

Upon completion of this chapter you will be able to:

- Discuss the objective, relevance and importance of corporate governance;

- Discuss the provisions of international codes of corporate governance;

- Describe good corporate governance requirements, including audit committees;

- Explain the importance of internal control and risk management;

- Compare the responsibilities of management and auditors for the design and operation of systems and controls;

- Discuss the factors to be taken into account when assessing the need for internal audit;

- Discuss the elements of best practice in the structure and operations of internal audit;

- Discuss the scope and limitations of internal audit;

- Discuss the nature and purpose of internal audit assignments including value for money, IT, best value and financial;

- Discuss the nature and purpose of operational internal audit assignments including procurement, marketing, treasury and human resources management;

- Describe and explain the format and content of internal audit review reports.

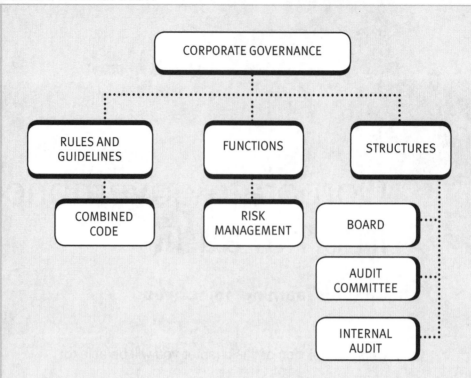

1 Introduction

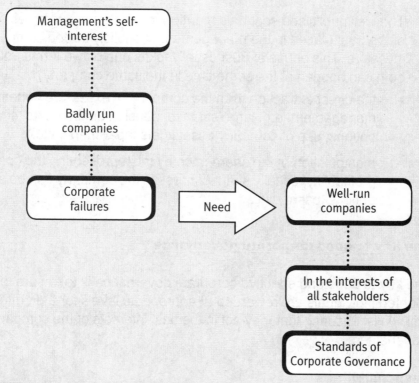

What is corporate governance?

Corporate governance is the means by which a company is operated and controlled.

It concerns such matters as:

- the responsibilities of directors
- the appropriate composition of the board of directors
- the necessity for good internal control – the necessity for an audit committee
- relationships with the external auditors.

Corporate governance is about ensuring that companies are run well in the interests of their shareholders and the wider community.

- The need to improve corporate governance came to prominence in the UK in the 1980s, following the high profile collapses of a number of large companies (Maxwell, Polly Peck, BCCI, etc).

- Poor standards of corporate governance also led to insufficient controls being in place to prevent the collapses of the likes of Enron and WorldCom in the US.

- Authorities - internationally - have been working for a number of years to improve standards of corporate governance.

- This is particularly important for publicly traded companies because large amounts of money are invested in them, either by 'small' shareholders, or from pension schemes and other financial institutions.

- The well publicised scandals mentioned above are examples of abuse of the trust placed in the management of publicly traded companies by investors. This abuse of trust usually takes one of two forms (although both can happen at the same time in the same company):
  - the direct extraction from the company of excessive benefits by management, e.g. large salaries, pension entitlements, share options, use of company assets (jets, apartments etc.)
  - manipulation of the share price by misrepresenting the company's profitability, usually so that shares in the company can be sold or options 'cashed in'.

The key to good corporate governance

The key to good and effective corporate governance is to ensure that talented individuals are rewarded at appropriate levels for their effort and skill, whilst ensuring that they act in the best interests of the company and its stakeholders.

Responsibilities

- Maintaining satisfactory standards of corporate governance is the responsibility of those operating a company – its management and those appointed for the purpose of ensuring that it is well managed.

- Whilst the external auditors do **not** have responsibility for standards of corporate governance at audit clients, they **do** have an interest in a company's attitude and approach to the subject because:
  - they are concerned with the risk that a company's financial statements might be misstated – we will consider the technical meaning of assurance and audit risk later, but for now let us accept that it simply means the likelihood that a company's financial statements will contain errors.
  - if a company has good standards of corporate governance and is well managed, the risk of errors in the financial statements is reduced.

KAPLAN PUBLISHING

Auditors responsibility for reporting on corporate governance

- Listed companies following the Combined Code in the UK, or other applicable guidance in respect of corporate governance, must include a corporate governance statement in the annual report.

- The auditors are not required to 'audit' this statement but must review it for inconsistencies with other information contained within the annual report.

- If inconsistencies are found, there may be an impact on the audit report in two ways:

  - if the inconsistency highlights an error in the financial statements and the directors refuse to amend the error, the auditor will issue a modified report

  - if the inconsistency highlights an error or misleading information in the corporate governance statement, the auditor will add an emphasis of matter paragraph to their report. This is not a modification to the opinion but to another part of the audit report. It is included to bring the reader's attention to the matter.

- In the US, the requirements are more stringent. Sarbanes Oxley states that the auditors must attest as to whether the company has complied with corporate governance requirements. Therefore, they must give an opinion as to the effectiveness of the company's internal control system amongst other things. Therefore there is significantly more risk involved with auditing US listed companies who are covered by Sarbanes Oxley.

2 The OECD Principles of Corporate Governance

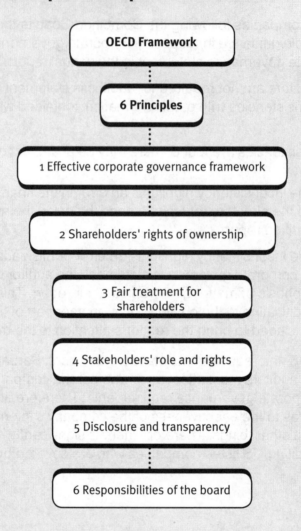

OECD Framework

6 Principles

1 Effective corporate governance framework

2 Shareholders' rights of ownership

3 Fair treatment for shareholders

4 Stakeholders' role and rights

5 Disclosure and transparency

6 Responsibilities of the board

Although there have always been well run companies as well as those where scandals have occurred, the fact that scandals **do** occur has led to the development of codes of practice for good corporate governance.

Often this is due to pressures exerted by stock exchanges. In 1999 the Organisation for Economic Co-operation and Development, OECD, assisted with the development of their 'Principles of Corporate Governance.' These were intended to:

- Assist member and non-member governments in their efforts to evaluate and improve the legal, institutional and regulatory framework for corporate governance in their countries

- Provide guidance and suggestions for stock exchanges, investors, corporations, and other parties that have a role in the process of developing good corporate governance.

The OECD principles were first published in 1999 and were revised in 2004. Their focus is on publicly traded companies. However, to the extent they are deemed applicable, they are a useful tool to improve corporate governance in non-traded companies.

There are six principles, each backed up by a number of sub principles. The principles, and those sub-principles relevant to the auditor, are reproduced below.

Expandable Text - Structure of the principles

Structure of the Principles

The six Principles:

(i) **Ensuring the basis for an effective corporate governance framework**

The corporate governance framework should promote transparent and efficient markets, be consistent with the rule of law and clearly articulate the division of responsibilities among different supervisory, regulatory and enforcement authorities. In other words, making sure everyone involved is aware of their individual responsibilities so no party is in doubt as to what they are accountable for.

(ii) **The rights of shareholders and key ownership functions**

The corporate governance framework should protect and facilitate the exercise of shareholders' rights. As we saw in chapter 1, the directors are the stewards of the company and should be acting in the best interests of the shareholders. However, the existence of the corporate collapses mentioned above proves that this isn't always the case and shareholders need protecting from such people.

(iii) **The equitable treatment of shareholders**

The corporate governance framework should ensure the equitable treatment of all shareholders, including minority and foreign shareholders. All shareholders should have the opportunity to obtain effective redress for violation of their rights.

(iv) The role of stakeholders in corporate governance

The corporate governance framework should recognise the rights of stakeholders established by law or through mutual agreements and encourage active co-operation between corporations and stakeholders in creating wealth, jobs, and the sustainability of financially sound enterprises.

(v) Disclosure and transparency

The corporate governance framework should ensure that timely and accurate disclosure is made on all material matters regarding the corporation, including the financial situation, performance, ownership and governance of the company. Therefore, the annual financial statements should be produced on a timely basis and include all matters of interest to the shareholders. For any matters of significance arising during the year, these should be communicated to the shareholders as appropriate.

(vi) The responsibilities of the board

The corporate governance framework should ensure the strategic guidance of the company, the effective monitoring of management by the board, and the board's accountability to the company and the shareholders. The introduction of audit committees and non executive directors on the board is the usual way for monitoring management. Non executive directors are not involved in the day to day running of the company and are therefore more independent. They can evaluate the effectiveness of the executive board on its merits and make sure they are carrying out their duties properly.

Expandable Text - The OECD principles and the audit

Sub principle VC

'An annual audit should be conducted by an independent, competent and qualified auditor in order to provide an external and objective assurance to the board and shareholders that the financial statements fairly represent the financial position and performance of the company in all material respects.'

Sub principle VD

'External auditors should be accountable to the shareholders and owe a duty to the company to exercise due professional care in the conduct of the audit.'

Expandable Text - The OECD principles and the board

Sub principle VI.D

- **Reviewing and guiding corporate strategy**, major plans of action, risk policy, annual budgets and business plans; setting performance objectives; monitoring implementation and corporate performance, and overseeing major capital expenditures, acquisitions and divestitures.

- **Monitoring the effectiveness of the company's governance practices** and making changes as needed.

- **Selecting, compensating, monitoring and, when necessary, replacing key executives** and overseeing succession planning.

- **Aligning key executive and board remuneration** with the longer term interests of the company and its shareholders ensuring a formal and transparent board nomination and election process.

- Monitoring and managing **potential conflicts of interest of management, board members and shareholders**, including misuse of corporate assets and abuse in related party transactions.

- Ensuring the **integrity of the corporation's accounting and financial reporting systems**, including the independent audit, and that appropriate systems of control are in place, in particular, systems for risk management, financial and operational control, and compliance with the law and relevant standards.

- Overseeing the process of **disclosure and communications**.

Expandable Text - The status of the OECD principles

The status of the OECD Principles

- The Principles represent a common basis that OECD Member countries consider essential for the development of good governance practice.

- They are intended to be concise, understandable and accessible to the international community.

- They are not intended to be a substitute for government or private sector initiatives to develop more detailed 'best practice' in governance.

3 How companies are run

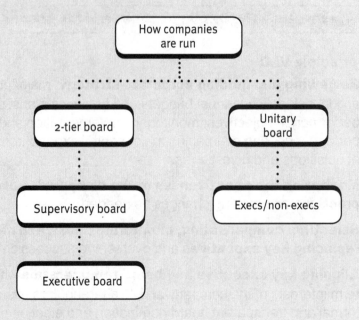

Boards of directors

Fundamentally corporate governance is about how a company is run by its management.

There are two basic models of board structure:

- The two tier board
- The unitary board.

Two tier board

In continental Europe, the 'two tier' board is common. This comprises:

- the executive board which takes day to day decisions in the running of the company.
- the supervisory board, which oversees the executive board and is made up of representatives of employees, investors and others. Major decisions are referred to the supervisory board for approval and which acts as a check on the actions of the executive board.

Disadvantage of this structure:

- The structure can be cumbersome and difficult to administer.
- The supervisory board may not have access to the information it needs on a sufficiently timely basis.
- It has been suggested that investors and some of the other stakeholders represented are reluctant to discuss many key issues in the presence of employees' representatives.

Unitary board

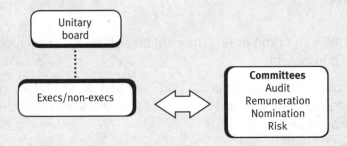

The structure of boards of directors is different in the UK and many other English-speaking countries.

The main points to note are:

- Single board of directors ('unitary' board).
- Distinction between executive and non-executive directors. (Executive directors are often referred to as 'management').
- Oversight of management's actions is by non-executive directors and by sub-committees, e.g. audit committee, remuneration committee.

Non-executive directors

Non-executive directors are usually employed on a part-time basis and do not take part in the routine executive management of the company.

Their role is as follows.

- Participation at board meetings.
- To provide experience and business contacts which strengthen the board.
- Membership of sub-committees, e.g. audit committee, which should be by independent and knowledgeable non-executive directors.

  Almost all listed companies in the UK and USA now have audit and remuneration committees as they are effectively a requirement of stock exchanges.

Advantages of participation by non-executive directors

- Oversight of the whole board.
- Often act as a 'corporate conscience'.
- They bring external expertise to the company.

Disadvantages

- They, and the sub-committees, may not be sufficiently well-informed or technically competent.

- They are subject to the accusation that they are staffed by an 'old boy' network and may fail to report significant problems and approve unjustified pay rises.

Enron provides a cautionary note as its audit committee proved incapable of preventing the wrongdoing of the executive directors.

4 Corporate governance in action

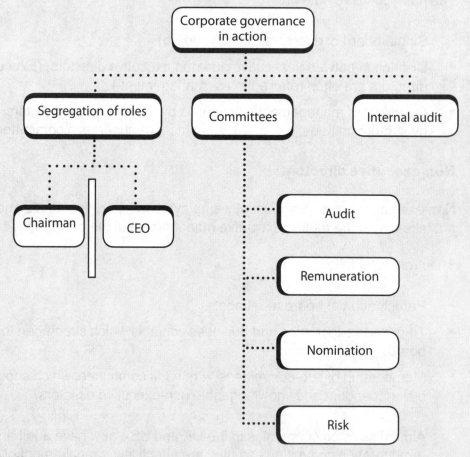

Challenges for companies

Some companies are struggling more than others to deal with an increasingly demanding corporate governance environment. For example:

- the need for an ongoing mechanism for managing risks presents challenges for the organisation

- no longer is it enough to send a checklist around once a year to meet corporate governance requirements, there must be evidence of an appropriate control culture and evidence of ongoing review

- this has resulted in increased importance of Audit Committees and the need for greater information to be made available to the Board and to the Audit Committee.

We will now look at four aspects of corporate governance in action which are regarded as crucial if public companies are to be well run.

- Segregation between the roles of chairman and chief executive officer (CEO).
- Audit (and other) committees.
- Risk management.
- Internal audit.

5 Segregation of Roles

Best practice and strongly recommended under corporate governance codes in many jurisdictions (e.g. the 'Combined Code' governing listed companies in the UK) is that the roles of:

- Chairman of the board and
- Chief executive officer.

should be held by different individuals.

The chairman's role

- Non executive.
- Ensures full information and full discussion at board meetings.
- Ensures satisfactory channels of communication with the external auditors.
- Runs the board of directors.
- Ensures the effective operation of sub-committees of the board.

The Chief executive's role

- Ensures the effective operational functioning of the company.
- It is important that there is a distinction between the chief executive and chairman as effectively one person assuming both roles is a conflict of interests. The chief executive heads up the executive directors and the chairman heads up the non executives.

- Not only that, but having one person in both roles means there is a lot of power vested in that one person. They would be able to sway the decisions taken by the board. Those decisions may not be made in the best interests of the shareholders but in the best interests of the directors.

6 Audit Committees

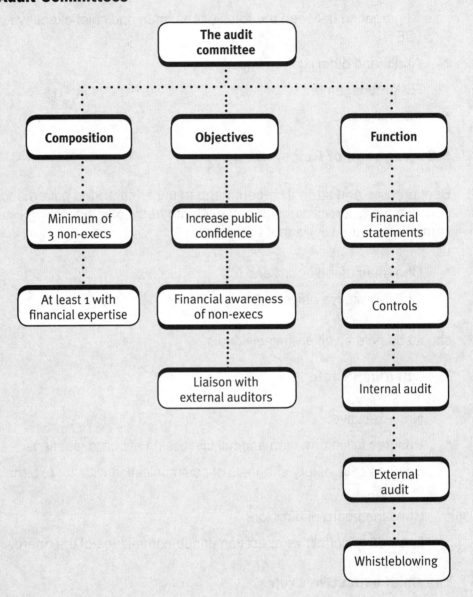

An audit committee is a committee consisting of non-executive directors which is able to view a company's affairs in a detached and independent way and liaise effectively between the main board of directors and the external auditors.

Best practice for listed companies:

- The company should have an audit committee of at least three non-executive directors (or, in the case of smaller companies, two).
- At least one member of the audit committee should have recent and relevant financial experience.

The objectives of the audit committee

- Increasing public confidence in the credibility and objectivity of published financial information (including unaudited interim statements).
- Assisting directors (particularly executive directors) in meeting their responsibilities in respect of financial reporting.
- Strengthening the independent position of a company's external auditor by providing an additional channel of communication.

The function of the audit committee

- Monitoring the integrity of the financial statements.
- Reviewing the company's internal financial controls.
- Monitoring and reviewing the effectiveness of the internal audit function.
- Making recommendations in relation to the appointment and removal of the external auditor and their remuneration.
- Reviewing and monitoring the external auditor's independence and objectivity and the effectiveness of the audit process.
- Developing and implementing policy on the engagement of the external auditor to supply non-audit services.
- Reviewing arrangements for confidential reporting by employees and investigation of possible improprieties (**'Whistleblowing'**).

Advantages

Advantages of having an audit committee:

- It provides the internal audit department with an independent reporting mechanism compared to reporting to the directors who may wish to hide or amend unfavourable internal audit reports.
- The audit committee will assist the internal auditor by ensuring that recommendations in internal audit reports are auctioned.
- Shareholder and public confidence in published financial information is enhanced because it has been reviewed by an independent committee.

- The committee helps the directors fulfil any obligations under corporate governance to implement and maintain an appropriate system of internal control within the company.

- The committee should assist in providing better communication between the directors, external auditors and management arranging meetings with the external auditor.

- Strengthens the independence of company's external auditor by providing a clear reporting structure and separate appointment mechanism from the board.

Disadvantages

Audit committees may lead to:

- fear that their purpose is to catch management out
- non-executive directors being over-burdened with detail
- a 'two-tier' board of directors
- additional cost in terms, at least, of time involved.

The audit committee and internal audit

Clearly, the functions of the audit committee are quite wide-reaching, therefore, it may be necessary to establish an internal audit function in order to help them fulfil their responsibilities.

Best practice is that the audit committee should:

- Ensure that the internal auditor has direct access to the board chairman and to the audit committee and is accountable to the audit committee.

- Review and assess the annual internal audit work plan.

- Receive periodic reports on the results of internal audit work.

- Review and monitor management's responsiveness to the internal auditor's findings and recommendations.

- Meet with the head of internal audit at least once a year without the presence of management.

- Monitor and assess the effectiveness of internal audit in the overall context of the company's risk management system.

Expandable Text - Other committees

Although not on the syllabus it is worth being aware that good corporate governance requires both a nomination and a remuneration committee.

The nomination committee

The function of the nomination committee is to suggest suitable candidates for appointment to the board and other senior posts. This should help to ensure that the best person is chosen for the job.

The remuneration committee

The function of the remuneration committee is to determine fair rates of pay and other compensation – bonuses, pension rights, share options etc – for directors, management and other senior employees.

7 Risk management

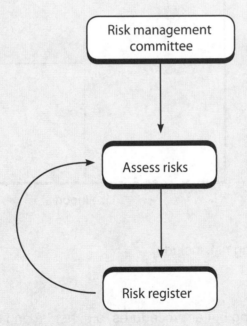

Business risk

All companies face risks of many kinds.

- The risk that products may become technologically obsolete.
- The risk of losing key staff.
- The risk of a catastrophic failure of IT systems.
- The risk of changes in government policy.
- The risk of fire or natural disaster.

Companies therefore need to:

* Identify potential risks and
* Decide on appropriate ways to minimise those risks.

Risk management in practice

Risks can arise from many sources and be of various natures, e.g. operational, financial, legal.

Companies need mechanisms in place to identify and then assess those risks. In so doing companies can rank risks in terms of their relative importance by scoring it on a combination of its likelihood and potential impact. This could take the form of a 'risk map'.

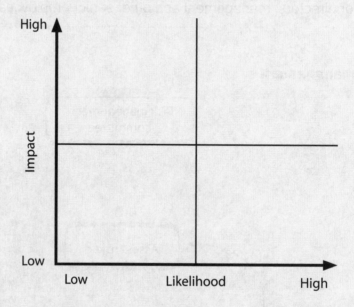

Ways of reducing risk include:

* insurance
* implementing better procedures, e.g. health and safety provisions outsourcing
* discontinuing especially risky activities
* improving staff training.

Sometimes the company may be forced to accept the risk as an inevitable part of its operations.

Internal controls and risk management

One way of minimising risk is to incorporate internal controls into a company's systems and procedures.

It is the director's responsibility to implement internal controls and the internal auditors role to monitor that these controls are being adhered to.

External auditors understand and test those systems to help confirm that the financial statements are produced from reliable sources.

We will look at internal controls in detail in chapter 8. Here it is sufficient for you to know that internal controls are mechanisms built into a company's systems and procedures to reduce the risk of error or fraud.

Examples might be as follows.

- one person checking another person's work.
- locking important documents in a safe.
- restricting access to places with security systems.
- restricting access to information held on computers through passwords.
- internal audit teams who assess the effectiveness of internal systems and controls.

In other words, internal controls are a means of minimising risk. They may not be able to:

- prevent an earthquake destroying a factory
- prevent a competitor coming up with a product which makes your product obsolete.

But they may be able to:

- reduce the risk that financial statements contain material errors
- reduce the risk of theft of the company's assets
- reduce the risk that your business secrets might be handed over to a competitor.

Test your understanding 1

(1) **What is meant by corporate governance?**

(3 marks)

(2) **Why are external auditors interested in corporate governance?**

(3 marks)

(3) **What are the key things the OECD principles are intended to deliver?**

(5 marks)

(4) **Explain the difference between a unitary board of directors and a two-tier board.**

(2 marks)

(5) **Who should make up a typical audit committee?**

(1 mark)

(6) **What is the committee's role?**

(2 marks)

(7) **Why would a company need an audit committee if it has a good relationship with its external auditors?**

(4 marks)

(8) **A company has identified one of its major risks as loss of key staff. Explain:**

(a) **what they should do as a result of this?**

(b) **how they might reduce or even eliminate the risk?**

(c) **why the auditor is interested in this, given that it is not a direct financial risk?**

(5 marks)

8 The requirement for internal audit

The need for internal audit

We have seen that Corporate Governance is about ensuring that companies are run well in the interest of all stakeholders. In order to achieve this companies must create a strong board of directors, structured according to the principles discussed on the preceding pages, who have clearly defined responsibilities for risk management.

However, it is not sufficient to simply have mechanisms in place to manage a business; their effectiveness must be regularly assessed. All systmes need some form of monitoring and feedback. This is the role of internal audit.

> ### Expandable Text - Introduction - The need for internal audit
>
> Having an internal audit department is generally considered to be 'best practice,' rather than being required by law. This allows flexibility in the way internal audit is established to suit the needs of a business.
>
> In small, or owner managed businesses there is unlikely to be a need for internal audit because the owners are able to exercise more direct control over operations, and are accountable to fewer stakeholders.
>
> The need for internal audit, therefore will depend on:
>
> * scale, diversity and complexity of activities;
>
> * number of employees;
>
> * cost/benefit considerations; and
>
> * the desire of senior management to have assurance and advice on risk and control.

What do internal auditors do?

In chapter 1 we explored the role of the external auditor, namely to provide assurance in the form of an opinion regarding the financial statements.

The role of internal audit can be much more varied, depending on the requirements of the business. However, the internal audit function may also provide assurance. They would provide this assurance to internal management on issues such as:

* the effectiveness of systems (financial, legal and operational);

* the effectiveness of internal controls;

- whether company procedures/manuals are being followed
- whether internally produced information is reliable; and
- whether the company is compliant with the OECD.

In addition to the above, internal audit will carry out ad hoc assignments, as required by management, e.g.: internal fraud investigations.

If the internal audit department is to be effective in providing assurance it needs to be :

- sufficiently resourced, both financially and in terms of qualified, experienced staff;
- well organised, so that it has well developed work practices; and
- independent and objective.

This last point needs some explanation. Internal auditors are (generally) employed by the company they are reporting on and are often managed as part of the finance function. They will therefore have to report upon the effectiveness of financial systems that they form a part of.

It is therefore difficult for internal audit to remain truly objective. However, acceptable levels of independence can be achieved through one, or more, of the following strategies:

- Reporting channels separate from the management of the main financial reporting function;
- Reviews of internal audit work by managers independent of the function under scrutiny; and
- Outsourcing the internal audit function to a professional third party.

Expandable Text - Organisation

How internal audit is organised will depend upon the scale of the organisation employing them, but usually it is necessary that:

- The head of internal audit has sufficient seniority within the organisation.
- Lines of communication ensure that internal audit reports, or at least a summary of them, are reviewed by the audit committee or some other body which is independent of management.
- There should be 'whistleblowing' arrangements so that, where circumstances demand - e.g. fraud, internal auditors can report directly to the company's chairman or the chair of the audit committee.

Limitations of the internal audit function

Reporting system

The chief internal auditor reports to the finance director. This limits the effectiveness of the internal audit reports as the finance director will also be responsible for some of the financial systems that the internal auditor is reporting on. Similarly, the chief internal auditor may soften or limit criticism in reports to avoid confrontation with the finance director.

To ensure independence, the internal audit should report to an audit committee.

Scope of work

The scope of work of internal audit is decided by the finance director in discussion with the chief internal auditor. This means that the finance director may try and influence the chief internal auditor regarding the areas that the internal audit department is auditing, possibly directing attention away from any contentious areas that the director does not want auditing.

To ensure independence, the scope of work of the internal audit department should be decided by the chief internal auditor, perhaps with the assistance of an audit committee.

Audit work

The chief internal auditor may audit their own work. This limits independence as the auditor is effectively auditing his own work, and may not therefore identify any mistakes.

To ensure independence, the chief internal auditor should not establish control systems in the company. However, where controls have already been established, another member of the internal audit should carry out the audit of that system to provide some limited independence.

Lengths of service of internal audit staff

All internal audit staff may have been employed for a long period of time. This may limit their effectiveness as they will be very familiar with the systems being reviewed and therefore may not be sufficiently objective to identify errors in those systems.

To ensure independence, the existing staff should be rotated into different areas of internal audit work and the chief internal auditor independently review the work carried out.

Appointment of chief internal auditor

The chief internal auditor is appointed by an executive director/CEO. Given that the CEO is responsible for the running of the company, it is possible that there will be bias in the appointment of the chief internal auditor; the CEO may appoint someone who he knows will not criticise his work or the company.

To ensure independence, the chief internal auditor should be appointed by an audit committee or at least the appointment agreed by the whole board.

Variation of standards

Standards of audit are not uniform across the profession. Compare this with external auditors who, on a global basis, have ISAs against which their performance can be measured.

Expectations gap

Like external audit there are inconsistencies in what the internal auditor's role is perceived to be.

Understanding of internal audit

Many people see internal audit negatively. It is perhaps seen as 'checking up' on employees on behalf of 'the bosses'.

Consideration of outsourcing the internal audit function

In common with other areas of a company's operations, the directors may consider that outsourcing the internal audit function represents better value than an in-house provision. Local government authorities are under particular pressure to ensure that all their services represent 'best value' and this may prompt them to decide to adopt a competitive tender approach.

Advantages

- Greater focus on cost and efficiency of the internal audit function.
- Staff may be drawn from a broader range of expertise.
- Risk of staff turnover is passed to the outsourcing firm.
- Specialist skills may be more readily available.
- Costs of employing permanent staff are avoided.
- May improve independence.
- Access to new market place technologies, e.g. audit methodology software without associated costs.
- Reduced management time in administering an in-house department.

Disadvantages

- Possible conflict of interest if provided by the external auditors (In some jurisdictions – e.g. the UK, the ethics rules specifically prohibit the external auditors from providing internal audit services).

- Pressure on the independence of the outsourced function due to, e.g. threat by management not to renew contract.

- Risk of lack of knowledge and understanding of the organisation's objectives, culture or business.

- The decision may be based on cost with the effectiveness of the function being reduced.

- Flexibility and availability may not be as high as with an in-house function.

- Lack of control over standard of service.

- Risk of blurring of roles between internal and external audit, losing credibility for both.

Minimising the risks of outsourcing

Some general procedures to minimise risks associated with outsourcing the internal audit function will include:

- Controls over acceptance of internal audit contracts to ensure no impact on independence or ethical issues.

- Regular reviews of the quality of audit work performed.

- Separate departments covering internal and external audit.

- Clearly agreed scope, responsibilities and reporting lines.

Performance measures, management information and risk reporting

- Procedure manuals for internal audit.

Expandable Text - The 4Cs

- **Challenge** – review internally the different options for providing services and question the status quo.

- **Compare** – compare with other service providers to review options for improving performance.

- **Consult** – consult all users of services and those affected by services.

- **Compete** – demonstrate through performance management and continuous improvement that the most efficient and effective service is being provided.

Best value is a requirement for local authorities to demonstrate achievement of the '4C' principles, as well as demonstrating service delivery and meeting customer needs through effective performance management systems.

9 Internal audit assignments

We consider below examples of Internal Audit assignments.

In this section we look at generic types of assignment:

- Value for money/best value assignments.
- Assignments dealing with IT.
- Project auditing.
- Financial audit.

In the next section we will consider operational assignments – those which examine particular aspects of a business' operations.

10 Value for money

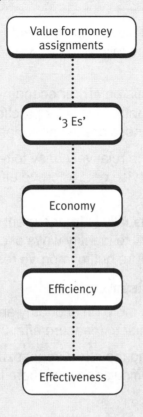

Value for money (VFM) is concerned with obtaining the best possible combination of services for the least resources. It is therefore the pursuit of 'Economy', 'Efficiency' and 'Effectiveness' – often referred to as the 3Es.

- **Economy** – least cost. Accomplishes objectives and goals at a cost commensurate with the risk.

- **Efficiency** – best use of resources. Accomplishes goals and objectives in an accurate and timely fashion with minimal use of resources.

- **Effectiveness** – best results. Providing assurance that the organisation objectives will be achieved.

Comparisons of value for money achieved by different organisations (or branches of the same organisation) are often made using performance indicators that provide a measure of economy, efficiency or effectiveness.

Examples of local government indicators are given below:

- Economy – cost of waste collection per local taxpayer.

- Efficiency – number of households (premises) covered per waste collector.

- Effectiveness – % of waste recycled measured against target for the year.

Expandable Text - Tensions between the three E's

It is not really possible to achieve improvements in these three aspects simultaneously. Consider the following:

- VFM audits tend to focus on **either** economy and efficiency **or** effectiveness, but not both. This is for practical reasons because economy and effectiveness are usually opposed to one another.

- For example, it would be relatively easy to reduce costs by providing a lower standard of service or to improve effectiveness by spending more.

- The solution to this is usually to treat current or target effectiveness levels as fixed and to try to identify ways of cutting costs or to aim to spend the same as before but to improve results in the process.

Measurement is also an issue:

- Audits frequently focus more on economy and efficiency. This is because it can be difficult to measure effectiveness.

- For example, measuring the effectiveness of a hospital department or a school might be difficult because there is no reliable measure of 'output'.

- Performance indicators such as the numbers of patients treated or the percentage of operations that are successful may be misleading.

- For example, one hospital might have a reputation for excellence in a particular area and have to treat the most seriously ill patients. Any statistical comparison with other hospitals might be affected by this.

- The push towards measuring and reporting performance has led to some unfortunate and unintended problems.

- For example, government targets to improve waiting times for hospital operations might mean that minor ailments are treated sooner than more serious ones, because the hospital managers may schedule treatments in the order that achieves the best statistics, rather than in order of clinical need.

KAPLAN PUBLISHING

Expandable Text - Best value in the context of current trends

Best value in the context of current trends

- Reviewing best value is a major trend within local government, following an increasing focus on tendering for contracts and ensuring 'best value' through regulation and political pressures.

- Best value is changing the local government operating environment and affecting all services and activities. It cannot, therefore, be ignored by internal audit; in fact, auditors can play a major role in providing assurance on best value.

- These approaches differ in detail and emphasis but they share an important common theme – that of assisting the organisation to achieve its objectives by identifying and managing the risks to which it may be exposed. These risks may inhibit the achievement of objectives.

- The 4Cs apply equally to internal auditors, who must demonstrate best value in the provision of their own service, including appropriate consultations with customers and effective performance management information.

Expandable Text - Audit of information technology

In chapter 8 we consider the different strengths and weaknesses of manual and IT based systems.

We do this mainly from the external auditor's point of view, which is to ascertain whether or not the company's systems provide a reliable basis for the preparation of financial statements, and whether there are internal controls – mechanisms built into the systems – which are effective in reducing the risk of misstatement.

The internal audit approach to IT will cover all of this but with some additional objectives.

- Does the system represent value for money/best value.

- Were the controls over awarding contracts for IT installations effective?

Project auditing

Best value and IT assignments are really about looking at **processes** within the organisation and asking:

- were things done well?
- did the organisation achieve value for money?

Project auditing is about looking at a specific project, such as commissioning a new factory or implementing new IT systems, and asking whether these were done well. The focus is different and has more to do with:

- were the objectives achieved?
- was the project implemented efficiently?
- what lessons can be learned from any mistakes made?

11 Operational internal audit assignments

Operational auditing covers:

- Examination and review of a business operation.
- The effectiveness of controls.
- Identification of areas for improvement in efficiency and performance including improving operational **economy**, **efficiency** and **effectiveness** – the **three Es** of value for money auditing.

We will now look at operational internal audit in practice, considering four of the main areas where such an approach is commonly used, namely:

- procurement
- marketing
- treasury
- human resources.

General approach

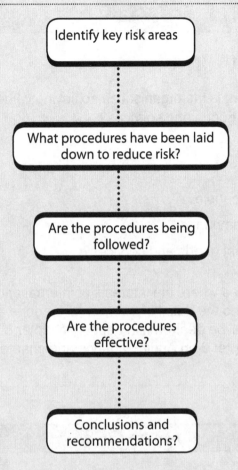

In all cases, the audit work should be based on an approach, which starts by identifying the objectives of the audit. These should focus on:

- the identification of the principal business risks involved which may prevent the organisation achieving its objectives

- the assessment of the extent to which controls are in place and are operating effectively in order to manage these risks.

The outcome of each assignment should be a report to management which appraises the control systems which are currently in place and which makes appropriate recommendations for improvement. This reporting aspect is dealt with later.

Expandable Text - Procurement

Procurement

Key question: Is the organisation achieving value for money in its purchases of goods and services?

Is it paying:

- the right people?
- the right amount?
- for the right goods and services?

This is one area where the interests of internal and external auditors are very similar and the detail of the work to be done and the issues to be considered will be dealt with in depth in chapter 8 on Systems and Controls, chapter 9 on Audit Evidence and chapter 10 on Audit Procedures.

Expandable Text - Marketing

Marketing

Definition

Marketing encompasses all aspects of the promotion and branding of an organisation, including branding and image management, product promotion and advertising and pricing.

Internal audit sometimes shies away from reviewing areas like marketing, because of the 'artistic' nature of the work carried out. However, there are significant risks associated with marketing that could damage the finances and/or reputation of the company or organisation.

For example, some major organisations have been significantly caught out by marketing campaigns offering free or reduced travel that have far outweighed the increased volume of sales. When organisations cannot meet the needs of such promotions, the damage to reputation can be enormous, as well as the impact on the bottom line.

KAPLAN PUBLISHING

An internal audit assignment into marketing activities will therefore consider:

- Did the campaign deliver on its objectives?

- Were the proper procedures followed in awarding any external contracts? (tenders, beauty parades etc).

- Possible breaches of regulatory requirements – this could be a particular risk in marketing campaigns that could result in fines or censure.

- Shareholder value lost or damage to reputation through poor brand image.

- Financial loss arising from poor cost control.

- Fraudulent practices.

- Excessive or inappropriate use of marketing entertainment.

Expandable Text - Treasury

Treasury management: the process of managing cashflow and investments within an organisation to maximise the use of available finances.

You are not expected to know the detail of treasury operations, but a simplified view of the possible risks would be to consider the organisation's exposure to:

- currency (forex) fluctuations

- interest rate fluctuations

- inflation (in some economies).

Treasury departments have ways of protecting against these risks – usually through a process known as **hedging**. Basically this means covering yourself so that if a particular currency or investment goes down in value you have an arrangement in place which will reduce your loss.

If these procedures are followed properly they should reduce the organisation's exposure to risk. If similar transactions are used speculatively, however, they can expose the organisation to additional, sometimes catastrophic risk, for example: Barings Bank and the famous Nick Leeson 'Rogue Trader' case.

As with all things, risk cannot be eliminated altogether, but the organisation should have a 'rulebook' of laid down procedures and the internal audit team will need to check that these procedures have been followed.

Alternatively, Internal Audit may be asked to check whether the procedures were appropriate in the first place.

Expandable Text - Human Resources

Human resources

HR consists of a number of key areas:

- policy
- recruitment
- pay and benefits administration
- performance management
- training and development
- disciplinary and grievance
- leavers.

Main areas of risk exposure include:

- failure to identify and recruit the right skills;
- excessive reliance on consultants or contractors, resulting in high costs;
- inaccurate or incomplete standing data on staff;
- failure to provide feedback to staff on performance;
- over-reliance on small number of key staff or loss of key staff;
- failure to provide appropriate training and development of staff;
- failure to understand underlying problems of staff morale;
- inappropriate payments made to staff; e.g. 'ghost employees' and leavers; and
- disciplinary procedures not carried out appropriately or in line with company or legal requirements.

The pattern of work for HR assignments will follow that of other assignments:

- are the organisation's procedures being applied properly?
- are the procedures appropriate?

12 Internal audit reports

Key principles

Who is the report for?

With any report the most important person in the process is the reader **not** the writer.

- If the report does not address the objective of the assignment.
- If the recipient of the report cannot understand its recommendations and the reasoning behind them, then the report might as well never have been written.

The report should be customer focused, meeting organisational needs. The internal auditor should always be conscious of the organisational philosophy, management styles and reporting objectives.

Purpose and structure of the report

Although it is possible to set out a format for reports which represents good practice (see below), the purpose of any report is to summarise the results of the work undertaken, so that lessons can be learned and appropriate action taken.

The content of any report will be determined by the nature of the assignment (see the section on Internal Audit assignments above).

Short and sweet

Clear, concise, easy to read format will mean it is more likely to be read and understood.

Measurable/quantifiable outcomes

It is easy to recommend in a report that something should be improved, but without:

- clear recommendations about how this is to be done
- some way of measuring whether the recommendations have been successfully implemented

it is less likely that improvements will actually happen.

Prioritisation

The important content needs to be readily accessible, not buried in the back of an appendix somewhere.

Avoid surprises

Discuss with management as points arise. This will mean less argument over facts or detail when the draft report is issued and will allow management to take steps promptly.

Fairness

Balanced and constructive reporting will be welcomed by management and the organisation. For example, recognising where controls are good and how they could be used elsewhere within the organisation.

Ensure consistency across reports, particularly where 'ratings' are used. If management feel unfairly treated or criticised, they will respond negatively to the report.

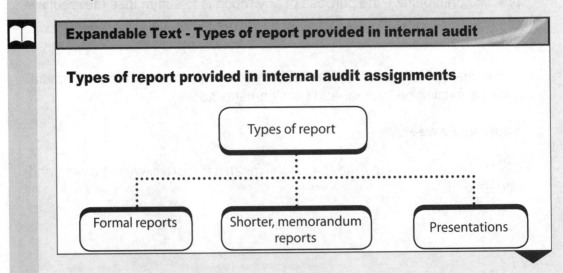

Expandable Text - Types of report provided in internal audit

Types of report provided in internal audit assignments

Formal reports

A formal written report is the traditional outcome from an internal audit assignment. A recommended structure for the report is set out in the following section.

Shorter memorandum reports

For:

- smaller scale assignments
- assignments where less depth is required
- assignments where results are required urgently
- a shorter, less formal report may be required.

Nevertheless, the same care needs to be taken with the contents of the report:

- **Addressees** – make sure it goes to the right people (especially reports delivered by email).
- **Subject matter** – make sure the purpose of the report is clear and that the objective is addressed by the content of the report.
- **Structure** – make sure the report is laid out well so that its message is communicated efficiently. Surprisingly, although this type of report is less formal, it still needs to be properly structured and lack of formality should not be taken as an excuse for sloppy drafting.

Presentations

- An oral presentation can have a greater impact than a written document.
- Usually, however, a presentation will be delivered as well as the main report and used to highlight the key findings.
- Although the delivery methods are clearly different, the structure of a presentation has much in common with the structure of a formal written report.

Structure of a formal report

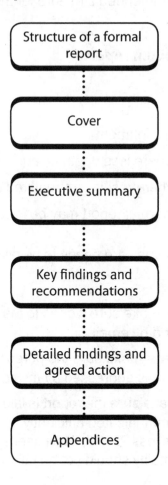

Cover of report

- Subject
- Distribution list
- Date of issue
- Any rating/evaluation.

The cover (or header for a shorter memorandum report) is surprisingly important:

- It makes sure the report goes to the right people.
- It can make the difference between the report being read or not – so the subject needs to be expressed carefully.

Detailed findings and agreed action

Setting out agreed actions, timescale for action and responsibilities for resolution will be the meat of the report for line management.

- Recommendations for solving the problem.
- Who is to carry out the necessary actions.
- Deadlines and timescales.

Executive Summary

The executive summary is like the whole report in miniature:

- It needs to grab the reader's attention to make sure they read the whole report.
- If the readers were only able to read the executive summary rather than all the detail of the whole report, they should still be able to come to the same conclusion and make the same decisions.

In a memorandum report, because it should be quite short to start with, there will usually be a summary of findings rather than a full executive summary.

In a presentation, a very early slide should give the equivalent of the executive summary.

If a question is asking you to demonstrate how a report should be structured always mention the executive summary, but it will probably be sufficient to state that its content would be a summary of the rest of the report.

Key findings and recommendations

Summary of key findings and recommendations

Short, clear summaries of the key findings and recommendations from the review.

- The main problems found.
- Breaches in procedures.
- Ineffective procedures.

Assessment gradings or ratings

In some organisations, internal auditors provide 'ratings' of the area under review, indicating the extent of concern over control or the level of risk, or the standard of performance in the area being reviewed.

This can be in various forms:

- colours – red/amber/green
- numbers/letters – A, B, C or 1, 2, 3
- wording such as 'acceptable' or 'satisfactory' and 'unacceptable' or 'unsatisfactory'
- star ratings ×, ××, ×××.

Such ratings can help senior management:

- form an overall opinion of the organisation
- identify trends
- facilitate high level reporting.

However, they can also be seen negatively if they result in management responding defensively to a report on their area that will result in a poor rating.

The most important consideration for rating a report is the basis on which any evaluation or measure will be carried out. This needs to be consistent and clear to ensure credibility of the ratings. The rating may be against a formal control or risk model that drives out the decision or opinion.

Alternative formats

The report can be set out either in:

- Paragraph format
- Tabular format.

Tabular format

Ref	Finding	Action:	Action by:	Date
1	Purchase invoices of 30 invoices reviewed, 10 had no evidence of being checked and had no supporting data to support payment.	All invoices will be supported by a corresponding purchase order and evidence of receipt of goods or service, with a check by the manager being evidenced prior to processing.	DCXX	By end of month

Risk

Fraudulent payment. Payment may be made for goods or services not received. Damage to reputation.

Appendices

- Explanations/further detail.
- Appropriate analysis to back up the matters referred to in the main body of the report.

Process for producing an internal audit report

```
   ┌──────────────────┐              ┌────────────────────────────┐
   │                  │              │  OBJECTIVES OF ASSIGNMENT   │
   │     PLANNING     │◄────────────►│     TERMS OF REFERENCE      │
   │                  │              │   WHAT IS REQUIRED FOR THE  │
   └────────┬─────────┘              │           REPORT           │
            │                        └────────────────────────────┘
            ▼                                      ▲
   ┌──────────────────┐                            │
   │  GATHER EVIDENCE │                            │
   └────────┬─────────┘                            │
            │                                      │
            ▼                                      │
   ┌──────────────────┐                            │
   │    SUMMARISE     │                            │
   │  RESULTS OF WORK │                            │
   │       DONE       │                            │
   └────────┬─────────┘                            │
            │                                      │
            ▼                                      │
   ┌──────────────────┐                            │
   │      DRAW        │                            │
   │   CONCLUSIONS    │                            │
   └────────┬─────────┘                            │
            │                                      │
            ▼                                      │
   ┌──────────────────┐                            │
   │    FORMULATE     │                            │
   │ RECOMMENDATIONS  │                            │
   └────────┬─────────┘                            │
            │                                      │
            ▼                                      │
   ┌──────────────────┐              ┌────────────────────────────┐
   │                  │              │                            │
   │   DRAFT REPORT   │◄────────────►│    OBJECTIVES ACHIEVED?    │
   │                  │              │                            │
   └──────────────────┘              └────────────────────────────┘
```

As we have seen, the report is the culmination of the assignment and without the report the assignment might as well never have happened.

However, it is equally true to say that if the assignment was not properly planned and executed, there could be no report.

So the production process for the report begins with the planning of the assignment itself:

- At the planning stage ensure that the work to be done:
    - will fulfil the objective of the assignment
    - will dovetail with the requirements for the report.

After all the work has been done the report needs to be drafted:

- It needs to be well structured.

- It needs to be clear and concise.

- Wherever possible, discuss it with those who will be affected by it so that there are no surprises.

- Check back with the original objectives/terms of reference of the assignment to make sure that the report delivers what it was supposed to.

Test your understanding 2

(1) **What is the role of internal audit in maintaining standards of corporate governance?**

(5 marks)

(2) **List the types of activities normally carried out by internal audit departments.**

(6 marks)

(3) **List and explain the limitations of internal audit.**

(4 marks)

(4) **List two types of internal audit report.**

(1 mark)

13 Chapter summary

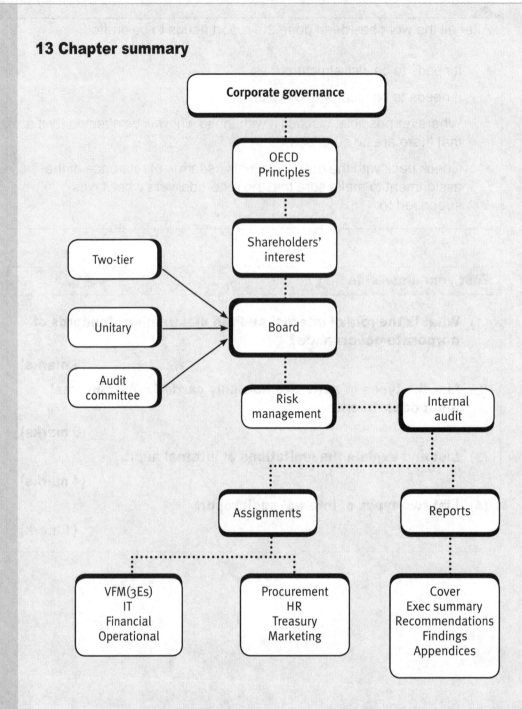

Test your understanding answers

Test your understanding 1

(1) What is meant by corporate governance?	The term corporate governance refers to the means by which a company is managed in the interests of all stakeholders. It will include consideration of:	
	(1) directors' responsibilities	
	(2) composition of the board of directors	1 mark
		1 mark
	(3) audit requirements (internal and external)	1 mark
(2) Why are the external auditors interested in corporate governance?	Corporate governance is the responsibility of the company's management and not its external auditors.	1 mark
	However, it is the responsibility of the external auditors to form an opinion on the truth and fairness of the company's financial statements.	1 mark
	If a company has good standards of corporate governance and is therefore managed well in the interests of all stakeholders, the auditors are likely to conclude that the risk of material misstatement in the financial statements is reduced.	1 mark
	As a result of this they may well be able to reduce the extent of the audit procedures they carry out.	1 mark

(3)	What are the key things the OECD principles are intended to deliver?	A framework so that companies are governed well which should be beneficial to financial markets.	1 mark
		Fair treatment of all shareholders	1 mark
		Companies to be run in the interests of all stakeholders.	1 mark
		Transparency of disclosure about the company's performance and state of affairs.	1 mark
		The management of the company should carry out its role in the interest of all stakeholders.	1 mark
(4)	Explain the difference between a unitary board of directors and a two-tier board?	**Unitary board** Single board of directors. Monitored by sub-committees and non-executive directors.	1 mark
		Two-tier board Two boards: Executive board (decision-makers) Monitored by supervisory board consisting of employees, investors etc.	1 mark
(5)	Who should make up a typical audit committee?	The audit committee should be made up of non-executive directors and include someone with relevant financial experience.	1 mark
(6)	What is the committee's role?	The audit committee provides a channel of communication between the internal workings of the company and the external auditor.	1 mark
		It also provides a channel of communication for employees who have concerns about the way the company is run.	1 mark

(7)	Why would a company need an audit committee if it has a good relationship with its external auditors?	A good relationship with external auditors is of immense help and support to an entity in complying with regulations, optimising controls and generally ensuring good corporate governance.	1 mark
		However, the existence of an audit committee will enhance the company's corporate governance profile by:	1 mark
		1 improving public confidence	1 mark
		2 providing further support to directors	
		3 strengthening the independence of the external auditor	1 mark
		4 improving internal procedures e.g. management accounting, & communication generally.	1 mark
			1 mark
(8)	A company has identified one of its major risks as loss of key staff. Explain • what they should do as a result of this? • how they might reduce or even eliminate the risk? • why the auditor is interested in this, given that it is not a direct financial risk?	The risk committee should discuss the issue and assess its seriousness in relation to its likelihood and potential impact. They should then decide what action is appropriate in order to manage the risk. This risk might be reduced by:	1 mark
		• ensuring favourable employment packages for such individuals	1 mark
		• ensuring training for other staff assists in case of succession issues	1 mark
		• ensure key tasks are not carried out by just one person.	1 mark
		The auditor must consider the possible impact of all significant risks as any of these could ultimately have financial consequences or going concern issues, hence impacting on the audit opinion.	1 mark

Test your understanding 2

(1) What is the role of internal audit in maintaining standards of corporate governance?	Internal audit is part of the organisational control of a business; it is one of the methods used by management to ensure the orderly and efficient running of the business as a whole and is part of the overall control environment.	1 mark
	A properly functioning internal audit department is part of good corporate governance, as recognised by national and international codes on corporate governance.	1 mark
	One of the objects of good corporate governance is to ensure that the needs of all stakeholders are met as far as possible and internal audit procedures meet the needs of the owners of the business, its employees, and the business community at large, as well as the needs of management. The main way in which internal audit exercises its functions is by enabling management to perform proper risk assessments in relation to corporate objectives by means of properly understanding the strengths and weaknesses in all of the control systems in the business.	2 marks
	The role of internal audit has expanded considerably in recent years and the scope of internal audit is no longer routine or low level; internal audit is involved at all levels of management and internal audit includes non-routine matters such as assisting in setting corporate objectives and assessing performance against them.	2 marks

(2) List the types of activities normally carried out by internal audit departments.	The review of management, organisational, operational, accounting, internal control and other business systems.	1 mark
	Making recommendations in relation to the improvement of systems and monitoring the performance of systems against targets.	1 mark
	Performing value for money (economy, efficiency and effectiveness), best value and similar audits.	1 mark
	Compliance work involving the review of compliance with legislation, regulations and codes of practices.	1 mark
	The detailed examination of financial and operating data.	1 mark
	Special investigations, such as fraud investigations.	1 mark
(3) List and explain the limitations of internal audit.	May not be independent.	1 mark
	There are no recognised standards for internal audit work.	1 mark
	There is an expectation gap in that internal audit cannot uncover every fraud or solve every problem, even though others in the organisation may wish it could.	1 mark
	Internal audit may be regarded as management's private police force, and as a result may not receive full co-operation from those whose work is being examined.	1 mark
(4) List two types of internal audit report.	Formal report.	½ mark
	Shorter memorandum reports.	½ mark
	Presentations.	½ mark

Responsibilities

Chapter learning objectives

Upon completion of this chapter you will be able to:

- Discuss the need for auditors to communicate with those charged with governance;

- Discuss the responsibilities of internal and external auditors for the prevention and detection of fraud and error;

- Compare and contrast the role of external and internal audit regarding audit planning and the collection of audit evidence; and

- Compare and contrast the types of report provided by internal and external audit.

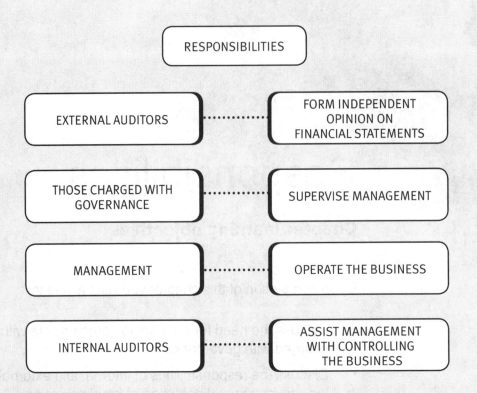

1 Introduction

The distinction between the responsibilities of a company's management and its external auditors should be clear.

However, as discussed previously, misconceptions, particularly about the role of audit, can lead to a phenomenon known as **the 'expectation gap'.** It is therefore crucial that clearly defined distinctions between the respective responsibilities of management and external auditors be established and that both parties understand (and agree upon) these prior to the commencement of work.

2 Control structure within the organisation

Corporate governance

A company's board of directors normally forms the highest level of management within a business and is responsible for operating the company in the interests of shareholders and other stakeholders.

To achieve this it must establish the mechanisms necessary for good corporate governance, as discussed in chapter 3.

Financial reporting

The board is responsible for preparing the company's financial statements, which give a true and fair view of the company's results for the period under review and its financial position at the year end.

In order to achieve this goal directors are required to:

- Select suitable accounting policies and apply them consistently;
- Make judgements and estimates that are reasonable and prudent; and
- Design and implement internal controls relevant to the preparation of financial statements and to prevent and detect fraud and error.

3 Responsibilities of the external auditors

The legal requirements for audit are presented in chapter 2.

The audit opinion

The auditors' main responsibility is to form an opinion on whether the company's financial statements give a true and fair view.

In some jurisdictions the external auditors have further reporting responsibilities, for example:

- The auditors of listed companies in the UK report on certain aspects of the disclosures of directors' remuneration.
- Auditors in the Republic of Ireland report on certain aspects of the adequacy of a company's capital.

Auditors are **not** responsible for:

- Preparing the financial statements;
- Choosing accounting policies;
- Implementing systems and controls; or
- Establishing the mechanisms for ensuring that good standards of corporate governance are maintained.

Other responsibilities and consequences

To enable them to offer an opinion, auditors are responsible for:

- Planning their work; and
- Gathering sufficient appropriate audit evidence to support their conclusions.

The more effectively the auditor performs these responsibilities the lower the risk that they come to the wrong conclusion.

To assist in planning and performing their work auditors must consider:

- The quality of accounting systems from which the financial statements are produced;

- The effectiveness of the internal controls operated by the company to ensure that its financial information is as complete and accurate as possible; and

- The standards of corporate governance, including the effectiveness of the internal audit function.

All of these factors affect the risk of misstatement and, for that reason, affect the risk of giving an inappropriate opinion.

However, it must be remembered that the establishment and maintenance of these systems is the responsibility of the company and its management, **not** its auditors.

4 Communicating with those charged with governance

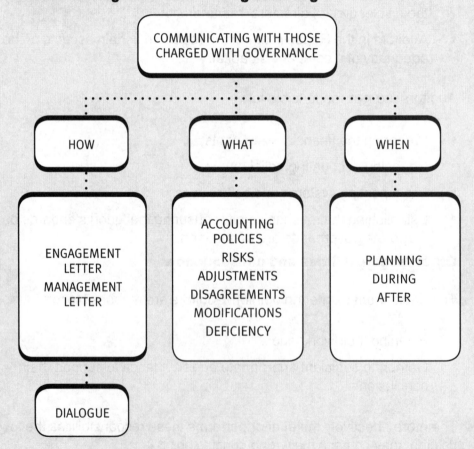

ISAs, in particular **ISA 260** *Communication with Those Charged with Governance and* **ISA 265** *Communicating Deficiencies in Internal Control to Those Charged with Governance and Management*, require the external auditors to engage in communications with management.

The main forms of formal communication between the auditors and management are: the engagement letter (see chapter 5); and another written communication, usually sent at the end of the audit, which is often referred to as 'the management letter.'

The objectives of these communications are:

- To communicate the responsibilities of the auditor and an overview of the scope and timing of the audit;

- To obtain, from those charged with governance, information relevant to the audit;

- To provide timely observations arising from the audit that are significant to the responsibilities of those charged with governance; and

- To promote effective two-way communication between the auditor and those charged with governance.

Whilst a formal communication is usually sent at the conclusion of the audit there may be a need to communicate particular matters at other times to help meet the third objective, for example; if a fraud is discovered.

Summary of responsibilities

Audit matters of governance interest include:

- Auditor independence;
- Effects of significant accounting policies and changes to them;
- Potential financial effect of risks/uncertainties;
- Material audit adjustments;
- Disagreements with management concerning the financial statements;
- Significant difficulties encountered during the audit;
- Expected modifications to the audit report; and
- Significant internal control deficiencies, including fraud.

Timing of communications

Stage of audit	Communication required
Planning	Practical matters concerning forthcoming audit.
	Independence of auditor.
	Expected fees.
	Nature and scope of audit work.
	Ensure letter of engagement is up to date.
During the audit	If any situation occurs and it would not be appropriate to delay communication until the audit is concluded.
Conclusion of audit	Major findings from audit work.
	Uncorrected misstatements.
	Qualitative aspects of accounting/reporting practices.
	Final draft of letter of representation.
	Expected modifications to audit report.
	Significant internal control deficiencies.

5 Responsibilities of internal auditors

As discussed in chapter 3, the internal auditors are either:

- employees of the organisation they are auditing; or
- contracted to provide internal audit services through an outsourcing arrangement.

It therefore follows that the precise responsibilities of internal auditors will be defined by whoever determines the objectives of the assignments they conduct. However, **ISA 610** *Using the Work of Internal Auditors* lists the main activities of the internal audit function as:

- Monitoring of internal control;
- Examination of financial and operating information;
- Review of the operating activities;
- Review of compliance with laws and regulations;
- Risk management; and
- Governance.

Whilst some of the work performed by internal and external auditors may be similar it must be remembered that the **external** auditor is **solely responsible** for the audit opinion. This responsibility can never be reduced by the use of the work of the internal auditors.

If the external auditor wishes, at any point, to use the work of internal audit to assist with their procedures, they must firstly determine:

- Whether the work of internal audit is adequate for the purposes of the audit;
- The effect of the work of internal auditors on the nature, timing and extent of the external auditor's own procedures;
- The objectivity of internal audit;
- The technical competence of internal audit;
- Whether the work of internal audit is carried out with due professional care; and
- Whether there is likely to be effective communication between the internal and external auditors.

6 Systems and controls

Directors need to establish and maintain suitable systems and controls to:

- Safeguard the company's assets;
- Enable financial statements that give a true and fair view to be produced; and
- Prevent and detect fraud.

External auditors need to:

- Ascertain and document how the company's systems, including any controls, should operate;
- Test those controls and document their findings;
- Assess whether the systems are effective, such that the risk of material misstatement in the financial statements is reduced;
- Consider the impact of this assessment on the nature, timing and scope and further audit procedures; and
- Report any significant deficiencies discovered to those charged with governance.

Internal auditors may be given assignments to review systems and controls and to report to management about their effectiveness. The nature of the work carried out by internal audit in these circumstances will be very similar to that performed by the external auditors and is covered in detail in chapter 8.

7 Fraud and error

What is fraud and error?

Major scandals that have affected the accounting profession in recent times have usually been as a result of fraud. Therefore, in order to maintain confidence in the profession it is important for auditors and directors to understand their role in the prevention and detection of fraud.

ISA 240 the *Auditor's Responsibilities Relating to Fraud in an Audit of Financial Statements* recognises that misstatement in the financial statements can arise from either fraud or error. The distinguishing factor is whether the underlying action that resulted in the misstatement was intentional or unintentional.

It is important to note that fraud is a criminal activity. It is not the role of an auditor to determine whether fraud has actually occurred. That is the responsibility of a country's legal system. Auditors must be aware of the impact of both fraud and error on the accuracy of the financial statements.

Fraud can be further split into two types:

*   fraudulent financial reporting – deliberately misstating the accounts to make the company look better/worse than it actually is

*   misappropriation of assets – the theft of the company's assets such as cash or inventory.

The external auditor's responsibilities

The external auditor is responsible for obtaining reasonable assurance that the financial statements, taken as a whole, are free from material misstatement, whether caused by fraud or error. Therefore, the external auditor has some responsibility for considering the risk of material misstatement due to fraud.

In order to achieve this auditors must maintain an attitude of **professional scepticism**. This means that the auditor must recognise the possibility that a material misstatement due to fraud could occur, regardless of the auditor's prior experience of the client's integrity and honesty.

ISA 315 *Identifying and Assessing the Risks of Material Misstatement Through Understanding the Entity and Its Environment* goes further than this general concept and requires that engagement teams discuss the susceptibility of their clients to fraud. The engagement team should also obtain information for use in identifying the risk of fraud when performing risk assessment procedures.

To be able to make such an assessment auditors must identify, through enquiry, how management assesses and responds to the risk of fraud. The auditor must also enquire of management, internal auditors and those charged with governance if they are aware of any actual or suspected fraudulent activity.

Despite these requirements, owing to the inherent limitations of an audit, there is an unavoidable risk that some material misstatements may not be detected, even when the audit is planned and performed in accordance with ISAs. The risks in respect of fraud are higher than those for error because fraud may involve sophisticated and carefully organised schemes designed to conceal it.

Reporting of fraud

If the auditor identifies a fraud they should communicate the matter on a timely basis to the appropriate level of management (i.e. those with the primary responsibility for prevention and detection of fraud). If the suspected fraud involves management the auditor shall communicate such matters to those charged with governance. If the auditor has doubts about the integrity of those charged with governance they should seek legal advice regarding an appropriate course of action.

In addition to these responsibilities the auditor must also consider whether they have a responsibility to report the occurrence of a suspicion to a party outside the entity. Whilst the auditor does have an ethical duty to maintain confidentiality, it is likely that any legal responsibility will take precedent. In these circumstances it is advisable to seek legal advice.

The directors' responsibilities

The **directors** have a primary responsibility for the prevention and detection of fraud. By implementing an effective system of internal control they should reduce the possibility of undetected fraud occurring to a minimum.

The directors should be aware of the potential for fraud and this should feature as an element of their risk assessment and corporate governance procedures. The audit committee should review these procedures to ensure that they are in place and working effectively. This will normally be done in conjunction with the internal auditors.

Internal auditors may be given an assignment:

- to assess the likelihood of fraud, or if a fraud has been discovered,
- to assess its consequences and
- to make recommendations for prevention in the future.

Expandable Text - Planning audit assignments

As assurance practitioners, both external and internal auditors will need to plan their work so that they gather sufficient appropriate audit evidence, in keeping with the objectives of the assignment.

External audit

The focus of external audit is on ensuring that the financial statements are: free from material misstatement; and properly prepared in accordance with a relevant reporting framework. Therefore the planning of external audit work will be done to achieve this objective.

All statutory audits must be planned in accordance with ISAs and other regulatory requirements.

Internal audit

Internal auditors plan their work so that they achieve the objectives of their assignments, as dictated by management.

Who does the planning?

As we know, external auditors are **independent** so they must be in control of planning their own work, in accordance with the objectives above.

Internal auditors' work may be programmed for them by management so that they focus on the areas thought to be most important by the board and those charged with governance.

However, it adds to the strength of corporate governance if the internal audit function has a degree of independence in the selection and objectives of its assignments.

Expandable Text - Evidence

Evidence

- The general rule for all assurance engagements is that the practitioner should gather sufficient appropriate evidence to support the opinion in the report which is the outcome of the assignment. Chapters 9 and 10 look at audit evidence and audit procedures in detail.

- ISA 330 states that under ISAs the auditor gathers evidence which addresses the risk of misstatement as assessed during the planning process and in the light of evidence gathered subsequently.

The external auditor, therefore is always governed by this when deciding what evidence is appropriate.

As we have seen above, the internal auditor may have different objectives, depending on the nature of the assignment.

For example, consider the auditor's approach to non-current assets:

- The **external auditor** is concerned with whether the figures for non current assets are materially misstated. So the auditor may check purchase prices against invoices, check depreciation is applied properly and physically inspect some assets, all on a test basis, and may therefore conclude that the figure for non current assets is materially correct.

- The **internal auditor** may have an assignment to ensure that the plant register at a particular factory is up to date, and so will need to check that every item recorded exists and that all machines on the factory floor are recorded. The auditor may or may not be concerned with values, depending on the nature of the assignment.

Expandable Text - Reporting

Reporting

We have seen in chapter 3 that the report produced by the internal auditor, is determined by the nature of the assignment (there is a bit of a theme developing here!).

The external auditor's report on financial statements is determined by statute and by ISAs (700, 705 & 706) and will be examined in depth in chapter 12.

The external auditor must also communicate to those charged with governance, as discussed earlier in the chapter.

Test your understanding 1

Whose responsibility are the following:

- **Preparation of accounts.**

(½ mark)

- **Undertaking the risk assessment exercise.**

(½ mark)

- **Detection of fraud.**

(½ mark)

- **Reporting on controls.**

(½ mark)

Test your understanding 2

List matters should be communicated to those charged with governance following the conclusion of the audit?

(3 marks)

8 Chapter summary

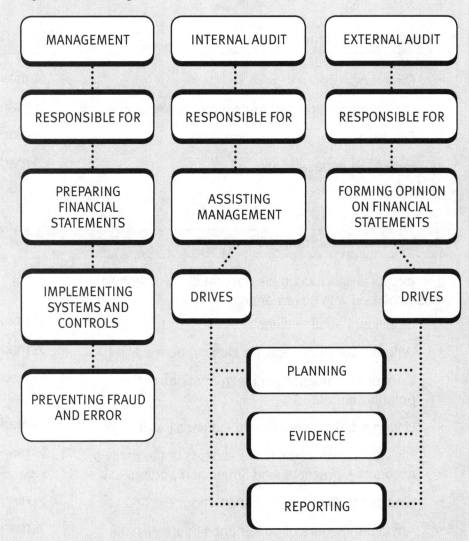

Test your understanding answers

Test your understanding 1

• Directors.	½ mark
• Directors/management/outsourced/internal auditors.	½ mark
• Directors.	½ mark
• External/internal auditor.	½ mark

Test your understanding 2

The auditor will include in his post-audit communication to those charged with governance:

• Significant audit findings.	½ mark
• Whether the audit report is likely to be modified.	½ mark
• Control weaknesses (with explanations of their potential impact).	½ mark
• Uncorrected misstatements – unless trivial.	½ mark
• His views on the qualitative aspects of the entity's accounting practices and financial reporting.	½ mark
• Final draft of letter of representation.	½ mark
• Any other matters of governance interest/issues required by other ISAs.	½ mark

KAPLAN PUBLISHING

5

Ethics and acceptance of appointment

Chapter learning objectives

When you complete this chapter you will be able to:

- Define and apply the fundamental principles of professional ethics;

- Define and apply the conceptual framework;

- Discuss the sources, and enforcement of, ACCA's Code of Ethics;

- Discuss the requirements of professional ethics and other requirements in relation to the acceptance of new audit engagements;

- Discuss the process by which an auditor obtains an audit engagement; and

- Explain the importance and state their contents of engagement letters.

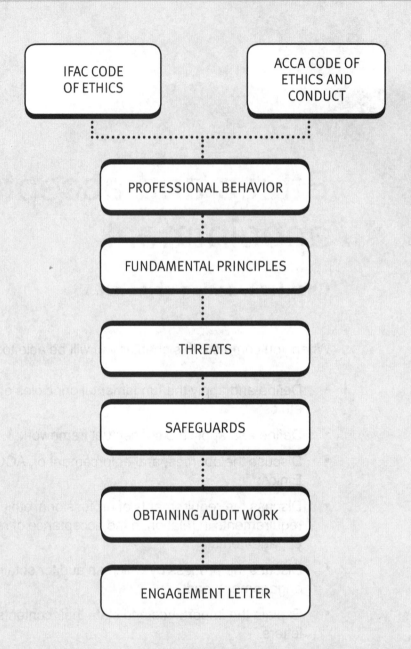

1 Introduction – the need for professional ethics

The purpose of assurance engagements is to increase the confidence of end users of information by reducing their level of risk.

It therefore follows that the user needs to trust the professional providing assurance. In order to be trusted the auditor needs to be **independent** of their client. Independence can be defined as having 'freedom from situations and relationships where objectivity would be perceived to be impaired by a reasonable and informed third party.'

Despite the need for trust the last thirty years has still witnessed a number of high profile corporate scandals that have had far reaching implications for companies, economies and accountancy firms. Enron and Worldcom are perhaps two of the most high profile examples from recent times.

To improve the image of the profession and to restore trust between users of accountancy services and the practitioners, it is vital that accountants operate (and are perceived to operate) according to an accepted code of ethics.

2 The IFAC and ACCA codes and the conceptual framework

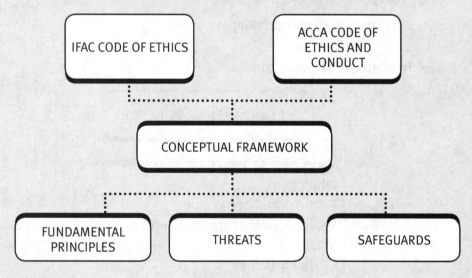

IFAC, through the International Ethics Standards Board for Accountants, has issued a code of ethics, as has the ACCA. The ACCA Code of Ethics is covered in this chapter however, both the IFAC and ACCA codes have the same roots and are, to all intents and purposes identical.

Both follow a conceptual framework which identifies:

- fundamental principles of ethical behaviour
- potential threats to ethical behaviour
- possible safeguards which can be implemented to counter the threats.

A conceptual framework relies on a principles rather than a rules based approach. This means that the spirit of the code is followed rather than a strict set of rules. It provides guidance so that the principles may be applied to wide ranging and - potentially - unique circumstances.

Giving the framework some teeth

The framework and principles would be of little use if they could not be enforced.

Professional bodies like the ACCA therefore reserve the right to discipline members who infringe the rules through a process of:

- Disciplinary hearings which can result in:
  - fines
  - suspension of membership
  - withdrawal of membership.

3 The fundamental principles

THE FUNDAMENTAL PRINCIPLES

Objectivity
Professional behaviour
Professional competence and due care
Integrity
Confidentiality

The formal definitions of the fundamental principles are as follows:

- **Objectivity**: Members should <u>not allow bias</u>, conflicts of interest or undue influence of others to override professional or business judgements.

- **Professional behaviour**: Members should comply with relevant laws and regulations and should avoid any action that <u>discredits</u> the profession.

- **Professional competence and due care**: Members have a continuing duty to maintain professional knowledge and skill at a level required to ensure that a client or employer receives competent professional service based on current developments in practice, legislation and techniques.

  Members should act diligently and in accordance with applicable technical and professional standards when providing professional services.

- **Integrity**: Members should be straightforward and honest in all professional and business relationships.

- **Confidentiality**: Members should respect the confidentiality of information acquired as a result of professional and business relationships and should not disclose any such information to third parties without proper and specific authority or unless there is a legal or professional right or duty to disclose. Confidential information acquired as a result of professional and business relationships should not be used for the personal advantage of members or third parties.

4 Threats and safeguards

Note: 6) Management – but this is an APB ethical standard.

Principles rather than rules based

Both the IFAC and ACCA codes have developed a 'principles approach' rather than a 'rules based' approach to ethical professional behaviour.

This has taken the form of identifying five potential threats to ethical behaviour and the suggestion of a number of safeguards which might be appropriate, including the possibility of ceasing to act for the client.

Throughout, the consideration is not simply the practitioner's view as to whether his or her integrity is under real threat, but how the situation might appear to a third party.

The practitioner needs to:

'behave **and be seen** to behave' in an ethical, professional manner.

Expandable text - Definitions of threats

Self Interest Threat

This can occur as a result of financial or other interests of auditors, or their close family, in clients. Examples include:

- When the auditor or a member of their family owns shares in a client. They would directly benefit from increases in client profits and would be reluctant to raise any concerns that could adversely affect the performance of the client.

- When there are significant outstanding fees from a client. This may make the auditor reluctant to raise issues for fear that the fees will not be paid.

- When a firm is dependent upon one client for a significant proportion of their total fee income. The firm may not raise issues with the client for fear of losing them.

- The acceptance of gifts and hospitality. This could be perceived as bribery to keep quiet about issues in the financial statements.

  As a result auditors should not accept gifts from clients unless they are clearly 'modest.' The definition of modest is not clear and is dependent upon who is receiving the gift and who the relevant observant third parties are. All judgements made regarding the acceptance of gifts and hospitality should be documented on the audit file.

Self Review Threat

A self-review threat occurs when an auditor has to re-evaluate work they have already completed. For example: if the external auditor prepared the financial statements and then audited them.

There is a risk that the auditor would not identify any shortcomings in their own work for fear of penalty (either financial or reputational).

Advocacy Threat

This can occur when the auditor is asked to promote or represent their client in some way. In this situation the auditor would have to be biased in favour of the client and therefore cannot be objective. This could happen if the client asked the auditor to promote their shares for a stock exchange listing or if the client asked the auditor to represent them in court.

Familiarity Threat

A familiarity threat occurs when the auditor is too sympathetic or trusting of the client because of a close relationship with them. This may be because a close friend or relative of the auditor works in a key role for the client. The auditor may trust their friend or relative to not make mistakes and therefore not review their work as thoroughly as they should and as a result allow material errors to go undetected in the financial statements. This can also arise after a long association with a client.

Intimidation Threat

Clients may try to harass or bully auditors into giving an preferential audit reports. They may use the fee as leverage. The auditor should not give in to such pressure and, in the circumstances, may choose to resign from such a client.

Identifying the threats

In order to guard against these threats, real or perceived, firms should establish procedures to enable them to:

* Identify possible threats;
* Evaluate the risk arising from the threat;
* Evaluate whether the necessary safeguards are in place; and
* Take corrective action if necessary.

Usually this will be done through the use of checklists. Whilst ethics should always be of paramount consideration it must be considered at these vital junctures:

- On acceptance of a new client;

- At the planning stage of any audit;

- At the completion stage of any audit;

- Whenever additional, non audit services are provided to an audit client; and

- If any event, or change in circumstance, occurs to either the auditor or the client.

The procedures operated by the firm will normally consist of the following:

- 'Fit and proper' or 'independence' forms to be completed by all staff on a regular basis, disclosing financial interests and other relevant factors.

- A checklist of procedures to be filled in when a new appointment is accepted covering such issues as:
  - proof of the client's identity; and
  - consideration of relationships with the firm, its staff, other clients etc.

- Consideration of independence issues when files are reviewed as part of the firm's quality control process.

- Appointment of a senior partner with responsibility for ethical issues.

Possible safeguards

General safeguards

- **Safeguards created by the profession**. These include: education; training and experience requirements for entry into the profession; continuing professional development requirements; corporate governance regulations; professional standards; monitoring; external review of work and reports; and disciplinary action.

- **Safeguards in the work environment**. These include: oversight structures; ethics and conduct programmes; recruitment procedures; internal controls; disciplinary procedures; strong ethical leadership; policies and procedures to promote quality control; and culture.

- **Safeguards created by individuals**. These include: complying with professional development requirements; keeping records of contentious issues; using a mentor; and keeping in contact with professional bodies.

Specific threats to objectivity

It is important to note that the safeguards listed below are generally well regarded principles that can be applied across a range of engagements and national boundaries. However, national regulatory authorities may have their own ethical standards (such as the UK's Audit Practice Board's Ethical Standards) which are enforceable nationally. In certain circumstances the limits and thresholds may be different

Self-Interest Threat

- To reduce fee dependency auditors should not accept appointment of clients if their total gross recurring fees exceed certain limits. For example, in the UK these limits are:
    - 10% of firms total fees (listed client); or
    - 15% of firms total fees (non-listed clients)
- Loans and guarantees should not be made to clients, unless in the normal course of business;
- Hospitality, gifts or other benefits should not be accepted unless considered 'modest.' Decisions as to whether such interests may be accepted must be made by partners and documented on audit files.
- Fees that are contingent upon achieving agreed goals (e.g. a commission basis) must not be accepted.
- Firms should publish 'prohibited shareholding lists;'
- Individuals with shares in a client must not be involved in their audit;
- Joint ventures with clients should not be entered into.

Self-Review Threat

- Auditors should not perform accountancy services for listed clients, unless it is an emergency;
- Where additional services are provided to audit clients separate engagement teams (including separate partners) should be used;
- Working files should be subject to review by a second partner, independent of either engagement.
- Individuals joining an assurance firm from a client should not be involved in that client's audit for at least two years.
- Internal audit services should not be provided to listed external audit clients, or where significant reliance will be placed upon the work of internal auditors.

Familiarity Threat

- Auditors should not have employment with audit clients (e.g. director - neither executive nor non-executive);

- Individuals joining an assurance firm from a client should not be involved in that client's audit for at least two years.

- Auditors should not be involved in an audit if a member of their immediate family is a director or officer of the client;

- If a partner joins a client and has been involved in the audit of that client in the previous two years (if allowed by law) the audit firm should resign;

- Senior audit team members should be removed from an audit after a period of association of between 5 and 10 years, depending on national custom (in the UK the period is 5 years for listed clients, 10 years for non-listed clients).

Advocacy Threat

- Auditors should not offer legal services to clients and defend them in any dispute or litigation which is material to the financial statements;

- Auditors should not enter into negotiations with banks, or other lenders, on behalf of clients;

- Auditors should not advise clients on debt restructuring as part of a corporate finance engagement.

Intimidation Threat

- Auditors should maintain the fee thresholds noted as a safeguard to self-interest threat;

- Auditors should always maintain an up-to-date engagement letter agreeing the basis of the fee, which has been signed by the client;

- If the relationship with the client breaks down irrevocably, the auditor should resign.

Management Threat

- Employees of accountancy firms (mainly partners and managers) should not serve on the board of a client in any capacity;

- Engagement letters should always specify that clients are responsible for their own decision making;

- Auditors should never make decisions for their clients.

Test your understanding 1

List and explain – the fundamental principles of the ACCA and IFAC Codes of Ethics?

(2 marks)

List the threats to objectivity.

(2 marks)

FIXED TEST 1 - JT & Co.

You are a manager in the audit firm of JT & Co; and this is your first time you have worked on one of the firm's established clients, Pink Co. The main activity of Pink Co is providing investment advice to individuals regarding saving for retirement, purchase of shares and securities and investing in tax efficient savings schemes. Pink is regulated by the relevant financial services authority.

You have been asked to start the audit planning for Pink Co, by Mrs Goodall, a partner in JT & Co. Mrs Goodall has been the engagement partner for Pink Co, for the previous six years and so has a sound knowledge of the client. Mrs Goodall has informed you that she would like her son Simon to be part of the audit team this year; Simon is currently studying for his first set of fundamentals papers for her ACCA qualification. Mrs Goodall also informs you that Mr Supper, the audit senior, received investment advice from Pink Co during the year and intends to do the same next year.

In an initial meeting with the finance director of Pink Co, you learn that the audit team will not be entertained on Pink Co's yacht this year as this could appear to be an attempt to influence the opinion of the audit. Instead, he has arranged a day at the horse races costing less than two fifth's of the expense of using the yacht and hopes this will be acceptable.

JT & Co have done some consultive work previously and the invoice is still outstanding.

Required:

(a) (i) Explain the ethical threats which may affect the auditor of Pink Co.

(6 marks)

(ii) For each ethical threat, discuss how the effect of the threat can be mitigated.

(6 marks)
(12 marks)

Expandable Text - Answer plan

You are a manager in the audit firm of JT & Co; and this is your first time you have worked on one of the firm's established clients, Pink Co. The main activity of Pink Co is providing investment advice to individuals regarding saving for retirement, purchase of shares and securities and investing in tax efficient savings schemes. Pink is regulated by the relevant financial services authority.

You have been asked to start the audit planning for Pink Co, by Mrs Goodall, a partner in JT & Co. Mrs Goodall has been the engagement partner for Pink Co, for the previous six years and so has a sound knowledge of the client. Mrs Goodall has informed you that she would like her son Simon to be part of the audit team this year; Simon is currently studying for his first set of fundamentals papers for her ACCA qualification. Mrs Goodall also informs you that Mr Supper, the audit senior, received investment advice from Pink Co during the year and intends to do the same next year.

In an initial meeting with the finance director of Pink Co, you learn that the audit team will not be entertained on Pink Co's yacht this year as this could appear to be an attempt to influence the opinion of the audit. Instead, he has arranged a day at the horse races costing less than two fifth's of the expense of using the yacht and hopes this will be acceptable.

JT & Co have done some consultive work previously and the invoice is still outstanding.

Required:

(a)   (i)   Explain the ethical threats which may affect the auditor of Pink Co.

(6 marks)

        (ii)   For each ethical threat, discuss how the effect of the threat can be mitigated.

(6 marks)
(12 marks)

Other issues

Opinion Shopping

Whilst shareholders appoint auditors, the Directors typically seek out a potential firm for the shareholders to vote on. The Board might be tempted to interview several firms until it found one that accepted its accounting methods.

Any firm of auditors aware that a potential client is engaged in this process should not accept nomination.

Confidentiality

External auditors are in a unique position of having a legal right of access to all information about their clients. It goes without saying that the client must be able to trust the auditor not to disclose anything about their business to anyone as it could be detrimental to their operations. As a basic rule, members of an audit team should not disclose any information to those outside of the audit team, whether or not they work for the same firm. There is little point using different teams for different work assignments if staff from different teams are disclosing information to each other!

Information should only be disclosed under certain circumstances.

- If the client has given their consent.

- If there is an obligation to disclose, e.g. if the client is suspected of money laundering, terrorism, drug trafficking.

- If it is required by a regulatory body, e.g. financial services legislation.

- If a court order has been obtained.

- If a member has to defend himself in court or at a disciplinary hearing.

- If it is in the public interest.

This latter point is difficult to prove and the audit must proceed with caution if thinking of disclosing information for this reason. Such examples could include fraud, environmental pollution, or simply companies acting against the public good.

Legal advice should be sought beforehand to avoid the risk of being sued. Matters to consider before disclosing information in the public interest are whether that matter is likely to be repeated and how serious the effects of the client's actions are.

Where an auditor feels the need to disclose information, they should consider disclosing to the company's Audit Committee (or Board of Directors, if there is no Audit Committee).

In certain circumstances auditors may be required by law to disclose information. For example, where money laundering is suspected, UK auditors must disclose their suspicions to the Serious Organised Crime Agency (SOCA).

On some occasions, auditors may come under pressure to disclose information (e.g. to customers, suppliers, tax authorities). There is no duty for the auditor to disclose to these parties therefore should only do so if a court order has been obtained.

Conflicts of interest

Members should place their clients' interests before their own and should not accept or continue engagements which threaten to give rise to conflicts of interest between the firm and the client. Any advice given should be in the best interests of the client. Where clients' interests conflict (for example, clients in the same line of business), the firm's work should be arranged to avoid the interests of one being adversely affected by those of another.

The steps to be taken by the auditor are:

- once a conflict is noted, you should advise both clients of the situation

- reassure the client that adequate safeguards will be implemented, e.g. separate engagement leaders for each, separate teams, 'Chinese walls' to prevent the transfer of client information between teams and a second partner review

- suggest they seek additional independent advice

- if adequate safeguards can't be implemented, the auditor should resign.

Safeguards can help to avoid or manage a problem situation, but problems are often hard to foresee as the auditor may have no knowledge that two clients are related in some way until a problem comes to light.

5 Accepting new audit engagements

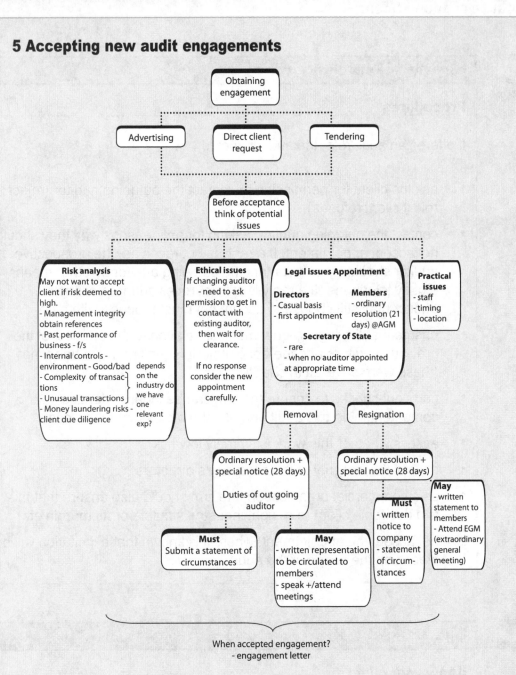

Obtaining engagement

- Advertising
- Direct client request
- Tendering

Before acceptance think of potential issues

Risk analysis
May not want to accept client if risk deemed to high.
- Management integrity obtain references
- Past performance of business - f/s
- Internal controls - environment - Good/bad
- Complexity of transactions
- Unusaual transactions
- Money laundering risks - client due diligence

depends on the industry do we have one relevant exp?

Ethical issues
If changing auditor - need to ask permission to get in contact with existing auditor, then wait for clearance.

If no response consider the new appointment carefully.

Legal issues Appointment

Directors
- Casual basis
- first appointment

Members
- ordinary resolution (21 days) @AGM

Secretary of State
- rare
- when no auditor appointed at appropriate time

Practical issues
- staff
- timing
- location

Removal

Ordinary resolution + special notice (28 days)

Duties of out going auditor

Must
Submit a statement of circumstances

May
- written representation to be circulated to members
- speak +/attend meetings

Resignation

Ordinary resolution + special notice (28 days)

Must
- written notice to company
- statement of circum-stances

May
- written statement to members
- Attend EGM (extraordinary general meeting)

When accepted engagement?
- engagement letter

Expandable Text - Procedures

Procedures

If offered an audit role, the auditor should:

- ask the client for permission to contact the outgoing auditor (reject role if client refuses)

- contact the outgoing auditor, asking for any reasons why they should not accept appointment. If a reply is not received, the prospective auditor should try and contact the outgoing auditor by other means e.g. by telephone. If a reply is still not received the prospective auditor may still choose to accept but must proceed with care.

- ensure that the legal requirements in relation to the removal of the previous auditors and the appointment of the firm have been met (these were covered in chapter 2)

- carry out checks to ensure the firm can be independent, is competent to do this audit and has the necessary resources

- assess whether this work is suitably low risk

- assess the integrity of the company's directors

- as a commercial organisation, the firm should also ensure that this is a desirable client (e.g. right industry, suitable profit margin etc)

- not accept the appointment, where it is known that a limitation will be placed on the scope of the audit.

Expandable text - Know your client

Know your client

Client screening procedures are designed to identify potentially high risk audit clients. A high risk client is one where total costs will exceed the benefits to the auditor.

Considerations which are relevant in deciding whether a client is high risk include the following.

- Evidence of client involvement in fraudulent or illegal activities.

- The state of the economic sector in which the client operates.

- The nature of the industry and the client's product lines or services.

- The client's previous audit history.

- The general abilities of the client's management team.

- Understanding, by the directors, of their own role and that of the auditor.

- Management permission or refusal to allow auditors to examine significant documents.

- Evidence of management intentionally failing to record a material transaction.

The review procedure is best carried out by means of a standard checklist. A client may exhibit some of the above risk factors and yet still be accepted due to the relatively high level of the proposed audit fee. It is very much a commercial decision to be made by the audit firm.

6 Obtaining new audit work

The most common way of obtaining an audit engagement is by recommendation. It is not uncommon for up to 90% of a firm's new business to come from its existing client base. The second most common way of obtaining new work is by submitting a successful tender.

'Tendering' is the process of quoting a fee for work before the work is carried out. It usually involves a number of firms competing by submitting tender proposals to the prospective client.

Risks associated with the tender process

In addition to the risk associated with any other new client the specific risks of being involved with the tender include:

- wasted time – if the audit tender is not accepted

- setting an uncommercially low fee in order to win the contract (lowballing, discussed above)

- making unrealistic claims or promises in order to win the contract.

Expandable Text - Before the tender

Before the tender

Prior to tendering, the auditor should establish:

- the specific needs of the prospective client

- an acceptable fee level.

The audit firm will want the following information before drawing up its proposal:

- precisely what does the company expect from the auditors?

- what timetable does the client expect, an interim audit followed by a final audit, or a longer final audit after the year end?

- by what date are the audited financial statements required?

- what are the company's future plans, e.g. public flotation, expansion, contraction, concentration on certain markets?

- what are the problems with the current auditors, if the company is seeking to replace them?

The contents of the proposal

The content of the proposal should include:

- the fee and how it has been calculated

- the nature, purpose and legal requirements of an audit (clients are often unclear about this)

- an assessment of the requirements of the client

- an outline of how the audit firm proposes to satisfy those requirements

- the assumptions made e.g. on geographical coverage, deadlines, work done by the client, availability of information etc.

- the proposed approach to the audit or audit methodology

- an outline of the firm and its personnel

- the ability of the firm to offer other services

The presentation will be in the format as required by the prospective client and should be dynamic and professional. Possible presentation requirements are:

- written

- oral presentation using visual aids, etc.

How will the proposal be judged?

After each of the prospective firms of auditors has made its presentation, the company must make its choice. Relevant criteria are likely to include:

- clarity

- relevance

- professionalism

- personal/standardised

- timeliness of delivery

- originality
- range of other services
- ability to deliver
- reputation.

7 Engagement letters

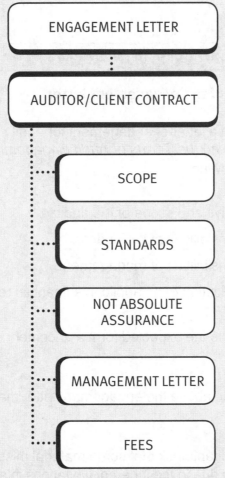

Engagement letters – main considerations

- The engagement letter will be sent before the audit.
- It specifies the nature of the contract between the audit firm and the client.
- It minimises the risk of any misunderstanding of the auditor's role.
- It should be reviewed every year to ensure that it is up to date but does not need to be reissued every year unless there are changes to the terms of the engagement.
- The auditor **must** issue a new engagement letter if the scope or context of the assignment changes after initial appointment.
- Many firms of auditors choose to send a new letter every year, to emphasise its importance to clients.

Expandable Text - Reasons for changes

Reasons for changes include:

- Changes to statutory duties due to new legislation.
- Changes to professional duties, perhaps due to new ISAs.
- Changes to 'other services' as requested by clients.

Expandable Text - Contents of the engagement letter

The contents of the engagement letter

The contents of a letter of engagement for audit services are listed in **ISA 210** *Agreeing the Terms of Audit Engagements*. They should include the following:

- The objective and scope of the audit;
- The responsibilities of the auditor;
- The responsibilities of management;
- The identification of an applicable financial reporting framework; and
- Reference to the expected form and content of any reports to be issued.

In addition to the above the engagement letter may also make reference to:

- The unavoidable risk that some material misstatements may go undetected due to the inherent limitations in an audit;
- Arrangements regarding the planning and performance of the audit;
- The expectation that management will provide written representations;
- The agreement of management to make available to the auditor draft financial statements and other information in time to complete the audit in accordance with the proposed timetable;
- The agreement of management to inform the auditor of facts that may affect the financial statements;
- The basis on which fees are computed and billing arrangements;
- A request for management to acknowledge receipt of the engagement letter and to agree the terms outlined;

- Agreements concerning the involvement of auditors experts and internal auditors; and

- Restrictions to the auditor's liability.

8 Chapter summary

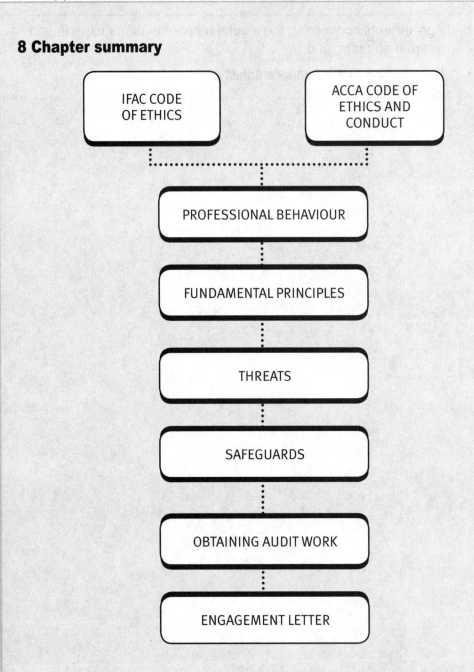

Test your understanding answers

Test your understanding 1

Objectivity: Members should not allow bias, conflicts of interest or undue influence of others to override professional or business judgements.	½ mark
	½ mark
Professional behaviour: Members should comply with relevant laws and regulations and should avoid any action that discredits the profession.	½ mark
	½ mark
Professional competence and due care: Members have a continuing duty to maintain professional knowledge and skill at a level required to ensure that a client or employer receives competent professional service based on current developments in practice, legislation and techniques. Members should act diligently and in accordance with applicable technical and professional standards when providing professional services.	½ mark ½ mark
Integrity: Members should be straightforward and honest in all professional and business relationships.	½ mark
	½ mark
Confidentiality: Members should respect the confidentiality of information acquired as a result of professional and business relationships and should not disclose any such information to third-parties without proper and specific authority or unless there is a legal or professional right or duty to disclose. Confidential information acquired as a result of professional and business relationships should not be used for the personal advantage of members or third parties.	½ mark ½ mark

FIXED TEST 1 - JT & Co.

THIS IS A FIXED TEST – Please answer the question in full (long form written). Then log on to en-gage at the following address: www.en-gage.co.uk. Follow the link to 'Fixed Test 1' and answer the questions based on your homework answer.

Once you have answered the questions on en-gage a model answer will be available for your reference.

6

Planning

Chapter learning objectives

When you have completed this chapter you will be able to:

- identify and explain the need for planning an audit

- identify and describe the contents of the overall audit strategy and the audit plan

- explain the difference between interim and final audit

- discuss the effect of fraud and misstatements on the audit strategy and extent of audit work

- explain and describe the relationship between the overall audit strategy and the audit plan

- explain how auditors obtain an initial understanding of the entity and knowledge of its business environment

- define and explain the concepts of materiality and tolerable error

- compute indicative materiality levels from financial information

- develop and document an audit plan

- describe and explain the nature and purpose of analytical procedures in planning.

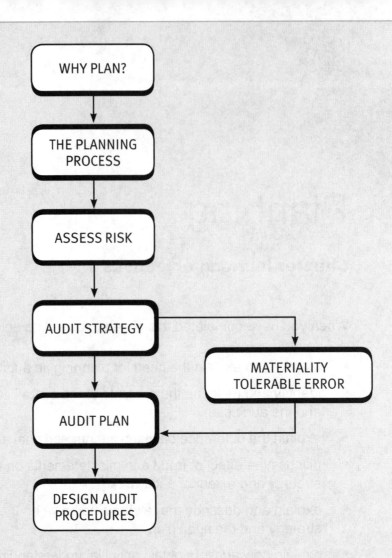

1 Why plan?

"The objective of the auditor is to plan the audit so that the audit so that it will be performed in an effective manner." (**ISA 300** *Planning and Audit of Financial Statements*).

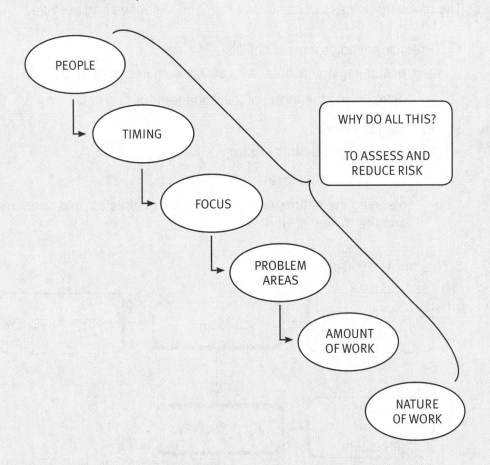

Audits are potentially complex, risky and expensive processes for an accountancy firm. Although firms have internal manuals and standardised procedures it is vital that engagements are planned to ensure that the auditor:

- Devotes appropriate attention to important areas of the audit;

- Identifies and resolves potential problems on a timely basis;

- Organises and manages the audit so that it is performed in an effective and efficient manner;

- Selects team members with appropriate capabilities and competencies;

- Directs and supervises the team and reviews their work; and

- Effectively coordinates the work of others, such as experts and internal audit.

The purpose of all this is to ensure that the risk of performing a poor quality audit (and ultimately giving an inappropriate audit opinion) is reduced to an acceptable level.

2 The planning process

The planning process consists of a number of phases and activities:

- Preliminary engagement activities:
    - evaluating compliance with ethical requirements; and
    - establishing the terms of the engagement.
- Planning activities:
    - developing the audit strategy;
    - developing an audit plan; and
    - planning the nature, timing and extent of direction and supervision and the review of work.

3 The audit strategy

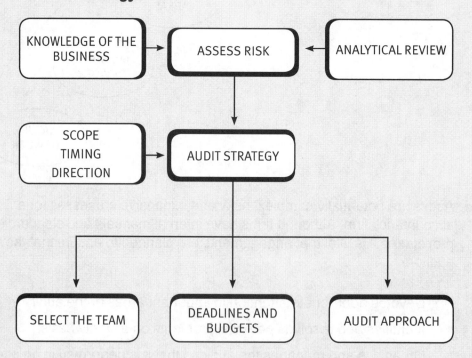

The audit strategy generally considers matters such as:

- the resources to deploy for specific audit areas (e.g. experience level, external experts);
- the amount of resources to allocate (e.g. number of team members);
- when the resources are to be deployed; and
- how the resources are managed, directed and supervised, including the timings of meetings, debriefs and reviews.

Considerations in Establishing the Overall Strategy

The following section provides examples of some of the considerations auditors make when devising an audit strategy. Whilst not exhaustive it should provide a broad range of matters that are likely to form the basis for strategy development.

Characteristics of the Engagement

- What is the financial reporting framework for the financial statements?
- Are there industry specific requirements? e.g. listed companies and charities;
- The number and locations of premises, branches, subsidiaries etc;
- The nature of the client and the need for specialised knowledge;
- The reporting currency;
- The effect of IT on audit procedures, including availability of data.

Reporting Objectives, Timing of the Audit, and Nature of Communication

- The timetable for interim and final reporting;
- The organisation of meetings with management;
- The expected types and timings of auditor's reports/communications;
- The expected nature and timing of communication amongst team members; and
- Whether there are any expected communications with third parties.

Significant Factors and Preliminary Engagement Activities

- Materiality;
- Results of risk assessment;
- Professional scepticism;
- Results of previous audits;
- Evidence of management's commitment to internal controls;
- Volume of transactions;
- Significant business developments/changes;
- Significant industry developments; and
- Significant financial reporting changes.

Nature, Timing and Extent of Resources

- The selection of and assignment of work to the engagement team; and
- Budgets.

4 Interim Versus Final Audits

The interim audit will normally focus on:

- documenting systems
- evaluating controls
- some tests of details – usually on individually material transactions, such as non-current asset acquisitions and disposals..

It may be possible to:

- attend an interim inventory count; or
- carry out an interim receivables circularisation,

These tests are only relevant when the results can be satisfactorily 'rolled forward' to the year-end. (A roll forward reconciles the movements between the date of the count or circularisation and the year end date.)

The final audit can then focus on remaining tests and areas that pose significant risk of material misstatement. This usually involves concentration on year-end valuations and areas where there is significant subjectivity.

For an interim audit to be justified the client normally needs to be of a sufficient size because this may increase costs. In argument to this, an interim audit should improve risk assessment and make final procedures more efficient. If there is to be an interim as well as a final audit the timing has to be:

- Early enough:
  - not to interfere with year-end procedures at the client and
  - to give adequate warning of specific problems.

- Late enough:
  - to enable sufficient work to be done to ease the pressure on the final audit.

5 The audit plan

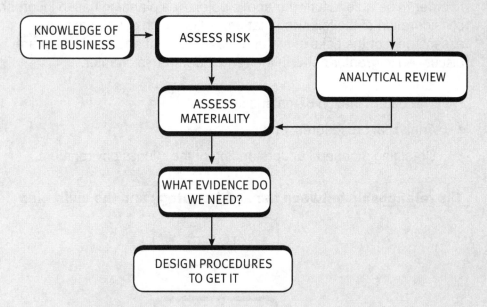

Once the audit strategy has been established, the next stage is to develop a plan to address the various matters identified in the overall strategy.

The audit plan is much more detailed than the overall strategy because it includes details of the nature, timing and extent of the specific audit procedures to be performed. Planning these procedures depends, largely, on the outcomes of the risk assessment process, which will be discussed later in this chapter.

The plan itself

The audit plan should include specific descriptions of:

- the nature, timing and extent of risk assessment procedures (considered in detail in chapter 7);
- the nature, timing and extent of further audit procedures, including:
  - **what** audit procedures are to be carried out
  - **who** should do them
  - **how much** work should be done (sample sizes, etc)
  - **when** the work should be done.
- any other procedures necessary to conform to ISA's.

In order to be able to fulfil the above objectives planning has to incorporate consideration of the following matters, all of which contribute to the assessment of the risks of material misstatement and all of which are discussed in greater detail in the remainder of this chapter:

- The determination of materiality;

- Analytical procedures; and

- Obtaining a general understanding of the client's environment.

The relationship between the audit strategy and the audit plan

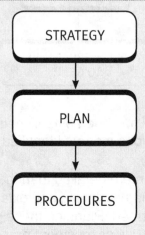

Whilst the strategy sets the overall approach to the audit, the plan fills in the operational details of how the strategy is to be achieved.

It is vital that both the strategy and the plan - and any consequent updates to them - are fully documented as part of audit working papers.

6 Materiality

What is the Significance of Materiality?

The bottom line is that the auditor is responsible for providing "an opinion on whether the financial statements are prepared, in all **material** respects, in accordance with an applicable financial reporting framework."

(**ISA 200** *Overall Objective of the Independent Auditor.......*)

If financial statements contain material misstatement they cannot be deemed to show a true and fair view and are therefore an unreliable basis for users' decision making.

As a result the focus of an audit is identifying the significant risks of misstatement in the financial statements and then designing procedures aimed at identifying and quantifying material misstatement.

What is materiality?

Materiality is a concept, a threshold, an intangible. What makes misstatement material to one user of the accounts may not be material to another user. The precise definition is as follows:

"Misstatement, including omissions, are considered to be material if they, individually or in the aggregate, could reasonably be expected to influence the economic decisions of users taken on the basis of the financial statements"

(**ISA 320** *Materiality in Planning and Performing an Audit*)

How is Materiality Determined?

The most significant misunderstanding about materiality is that it is a purely financial concern. However, disclosures in the financial statements pertaining to possible future legal claims, for example, could influence users' decisions and may be purely narrative. In this case a numerical calculation is not relevant.

The guidance in ISA 320 states that the determination of materiality is a matter of professional judgement and that the auditor must consider:

- The circumstances surrounding the entity;
- Both the size and nature of misstatements; and
- The information needs of the users as a group.

This is an obviously subjective and potentially complex process but is vital in ensuring that materiality is considered in light of the client instead of just applying an arbitrary calculation. However, ISA 320 does recognise the need to establish a financial threshold to guide audit planning and procedures. For this reason it does allow the use of standard benchmarks but only as a starting point. The auditor must then consider all the factors listed above. Traditional benchmarks include:

- ½ – 1% of turnover
- 5 – 10% of profit before tax
- 1 – 2% of gross assets

Material by Nature

Examples of items which could be, or are generally accepted to be, material by nature include:

- Misstatements that, when adjusted, would turn a reported profit into a loss for the year.

- Transactions with directors e.g. salary and benefits, personal use of assets, etc.

- Related party transactions.

The Practical Application of Materiality

It is unlikely, in practice, that auditors will be able to design tests that identify individually material misstatements. It is much more common that misstatements in aggregate (i.e. in combination) become material. Auditors also have to consider that they can only test on a sample basis, so they have to evaluate their findings and determine how likely it is that errors identified in the sample are representative of errors in the whole population under scrutiny.

For this reason materiality, as determined for the financial statements as a whole, may not be the best guide in determining the nature and extent of further procedures. To assist ISA's introduce two further concepts: performance materiality and tolerable misstatement.

Performance Materiality

This is defined in ISA 320 as:

"The amount set by the auditor at less than materiality for the financial statements as a whole to reduce to an appropriately low level the probability that the aggregate of uncorrected and undetected misstatements exceeds materiality for the financial statements as a whole."

In using this lower threshold to perform audit procedures the auditor is more likely to identify misstatements, the effect of which can be considered in combination.

Tolerable Misstatement

This is defined in **ISA 530** *Audit Sampling as:*

"A monetary amount set by the auditor in respect of which the auditor seeks to obtain an appropriate level of assurance that the monetary amount set by the auditor is not exceeded by the actual misstatement in the population."

Although it sounds complex it is simply the practical application of performance materiality to an audit sample. If the total of errors in the sample selected exceeds tolerable misstatement the auditor considers that the risk of a material misstatement from the whole population is high and therefore tests a greater sample size. If the total of errors in the sample is less than tolerable misstatement then the auditor may be reasonably confident that the risk of material misstatement in the whole population is low and no further testing will be required.

7 Analytical Procedures

Analytical procedures are fundamental to the auditing process and are used at the planning, performance and review stage of the audit. They are defined in **ISA 520** *Analytical Procedures* as:

"The evaluation of financial information through analysis of plausible relationships among both financial and non-financial data."

Traditionally they incorporate the comparison of:

- Current and prior year figures;
- Current and budgeted/forecast figures; and
- Client and industry average figures.

At the planning stage analytical procedures are useful for helping to gain an understanding of the client's performance over the last twelve months and to identify any significant changes to the business, for example: the disposal of significant land and buildings. In addition, analytical procedures are also used to identify peculiar deviations (from either prior year figures, budget or the auditor's knowledge) that could indicate misstatement in the reported figures. These must then be investigated during final audit procedures.

For example; when conducting an analytical review of a current audit client you notice that turnover had increased by 20% in comparison to last year but delivery costs have increased by 50%. Normally you would expect costs to rise in line with changes in activity but clearly delivery costs have increased at a much higher rate. Plausible reasons for this variance include:

- Increasing sales by attracting customers from more distant geographical locations;
- Reducing delivery waiting times by making more frequent deliveries; or
- There is an error in either sales or delivery costs.

The reason for the variance will be investigated during the audit until a satisfactory explanation is obtained.

More recently, computer aided auditing techniques have been used to perform data analysis.

8 Obtaining a General Understanding of the Client

Auditors are required to obtain an understanding of: their clients; their clients' environments; and their clients' internal controls. This is often referred to as *Knowledge of the Business*, or *"KOB."* This generally includes:

- Relevant industry, regulatory and other external factors (including the financial reporting framework);
- The nature of the entity, including:
  - its operations;
  - its ownership and governance structures;
  - the types of investment it makes; and
  - the way it is structured and financed.
- The entity's selection and application of accounting policies;
- The entity's objectives, strategies and related business risks;
- The measurement and review of the entity's financial performance; and
- The internal controls relevant to the audit.

(**ISA 315** *Identifying and Assessing the Risks of Material Misstatement...*)

The purpose of acquiring this knowledge is to identify the risks that the business is exposed to and, ultimately, how could these lead to a risk of material misstatement in the financial statements.

What Tools can the Auditor Use?

Methods of risk assessment are discussed further in chapter 7. However, it is useful to know that auditors can use relatively simple and well known tools to frame their knowledge of clients, including:

- PEST analysis: this helps to assess a company's external environment by considering the significant political, economical, social and technological factors affecting it;
- Michael Porter's '5 Forces' analysis: this is another external analysis tool that considers the power of buyers, the power of suppliers, the threat of existing competitors, the threat of new entrants to the market and the threat posed by substitute products.
- SWOT analysis: this considers a business from a more internal perspective and requires the assessor to consider the businesses strengths, weaknesses, opportunities and threats.

The information used to complete these references can come from a wide range of sources, including:

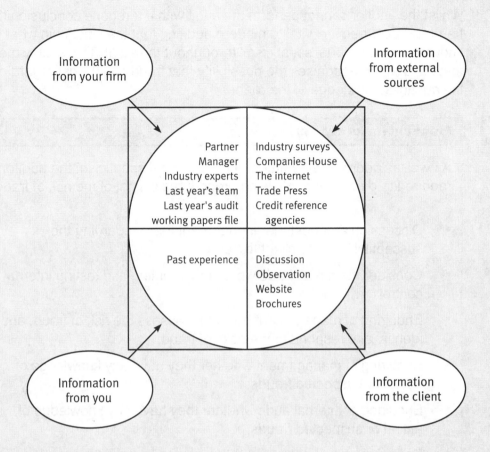

9 The impact of fraud on the audit strategy

Whilst the director's of a company are charged with safeguarding a company's assets (and are therefore responsible for the prevention and detection of fraud) the auditors also have a responsibility for detecting fraud. Namely, auditors are responsible for giving an opinion that the financial statements are free from material misstatement, whether caused by fraud or error.

Therefore when planning and performing an audit the auditor must take fraud into account. Most importantly the auditor must:

- Identify and assess the risk of material misstatement due to fraud;

- Obtain sufficient appropriate evidence in response to the assessed risk of material misstatement due to fraud; and

- Respond appropriately to fraud or suspected fraud identified during the audit.

(**ISA 240** *The Auditor's Responsibility Relating to Fraud in an Audit of Financial Statements*)

Whilst the auditor cannot perform the audit with a foregone conclusion that fraud has occurred it is vital to modern auditing that they maintain what is known as 'professional scepticism' throughout the audit. This simply means that the auditor recognises the possibility that fraud could exist regardless of the auditor's knowledge of the client.

Practical Imact of Fraud

As well as adopting an attitude of professional scepticism the auditor is required to perform the following procedures in light of the risk of fraud:

- Discussion amongst the engagement team regarding the susceptibility of the client to fraud;

- Consider the risk of fraud when documenting and testing internal controls;

- Enquiring of management how they: assess the risk of fraud; and identify and respond to the risks of fraud;

- Enquiring of management whether they have any knowledge of actual or suspected frauds;

- Enquiring of internal audit whether they have any knowledge of actual or suspected frauds;

- Enquiring of those charged with governance how they exercise oversight of management's process for identifying and responding to the risk of fraud; and

- Enquiring of those charged with governance whether they have any knowledge of actual or suspected frauds;

10 Audit Documentation

As per **ISA 230** *Audit Documentation,* auditors are required to prepare and retain written documentation that provides: a sufficient appropriate record of the basis for the audit report; and evidence that the audit was planned and performed in accordance with ISA's and other regulatory requirements.

As a general rule of thumb documentation should be sufficient to enable an experienced auditor, with no previous connection to the audit, to understand:

- The nature, timing and extent of audit procedures performed;

- The results of the procedures performed and the evidence obtained; and

- The significant matters arising during the course of the audit and the conclusions reached thereon, and significant professional judgements made in reaching those conclusions.

In so doing auditors must document: the characteristics of items/matters tested; who performed the work; the date work was completed; who reviewed the work; and the dates reviews took place.

A final requirement is that the auditor must document all discussions of significant matters with management and those charged with governance.

It is vital that documentation is retained in an audit file, which should be completed in a timely fashion after the date of the audit report (normally not more than 60 days after) and retained for the period required by national regulatory requirements. Ordinarily this is no shorter than five years from the date of the auditor's report.

Types of Audit Documentation

Audit documentation includes:

- Planning documentation:
    - Overall audit strategy;
    - Audit plan;
    - Risk analysis;
- Audit programmes;
- Issues memoranda
- Summary of significant matters;
- Letter of confirmation and representation;
- Checklists;
- Correspondence; and
- Abstracts/copies of client records.

Variations on the theme

- For large audits much of the KOB information may be kept on a permanent file and the audit plan may contain a summary or simply cross refer to the permanent file.

- Increasingly KOB is being summarised in a planning memorandum which is updated each year.

- With computerised audit systems where all background documents may be scanned in, the distinction between current and permanent audit files is being eroded.

- For large audits, the planning may be so complex that it needs to be summarised in a separate memorandum.

- For small audits the summary may be all that is necessary.

Permanent file – a file of information which is relevant for more than one year's audit, e.g.

- Names of management, those charged with governance, shareholders.

- Systems information.

- Background to the industry and the client's business.

- Title deeds.

- Directors' service agreements

- Copies of contract and agreements.

Current file – a file containing the documentation and evidence for the current audit.

Example Contents of an Audit File

Typically, there are at least three sections, as follows:

- planning;
- performance; and
- completion .

Planning

The main element of this section is likely to be the Audit Planning Memorandum.

This document is the written audit plan and will be read by all members of the audit team before work starts. Its contents are likely to include:

- background information about the client, including recent performance
- changes since last year's audit (for recurring clients)
- key accounting policies
- important laws and regulations affecting the company
- client's trial balance (or draft Financial Statements)
- preliminary analytical review
- key audit risks
- overall audit strategy
- materiality assessment
- timetable of procedures
- deadlines
- staffing and a budget (hours to be worked x charge-out rates)
- locations to be visited.

Performance

Working papers are likely to consist of:

- Lead Schedule – showing total figures, which agree to the financial statements
- Back-up schedules – breakdowns of totals into relevant sub-totals
- Audit work programme detailing:
  - the objectives being tested
  - work completed
  - how sampled items selected
  - conclusions drawn
  - who did the work
  - date work completed
  - who reviewed it

Completion

The completion (also known as review) stage of an audit has a number of standard components:

- Going concern review
- Subsequent events review
- Final analytical review

- Accounting standards (disclosure) checklist
- Letter of representation
- Summary of adjustments made since trial balance produced
- Summary of unadjusted errors
- Draft final financial statements
- Draft report to those charged with governance (management letter).

Test your understanding 1

(a) With reference to ISA 520 *Analytical Procedures* explain

    (i)   what is meant by the term 'analytical procedures';

(2 marks)

    (ii) the different types of analytical procedures available to the auditor; and

(3 marks)

    (iii) the situations in the audit when analytical procedures can be used.

(3 marks)

Tribe Co sells bathrooms from 15 retail outlets. Sales are made to individuals, with income being in the form of cash and debit cards. All items purchased are delivered to the customer using Tribe's own delivery vans; most bathrooms are too big for individual's to transport in their own motor vehicles. The directors of Tribe indicate that the company has had a difficult year, but are pleased to present some acceptable results to the members.

The income statements for the last two financial years are shown below:

Income statement

	31 March 2009	31 March 2008
	$000	$000
Revenue	11,223	9,546
Cost of sales	(5,280)	(6,380)
	5,943	3,166
Operating expenses		
Administration	(1,853)	(1,980)
Selling and distribution	(1,472)	(1,034)
Interest payable	(152)	(158)
Investment income	218	–
	2,684	(6)

Financial statement extract

Cash and bank	380	(1,425)

Required:

(b) As part of your risk assessment procedures for Tribe Co, identify and provide a possible explanation for unusual changes in the income statement.

(9 marks)

Test your understanding 2

Amongst the matters the auditor is required to consider when planning an audit (in accordance with the requirements of **ISA 300** *Planning an Audit of Financial Statements)* are those of 'materiality' and the 'direction, supervision and review' of the audit.

Required:

(a) Explain the concept of materiality and how materiality is assessed when planning the audit. Your answer should include consideration of materiality at the overall financial statement level and in relation to individual account balances.

(6 marks)

(b) Explain the nature and significance of direction, supervision and review both in planning the audit and subsequently during the performance of the audit on a particular engagement.

(6 marks)

Test your understanding 3

(1) Discuss the issues to be considered as part of the planning process for an audit.

(5 marks)

(2) List four things which need to be done during the planning process.

(2 marks)

(3) List two sources of information which enable the auditor to assess risk.

(1 mark)

(4) What is the difference between the audit strategy and the audit plan?

(1 mark)

(5) Discuss aspects of the client's business which need to be explained in the audit plan.

(1 mark)

(6) List possible sources of knowledge of the business.

(4 marks)

(7) What is the difference between materiality and tolerable misstatement?

(1 mark)

(8) List eight stages of the audit plan.

(4 marks)

(9) Why is it important for the auditor to plan?

(5 marks)

11 Chapter summary

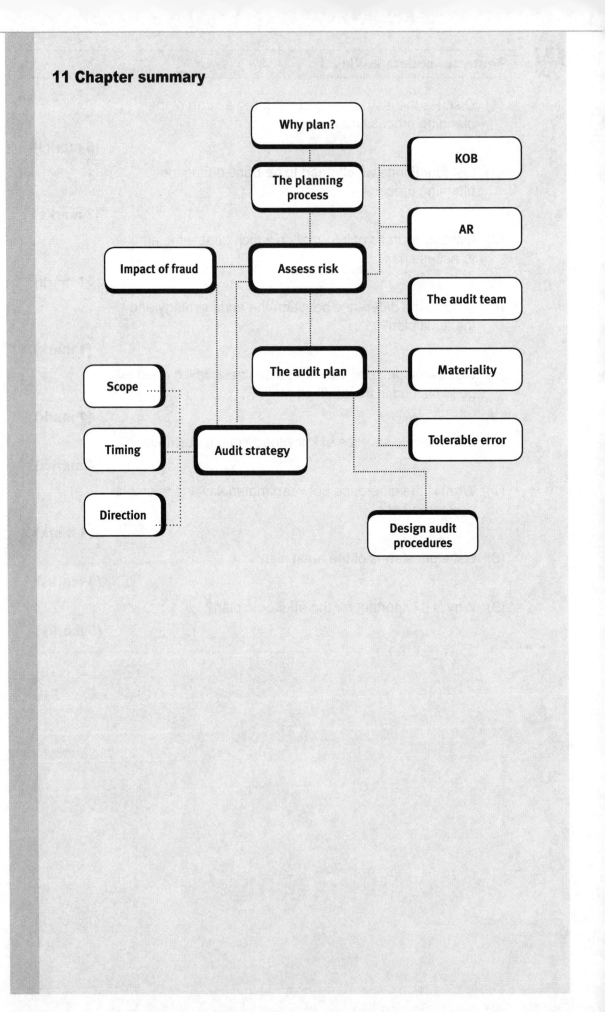

Test your understanding answers

(a) (i) Explanation of analytical procedures

Analytical procedures are used in obtaining an understanding of an entity and its environment and in the overall review at the end of the audit.   1 mark

'Analytical procedures' actually means the evaluation of financial and other information and the review of plausible relationships in that information. The review also includes identifying fluctuations and relationships that do not appear consistent with other relevant information or results.   1 mark

(ii) Types of analytical procedures

Analytical procedures can be used as:

– Comparison of comparable information to prior periods to identify unusual changes or fluctuations in amounts.   1 mark

– Comparison of actual or anticipated results of the entity with budgets and/or forecasts, or the expectations of the auditor in order to determine the potential accuracy of those results.   1 mark

– Comparison to industry information either for the industry as a whole or by comparison to entities of similar size to the client to determine whether receivable days, for example, are reasonable.   1 mark

(iii) Use of analytical procedures

Risk assessment procedures

Analytical procedures are used at the beginning of the audit to help the auditor obtain an understanding of the entity and assess the risk of material misstatement. Audit procedures can then be directed to these 'risky' areas.   1 mark

Analytical procedures are substantive procedures.

Analytical procedures can be used as substantive procedures in determining the risk of material misstatement at the assertion level during work on the income statement and statement of financial position (balance sheet). — 1 mark

Analytical procedures in the overall review at the end of the audit.

Analytical procedures help the auditor at the end of the audit in forming an overall conclusion as to whether the financial statements as a whole are consistent with the auditor's understanding of the entity. — 1 mark

(b) Net profit — ½ mark

Overall, Tribe's result has changed from a net loss to a net profit. Given that sales have only increased by 17% and that expenses, at least administration expenses, appear low, then there is the possibility that expenditure may be understated. — 1 mark

Sales – increase 17% — ½ mark

According to the directors, Tribe has had a 'difficult year'. Reasons for the increase in sales income must be ascertained as the change does not conform to the directors' comments. it is possible that the industry as a whole, has been growing allowing Tribe to produce this good result. — 1 mark

Cost of sales – fall 17% — ½ mark

A fall in cost of sales in unusual given that sales have increased significantly. This may have been caused by an incorrect inventory valuation and the use of different (cheaper) suppliers which may cause problems with faulty goods in the next year. — 1 mark

Gross profit (GP) – increase 88% — ½ mark

This is significant increase with the GP% changing from 33% last year to 53% in 2008. Identifying reasons for this change will need to focus initially on the change in sales and cost of sales. — 1 mark

Administration – fall 6%	½ mark

A fall is unusual given that sales are increasing and so an increase in administration to support those sales would be expected. Expenditure may be understated, or there has been a decrease in the number of administration staff. — 1 mark

Selling and distribution – increase 42% — ½ mark

This increase does not appear to be in line with the increase in sales – selling and distribution would be expected to increase in line with sales. There may be mis-allocation of expenses from administration or the age of Tribe's delivery vans is increasing resulting in additional service costs. — 1 mark

Interest payable – small fall — ½ mark

Given that Tribe has a considerable cash surplus this year, continuing to pay interest is surprising. The amount may be overstated – reasons for lack of fall in interest payment e.g. loans that cannot be repaid early, must be determined. — 1 mark

Investment income – new this year — ½ mark

This is expected given cash surplus on the year, although the amount is still very high indicating possible errors in the amount or other income generating assets not disclosed on the statement of financial position extract. — 1 mark

Test your understanding 2

(a) Materiality

Financial statements may be misstated due to either: fraud; error; or omission. Materiality is the measure of when those misstatements, either individually or in the aggregate, affect the decision making processes of the users of the financial statements. Therefore, if the financial statements contain material misstatement they cannot be considered to be fairly presented (or true and fair).

ISA 320 *Audit Materiality*, requires auditors to consider materiality when determining the nature, timing and extent of audit procedures.

Materiality at the overall financial statement level

There may be more than one level of materiality relating to the financial statements. For the income statement, materiality could be related to revenue or to profit (usually before tax). For the statement of financial position, materiality could be based on shareholders' equity, assets or liability class totals.

Standard benchmarks are a widely accepted basis for preliminary materiality assessments. A typical example is:

- ½ – 1% of turnover
- 5 – 10% of profit before tax
- 1 – 2% of gross assets

However, the auditor must only use this as a starting point. The final materiality assessment must be based upon professional judgement and include consideration of:

- The circumstances surrounding the entity;
- Both the size and nature of misstatements; and
- The information needs of the users as a group.

Materiality at the account balance or transaction class level

Using materiality (as calculated for the financial statements as a whole) when considering specific transactions, balances and samples is likely to be misleading. If all samples were tested and all errors assessed purely on a consideration of materiality, then many smaller misstatements, which could become material in aggregate, would be ignored. Therefore when designing procedures they auditor uses a second measure of performance materiality.

This is defined in ISA 320 as:

"The amount set by the auditor at less than materiality for the financial statements as a whole to reduce to an appropriately low level the probability that the aggregate of uncorrected and undetected misstatements exceeds materiality for the financial statements as a whole."

In using this lower threshold to perform audit procedures the auditor is more likely to identify misstatements, the effect of which can be considered in combination.

When assessing the results of testing, performed on a sample basis, the auditor must also consider if the total of errors identified (again unlikely to be material to the financial statements as a whole) could be indicative of a material misstatement in the population as a whole. To evaluate this the auditor uses a third measure known as tolerable misstatement.

Tolerable misstatement (as per ISA 530) is the maximum misstatement that can exist in a sample before the auditor considers the risk of material misstatement in the population as a whole to be significant. As long as the identified misstatements within the sample tested are less than this balance, the auditor need do no further testing.

(b) **Direction, supervision and review**

Direction

An important function in planning the audit is the generation of material necessary for the direction of staff assigned to the audit. Staff need to receive adequate guidance as to the nature of the business and, in particular as to any specific matters affecting the audit determined during the planning phase, such as recent or proposed changes in the nature of the business, its management or its financial structure. Assistants assigned to an audit must receive direction as to such matters to enable them to carry out the audit work delegated to them.

A principal purpose of planning is determining the mix of tests of controls and substantive procedures and the nature, timing and extent of those procedures. The results of the plan are documented in an audit program which specifies the individual procedures to be performed in sufficient detail relative to the experience of the staff assigned to the engagement.

Supervision

The assignment of staff to the audit as part of the planning process should ensure that they are subject to an appropriate level of supervision. The more junior or inexperienced the staff, the more supervision they will require. On small audits supervision is usually in the form of daily contact with the staff members at the client's premises by a supervisor, usually the audit manager; with regular visits to the clients' premises during the course of the audit.

On larger audits there will be a hierarchy of staff at different levels each with responsibility for supervising the work of assistants assigned to them. During the course of the audit supervisory staff should regularly monitor the work of assistants to ensure that:

- they understand the requirements of each procedure in the audit programme to which they are assigned

- they have the necessary skills and competence to perform their assigned tasks

- the work performed is in accordance with the requirements of the audit programme.

In addition, supervision should ensure that any important matters discovered during the audit are promptly dealt with and the audit programme modified as necessary. The supervisor should also monitor the time spent on each phase of the audit against time budgeted during the planning phase. Significant variances could indicate problems in the performance of the audit.

Review

Supervision also involves review of the work performed. All work must be reviewed to ensure that:

- the work has been performed in accordance with the programme

- the evidence has been properly documented

- all outstanding matters have been satisfactorily resolved

- conclusions drawn are consistent with the evidence and support the audit opinion.

In addition to the review of evidence obtained in accordance with the audit programme, there needs to be a review at a higher level of more significant audit decisions made. These include a review of:

- the audit plan and audit programme

- the assessment of inherent and control risk and the proposed audit strategy

- reviews of the working papers undertaken by staff at an appropriate level of responsibility

- the proposed audit opinion based on the overall results of the audit process.

On smaller engagements this review may be undertaken by the manager; with oversight by the engagement partner that the review has been properly conducted. On larger audits the final review will be carried out by the partner. On certain audits it is considered desirable for a second partner, not otherwise involved in the audit, to perform an additional review before issuing the auditors' report. This is sometimes referred to as a hot review.

Test your understanding 3

1.	**People** – Who should make up the audit team?	1 mark
	Timing – What are the deadlines?	1 mark
	Focus – What are the key aspects of the audit?	1 mark
	Problem areas – What issues are likely to cause difficulties and how should they be addressed?	1 mark
		1 mark
	Nature of work – What audit approach should be used and what types of procedures are appropriate?	1 mark
	Amount of work – Sample sizes, number of tests etc. all driven by assessment of risk and materiality.	
2.	Assess risk.	½ mark
	Develop the audit strategy.	½ mark
	Select the audit team.	½ mark
	Assess materiality.	½ mark
	Select appropriate audit procedures.	½ mark
3.	Knowledge of the business.	½ mark
	Analytical review.	½ mark
4.	Whilst the strategy sets the overall approach to the audit, the plan fills in the operational details of how the strategy is to be achieved.	1 mark

KAPLAN PUBLISHING

5.	Choose from:	
	• The industry • The competition • Technology • Laws and regulations • Stakeholders • Acquisitions • Disposals • Financing • Trading partners • Related parties • What the client does • Management • Systems • Controls • Significant risks • Accounting policies.	1 mark per point
6.	Choose from:	
	• The engagement partner • The engagement manager • Your firm's industry experts • Last year's audit team • Industry surveys • The company's registry • The internet • Trade press • Credit reference agencies . • Discussions with client's staff • Observation of events and processes at the client's premises • The client's website • Brochures and other publicity material.	½ mark per point

7.	**Materiality** concerns the financial statements as a whole.	
	Tolerable error only concerns the population being tested.	1 mark
8.	Knowledge of the business.	½ mark
	Preliminary analytical review.	½ mark
	Risk assessment.	½ mark
	Materiality.	½ mark
	Tolerable error.	½ mark
	Audit approach.	½ mark
	Independence.	½ mark
	Budget and staffing.	½ mark
	Timetable and deadlines.	½ mark
9.	To decide on the audit approach.	1 mark
	To decide how much work to do.	1 mark
	To decide what type of work to do.	1 mark
	To decide on the composition of the audit team.	1 mark
	To ensure that risk is reduced to an acceptable level.	
		1 mark

Risk

Chapter learning objectives

Upon completion of this chapter you will be able to:

- identify and describe the need to plan and perform audits with an attitude of professional scepticism

- compare and contrast risk-based, procedural and other approaches to audit work

- discuss the importance of risk analysis

- describe the use of information technology in risk analysis

- identify and describe engagement risks affecting the audit of an entity

- explain the components of audit risk.

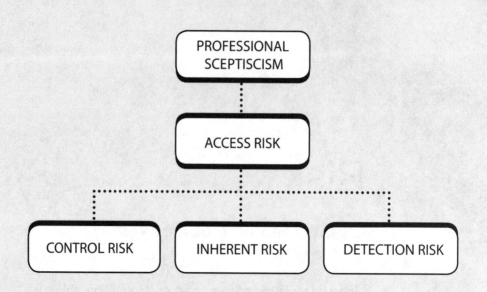

1 Risk-based and procedural approaches to auditing

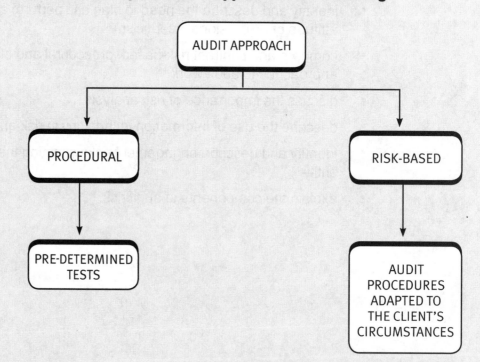

When doing an audit, auditors can take one of two basic approaches:

- procedural
- risk-based.

Procedural

The auditor carries out a set of standard procedures and tests regardless of the particular nature of the client.

KAPLAN PUBLISHING

Illustration – Risk-based and procedural approaches

Possible examples are:

- the auditors execute pre-defined procedures to determine how shared costs should be determined and allocated between the owners of apartments in an apartment block

- procedures determined by legislation or regulation – e.g. in the UK auditors have to perform certain procedures to ensure that lawyers are dealing with client's money in accordance with the rules.

Risk-based

The auditor plans the audit around the risks that the client's financial statements may contain material misstatements, whether as a result of fraud or error. As such, each audit will involve different priorities, different tests, and will take different lengths of time.

Traditionally, auditors have followed a risk-based approach, as this should minimise the chance of them giving the wrong opinion. It also helps to ensure that audit work is carried out as efficiently as possible, as assurance is obtained using the most effective tests.

2 Risk assessment as part of the audit process

Auditors are required to perform audits with an attitude of 'professional scepticism' This is defined as:

"An attitude that includes a questioning mind, being alert to conditions which may indicate possible misstatement due to fraud or error, and a critical assessment of audit evidence." (**ISA 200** *Overall Objectives of the Independent Auditor and the Conduct of an Audit in Accordance with International Standards of Auditing*).

Having an enquiring mind in itself is not sufficient to comply with a risk based method of auditing. In order to fulfil this responsibility auditors must also use professional judgement. This means the application of relevant training, knowledge and experience in making informed decisions about the courses of action that are appropriate to the unique circumstances of the audit engagement.

Therefore the use of a risk based approach requires skill, knowledge, experience and an inquisitive, open mind; something that is neither gained quickly nor easily.

Expandable Text

Although approaches other than this risk-based approach to auditing are possible, since the introduction of ISAs and ISA 315 in particular, its use is compulsory for statutory audits.

We will see how audit risk breaks down into its three components:

- inherent risk
- control risk
- detection risk.

3 The importance of risk analysis

Risk analysis is an important stage of the audit. In conducting a thorough assessment of risk auditors will be able to:

- Identify areas of the financial statements where misstatements are likely to occur early in the audit;
- Plan procedures that address the significant risk areas identified;
- Carry out an efficient, focussed and effective audit;
- Minimise the risk of issuing an inappropriate audit opinion to an acceptable level;
- Reduce the risk of reputational and punitive damage;

Although risk assessment is a fundamental element of the planning process, it is important to understand that risks can be uncovered at any stage of the audit and that procedures must be adapted in light of revelations that indicate further risks of material misstatement. It is, ultimately, the responsibility of the most senior reviewer (usually the engagement partner) to confirm that the risk of material misstatement has been reduced to an acceptable level.

Expandable Text - The role of information technology

The role of information technology (IT)

IT can play an important part in risk analysis because it enables auditors to carry out analytical procedures (see the sessions on audit procedures) in a cost effective way to highlight:

- unusual relationships
- unusual trends

in the components of financial statements.

The use of IT also enables the auditor to process high volumes of data through computer-assisted audit techniques (CAATS), to screen for unusual relationships or unexpected repetition of data in a way which would be impossible without such technology. See chapter 10 Audit procedures for more on CAATS.

The impact of ISA 315

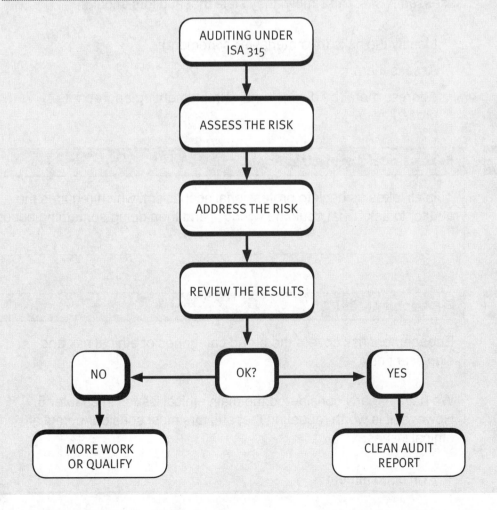

Audits conducted under ISAs **must** follow the risk-based approach

It is difficult to overstate how important this is. It affects:

- how audits are planned
- the nature of audit evidence gathered by the auditor
- the nature of the procedures carried out by the auditor
- the amount of evidence gathered.

We consider all of these aspects in the chapters on planning, systems and controls, audit evidence and audit procedures.

Exam hint

It is also important for your approach to exam questions. Where there is a scenario given, you **must adapt** your answer to the facts of the scenario, the nature of the business, systems in operation, etc.

The major drivers behind this approach are **ISA 315** *Identifying and Assessing the Risks of Material Misstatement Through Understanding the Entity and its Environment* and **ISA 330** *The Auditor's Response to Assessed Risks.* Put simply, they state that auditors should:

- Identify the risks (of material misstatement);
- Assess them;
- Address them (by designing and implementing appropriate procedures).

Professional Scepticism Again!

This all takes us back to professional scepticism, which requires the auditor to ask "what could go wrong?" and then doing something about it.

Engagement Risk

Engagement risk covers the broad categories of ethical risk and significant risk.

We have already considered the main ethical issues in chapter 5. However it is worth repeating that auditors must consider potential ethical issues:

- on appointment

- when planning the engagement
- when completing the engagement
- when accepting engagements to provide non-audit services.

It is vital that the auditor identifies any potential threat to independence and that they establish appropriate safeguards against these threats (including resignation from/refusal of the engagement).

ISA 315 simply defines significant risk as:

'An identified and assessed risk of material misstatement that, in the auditor's judgement, requires special audit consideration.'

Examples of Engagement Risks

These could include such things as:

- going concern problems
- imminent takeovers
- key staff leaving
- impact of laws and regulations
- limited availability of audit staff
- inexperienced audit staff
- tight deadlines.

4 Audit risk

Audit risk defined

Audit risk is the risk of that the auditor expresses an **inappropriate audit opinion**, i.e. that they give an unmodified audit opinion when the financial statements contain a material misstatement.

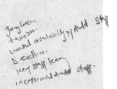

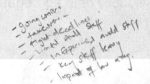

It can be further defined by way of the following formula:

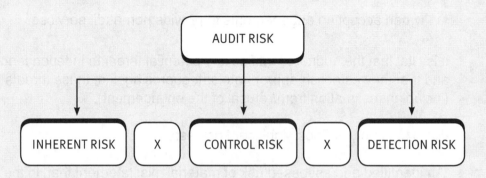

Inherent risk

This is the susceptibility of a class of transaction, account balance or disclosure to a misstatement that could be material, either individually or in aggregate, before consideration of related controls. In other words this is the risk that a misstatement occurs in the first instance.

Inherent risk is often considered in relation to business risk. These are the risks resulting from conditions, events, circumstances, actions or inactions that could adversely affect an entity's ability to achieve its business objectives and goals. Ultimately these business risks can lead to complications and deficiencies in the accounting process, which could lead to fraud, error or omission.

Clearly this requires the audit team to have a good knowledge of how the client's activities are likely to affect its financial statements, and the audit team should discuss these matters in a **planning meeting** before deciding on the detailed approach and audit work to be used. This was discussed further in chapter 6.

Control risk

Control risk is that a misstatement will not be prevented, or detected and corrected on a timely basis by the entity's internal controls. This is either due to the internal control system being insufficient in the circumstances of the business or because the controls have not been applied effectively during the period.

We will consider internal control in depth in chapter 8.

Detection risk

This is the risk that the procedures performed by the auditor to reduce audit risk to an acceptable level will not detect potentially material misstatements, either individually or in aggregate.

Sampling risk

Detection risk includes sampling risk, which is defined as the risk that the auditor's conclusions based on a sample may be different from the conclusion if the entire population were subjected to the same audit procedure (**ISA 530**).

In other words it is the risk that the sample may not be representative.

The risk that the auditor may come to the wrong conclusion for any reason not related to sampling risk is called non-sampling risk. Examples include:

- misinterpreting the results of a test
- using inappropriate procedures
- failing to investigate a particular balance or transaction
- because a member of the client's staff misleads the auditor

5 Assessing the risk

The audit risk model requires the auditor to assess the risks of material misstatement arising from inherent and control risk. These are entirely outside of the control of the auditor and cannot be altered (at least in the short term).

The only tool at the auditor's disposal is the design of the nature, extent and timing of audit procedures. Through manipulation of these the auditor can either increase or decrease their detection risk.

If the auditor concludes that there is a high risk of material misstatement in, say, inventory they can increase the quantity of detailed procedures they perform in this area (and perhaps assign testing to an experienced member of the team) and hence reduce the risk that they fail to detect material misstatement.

Conversely, if the auditor considers that there is a low risk of material misstatement in a balance, cash for example, they can reduce the quantity of detailed procedures in this area and perhaps assign testing to a less experienced member of staff.

It is through manipulation of detection risk that the auditor focuses on those significant risks, streamlining the audit and ensuring that it is efficient and effective.

Example Risks

Factor/Identify	Audit risk	Work we need to perform/effect on the audit	Type of risk
Lack of physical controls, e.g. • physical security of assets • restriction of access • no CCTV	Increased risk of theft and damage of assets. Incorrect valuation of assets in statement of financial position.	Physical checks of the assets required to determine completeness and value. Analytical review to see any unusual trends over excess ordering etc.....	Control risk
Lack of IT based controls • lack of password protection.	Computer systems and financial information could be changed or modified without suitable authorisation.	Analytical procedures to be performed to see if any unusual trends are happening. Ascertain and test the systems to see if changes will go undetected.	Control risk

Factor/Identify	Audit risk	Work we need to perform/effect on the audit	Type of risk
Lack of authorisation controls.	Unnecessary expenditure incurred or even non business expenditure. Sales completed on credit to high risk customers. New staff employed without authorisation that may not be necessary.	Ascertain and test the systems to determine the likelihood of this happening. Review the old balances and credit limited and see what other controls the company have in place. Review the organisation chart for reasonableness and understand the roles within the company.	Control risk
Lack of segregation of duties.	Not identifying errors and fraud as only one person doing the job therefore concealment easier to perform.	Increase the substantive testing to ensure that the statements are true and fair.	Control risk
Account balances for complex, judgemental areas of accounting, e.g. provisions.	Due to the natures of these transactions a high degree of judgement or estimation is involved and is therefore open to manipulation or error.	Detailed substantive procedures required, including recalculations, inspections of supporting documents and obtaining written representations from management.	Inherent risk
Client operates in a high tech or fast moving industry	Inventory may become obsolete Obsolete inventory may be overstated in the financial statements	Review events after the reporting period to determine the net realisable value of inventory Use an independent valuer to value inventory	Inherent risk

Factor/Identify	Audit risk	Work we need to perform/effect on the audit	Type of risk
Client is based in multiple locations	Inventory held at other locations may be omitted from year-end inventory Controls may be less effective	Attend inventory takes at all locations Review control procedures to ensure they are adequate Consider using a substantive approach	Control risk + Detection risk
Bank is relying on the financial statements or Directors are paid a bonus based on profits	Risk of management bias	Pay more attention • accounting estimates • cut-off Obtain independent estimates re valuation of year-end inventory etc	Inherent risk
It is cash-based business	Cash may be misappropriated, causing turnover to be understated	Consider the adequacy of internal controls over sales (possible limitation in scope if we cannot verify the completeness of sales and internal controls are inadequate)	Inherent risk + Potentially control risk
The company trades overseas	Transactions in foreign currency may not be translated at the correct rate The company may make foreign exchange losses	Ensure foreign currency is correctly accounted for Review procedures to mitigate exchange loss risk, e.g. hedging	Inherent risk

Factor/Identify	Audit risk	Work we need to perform/effect on the audit	Type of risk
New computer systems	Errors in transferring the data from one system to another There may be inherent errors in the new system that have not yet been discovered	Review controls over the changeover: • parallel run • check opening balances transferred properly Use test data on the system to ensure it operates correctly	Control risk + Inherent
New audit client	Lack of cumulative audit knowledge and experience may lead to increased detection risk	Use an audit team that is experienced in the industry Gather knowledge of the company Check opening balances are correct	Detection risk
Tight audit deadline imposed by client	Staff working quickly to a tight deadline are more likely to make errors There is a shorter post statement of financial position period that we can use to help with our audit	Increase substantive testing Perform an interim visit to complete some audit work before the end of the year Agree a timetable re: • reporting deadline • client schedules to be available	Detection risk
Temporary staff used during the year	Errors more likely as staff are not familiar with the client's systems	Increase substantive testing	Control risk

A client in a specialised industry	Errors more likely or fraud more likely to be missed because of the complexity of the work	Ensure that the auditors understand the system, increase testing	Inherent risk

FIXED TEST 2

(a) Explain the term 'audit risk'.

(4 marks)

(b) You are the audit manager for Parker, a limited liability company which sells books, CDs, DVDs and similar items via two divisions: mail order and on-line ordering on the Internet. Parker is a new audit client. You are commencing the planning of the audit for the year-ended 31 May 20X5. An initial meeting with the directors has provided the information below.

The company's sales revenue is in excess of $85 million with net profits of $4 million. All profits are currently earned in the mail order division, although the Internet division is expected to return a small net profit next year. Sales revenue is growing at the rate of 20% p.a. net profit has remained almost the same for the last four years.

In the next year, the directors plan to expand the range of goods sold through the Internet division to include toys, garden furniture and fashion clothes. The directors believe that when one product has been sold on the Internet, then any other product can be as well.

The accounting system to record sales by the mail order division is relatively old. It relies on extensive manual input to transfer orders received in the post onto Parker's computer systems. Recently errors have been known to occur, in the input of orders, and in the invoicing of goods following despatch. The directors maintain that the accounting system produces materially correct figures and they cannot waste time in identifying relatively minor errors. The company accountant, who is not qualified and was appointed because he is a personal friend of the directors, agrees with this view.

The directors estimate that their expansion plans will require a bank loan of approximately $30 million, partly to finance the enhanced web site but also to provide working capital to increase inventory levels. A meeting with the bank has been scheduled for three months after the year end. The directors expect an unmodified auditor's report to be signed prior to this time.

Required:

Identify and describe the matters that give rise to audit risks associated with Parker.

(10 marks)

6 Chapter summary

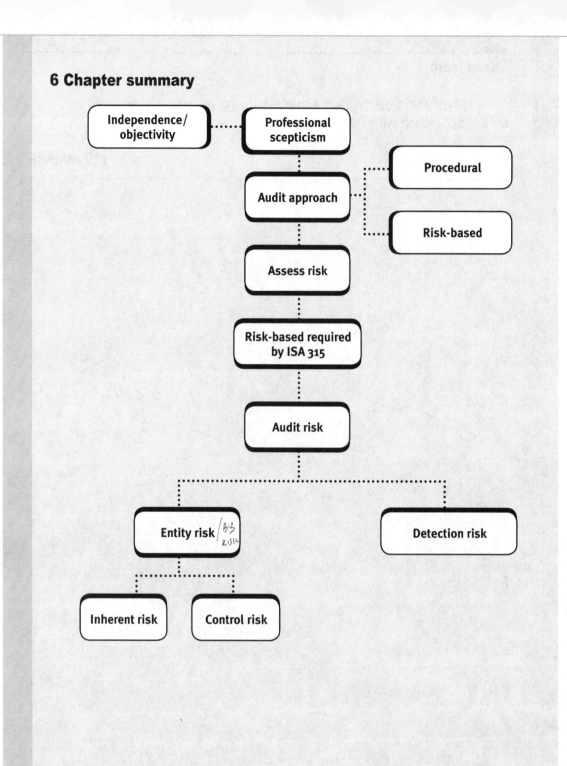

Test your understanding answers

FIXED TEST 2

THIS IS A FIXED TEST – Please answer the question in full (long form written). Then log on to en-gage at the following address: <u>www.en-gage.co.uk</u>. Follow the link to 'Fixed Test 2' and answer the questions based on your homework answer.

Once you have answered the questions on en-gage a model answer will be available for your reference.

Systems and controls

Chapter learning objectives

Upon completion of this chapter you will be able to:

- explain why an auditor needs to obtain an understanding of internal control activities

- describe and explain the key components of an internal control system

- discuss the difference between tests of control and substantive procedures

- identify and describe the important elements of internal controls

- explain how auditors identify weaknesses in internal control systems

- provide examples of application and general IT controls

- analyse the limitations of internal control components in the context of fraud and error

- identify and explain management's risk assessment process

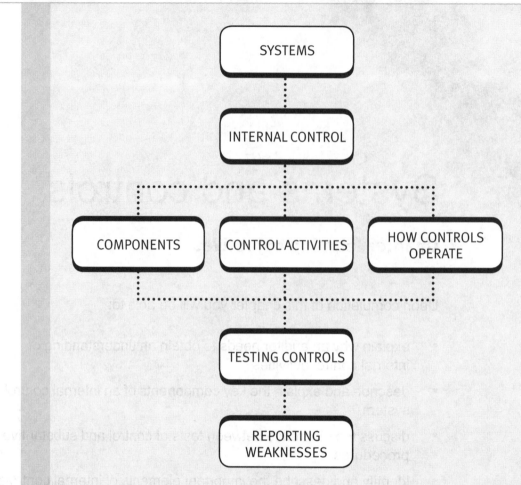

1 The importance of internal control systems

Audit risk = inherent risk x **control risk** x detection risk!!

In order to design further audit procedures auditors need to be able to assess the risk of material misstatement in the financial statements. They then focus their remaining efforts on those significant risk areas.

Internal controls are a vital component of this risk model because they are the mechanisms that clients design in an attempt to prevent, detect and correct misstatement. This is not only necessary for good financial reporting it is necessary to safeguard the assets of the shareholders and is a requirement of corporate governance.

The fundamental principle is: the stronger the control system the lower the risk of material misstatement in the financial statements.

Therefore auditors can seek to place some reliance on internal control systems and, as a result, reduce the substantive testing performed. In order to be able to do this they need to:

- Ascertain how the system operates;
- Document the system in audit working papers;
- Test the operation of the system;
- Assess the effectiveness of the control system; and
- Determine the impact on the audit approach for specific classes of transactions, account balances and disclosures.

This chapter considers the basic components of control systems and how the auditor fulfils their objectives for assessing control risk.

Control systems - basic principles

The auditor's main focus is on those systems relevant to the financial statements and, therefore, the audit. The basic objectives of these systems are to:

- measure the effects of transactions and other relevant issues;
- record those transactions and effects;
- summarise them into a useable form; and
- publish those summaries to the relevant users of the information to assist decision making.

This can be illustrated as follows:

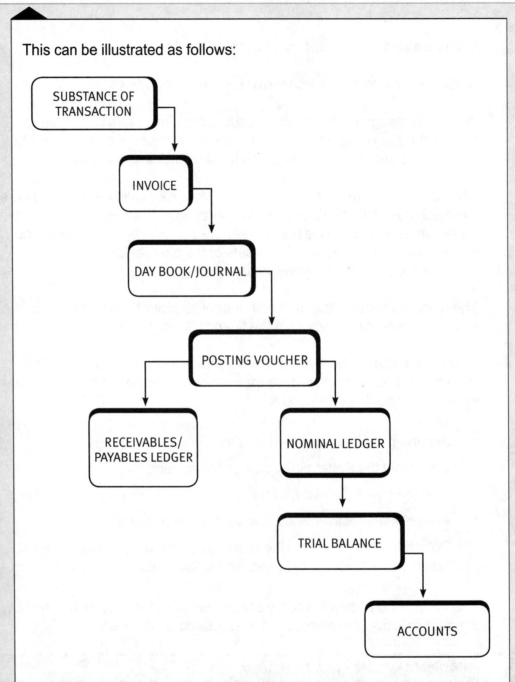

It should be noted that the above illustration represents a typical manual accounting system. These are rare nowadays due to the use of readily available (and cheap) accounting software. However, the basic principles of those systems are still the same and it is worth understanding how the flow of information in a system works.

Computerised systems

There are a number of things to understand about the impact of computerised accounting systems:

- The need to transfer information from one piece of paper to another is greatly reduced.

- The outputs from the system – the listings, trial balances, even the financial statements themselves – usually do not form part of a strict chronological sequence. So once an invoice is entered into the system, the TB, the ledger, the financial statements are all updated. There is no delay waiting for the purchase ledger clerk to 'do the postings'.

- Once a transaction is entered into the system it **will** be processed.

- Calculations **will** be accurate (unless someone has programmed them otherwise).

2 How do internal control systems operate?

The components of an internal control system

ISA 315 states that auditors need to understand an entity's internal controls. To assist this process it identifies **five** components of an internal control system:

- the control environment;
- the entity's risk assessment process;
- the information system;
- the control activities; and
- the monitoring of controls.

i. The control environment

The control environment includes the governance and management function of an organisation. It focuses largely on the attitude, awareness and actions of those responsible for designing, implementing and monitoring internal controls. Elements of the control environment that are relevant when the auditor obtains an understanding include the following:

- communication and enforcement of integrity and ethical values;
- commitment to competence;
- participation by those charged with governance;
- management's philosophy and operating style;
- organisational structure;
- assignment of authority and responsibility; and
- human resource policies and practices.

Evidence regarding the control environment is usually obtained through a mixture of enquiry and observation, although inspection of key internal documents (e.g. codes of conduct and organisation charts) is possible.

ii. The risk assessment process

The forms the basis for how management determines the risks to be managed. These processes will vary hugely depending upon the nature, size and complexity of the organisation. However, larger organisations (usually listed ones) will have internal audit departments, whose roles focus heavily on risk identification and assessment.

If the client has robust procedures for assessing the business risks it faces, the risk of misstatement, overall, will be lower.

iii. The information system

The information systems relevant to financial reporting objectives include all the procedures and records which are designed to:

- Initiate, record, process and report transactions;
- Maintain accountability for assets, liabilities and equity;
- Resolve incorrect processing of transactions;
- Process and account for system overrides;
- Transfer information to the general/nominal ledger;
- Capture information relevant to financial reporting for other events and conditions; and
- Ensure information required to be disclosed is appropriately reported.

iv. Control Activities

The control activities include all policies and procedures designed to ensure that management directives are carried out throughout the organisation. Examples of specific control activities include those relating to:

- Authorisation;
- Performance review;
- Information processing;
- Physical controls; and
- Segregation of duties.

IT affects the way in which control activities are implemented. It is important that auditors assess how controls over IT maintain the integrity and security of information held on them. Such controls are normally divided into two categories:

- Application; and
- General.

Application controls

Application controls are either manual or automated and typically operate at the business process level and apply to the processing of transactions. Examples include:

- batch total checks;
- sequence checks;
- matching master files to transaction records;
- arithmetic checks;
- range checks (to ensure that data stays within reasonable ranges);
- existence checks (e.g. to check employees exist);
- authorisation of transaction entries
- exception reporting

An example is that Quickbooks, a small business accounting package, will not let you enter a sale until you have set up an 'item', which means you have to allocate the sale to a revenue account, set up the customer as a receivable, decide on VAT treatment, etc.

General controls

General IT controls are policies and procedures that relate to many applications and support the effective functioning of application controls by helping to ensure the continued proper operation of information systems, e.g. controls over:

- data centre and network operations
- system software acquisition
- program change and maintenance
- access security – passwords, door locks, swipe cards
- backup procedures.

A healthy IT system should include both application and general control procedures.

Control Examples

One way to try and remember the typical controls that a business operates is by using the mnemonic ACCAMAPS:

A uthorisation – e.g. of expense claims, of purchases, of cash transfers.

C omputer controls – e.g. passwords, backups, virus checks, maintenance.

C omparison – e.g. comparing budget versus actual and reviewing for variances.

A rithmetic controls – e.g. recalculating hours worked on time sheets.

M aintain and review control accounts – e.g. sales/purchase ledger control account, bank.

A ccount reconciliations – e.g. bank reconciliation, sales/purchase ledger reconciliation

P hysical controls – e.g. locking mechanisms, CCTV, safes.

S egregation of duties – e.g. purchase ledger clerk does not process payments to suppliers (to reduce risk of false supplier fraud).

Expandable text - A changing world

Rapid developments in IT have implications for systems and controls. Examples of such issues include:

- Transactions automatically triggered by predetermined system criteria, e.g. stock purchases, automated utility billing;

- High volume transactions enabled through the use of barcodes and scanning, e.g. supermarkets;

- On-line purchasing

- On-line account management

- Automated goods delivery, e.g. Amazon

- Automated cash collection, e.g. Amazon

- On-line/virtual products, e.g. on-line gambling.

All of these modern business practices require systems that operate effectively and use the most up to date information available. Without excellence in IT systems and controls these businesses would simply not be possible.

v. Monitoring of controls

This is the process of assessing the effectiveness of controls over time and taking necessary remedial action. Clearly if a control is not implemented properly or is simply considered ineffective then misstatements may pass undetected into the financial statements.

Monitoring can either be ongoing or performed on a separate evaluation basis. Either way, it needs to be effective for the system to work. Monitoring of internal controls is often the key role of internal auditors.

3 Ascertaining the systems

Procedures used to obtain evidence regarding the design and implementation of controls include:

- enquiries of relevant personnel;
- observing the application of controls;
- tracing transactions through systems; and
- inspecting documents, such as internal procedure manuals.

In addition to this, auditor's can also use their prior knowledge of the client and the operation of the systems in prior years. However, it must be noted, that auditors cannot simply rely on their systems knowledge from the prior year's audit; much can happen in a year and systems knowledge must be updated and the systems tested once more.

It should also be noted that ISA 315 specifies that enquiry, alone, is not sufficient to understand the nature and extent of controls.

4 Documenting the systems

Possible ways of documenting systems include:

- narrative notes (which can prove bulky if systems are large or complex)
- flowcharts (which can make a complex system easier to follow)
- organisation charts – showing roles, responsibilities, and reporting lines
- Internal Control Questionnaire (**ICQ**)
- Internal Control Evaluation Questionnaire (**ICE**).

ISA 315 states that the method adopted is a matter of auditor judgement.

ICQs

An **ICQ** is a list of possible controls for each area of the Financial Statements. The client is asked to review the list and confirm which are applicable to their system.

ICEs

In contrast to ICQ's an **ICE** lists for control objective. Client's are then asked to confirm how they meet that objective.

For example; an ICQ might ask a client: "does a supervisor authorise all weekly timesheets?" An ICE would ask "how does the company ensure that only hours worked are recorded on timesheets?"

5 Testing the system

Tests of control vs substantive procedures

Having documented the systems the auditor needs to assess whether:

- they are actually implemented; and
- they are effective.

In order to assess the operating effectiveness of controls in preventing and detecting material misstatement the auditor performs tests of controls. These are designed to gather evidence concerning:

- how controls were applied during the period;
- the consistency of application; and
- who (or what) they were applied by.

Typical methods of controls testing include:

- walkthrough tests, where a transaction is followed through the system;
- observation of control activities, e.g. the inventory count; and
- computer aided audit techniques (see chapter 10 for more detail).

Substantive procedures, on the other hand, are those procedures designed to detect material misstatement. They include both tests of detail and analytical procedures. These will be covered in more detail in chapter 9.

6 The impact on the audit approach

The principle is simple: the auditor amends the audit approach in response to risk assessment. They can achieve this by:

- emphasising the need for professional scepticism;
- assigning more experienced staff to risk areas;
- increasing supervision levels;

- increasing the element of unpredictability in sample selection;
- changing the nature, timing and extent of procedures.
- increasing the emphasis on substantive tests of detail.

If the risk assessment indicates significant risk of material misstatement due to deficiencies in internal controls the auditor should respond by:

- increasing procedures conducted at and after the year-end;
- increasing substantive procedures; and
- increasing the locations included in the audit scope.

An effective control environment may allow the auditor to place more reliance on internal controls and evidence generated internally within the entity. Typically this increases the appropriateness of interim testing and allows the auditor to reduce the quantity of detailed substantive procedures performed. Whilst this is true to a certain extent the auditor can never eliminate the need for substantive procedures entirely because there are inherent limitations to the reliance that can be placed on internal control due to:

- human error in the use of judgement;
- simple processing errors and mistakes;
- collusion of staff in circumventing controls; and
- the abuse of power by those will ultimate controlling responsibility.

Expandable Text - Problems with fraud

Fraud is specifically designed to mislead people. Consider the following example:

- A company only deals with suppliers on a list authorised by the Finance Director (FD).
- Payments to suppliers are made after the purchases clerk identifies the monthly payments to be made and prepares the cheques.
- The cheques are signed by the FD, who confirms the amounts paid and supplier names to supporting documentation; and
- The cheques are countersigned by the Managing Director, who does not check the details but has a good knowledge of who the suppliers are.

This appears like a sensible combination of authorisation controls and segregation of duties.

> However, now consider the implication if one of the suppliers is actually controlled by the FD. The supplier regularly overcharges and the purchases clerk is being bribed by the FD in return for her silence.
>
> Of course, this is a potentially criminal scheme, but that is what a fraud is. The auditor, unfortunately, would place reliance on the control system and reduce substantive testing of purchases. It is for this reason that the auditor must always perform some substantive procedures and must always maintain an attitude of professional scepticism.

7 The sales cycle

Objectives

The objectives of controls in the revenue cycle are to <u>ensure</u> that:

- sales are made to valid customers
- sales are recorded accurately
- all sales are recorded
- cash is collected within a reasonable period.

This is a summary of the sales cycle, showing the possible problems and the related controls:

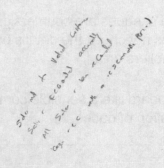

Stage	Risks	Control Objective	Control procedures
Order received	Orders not recorded accurately. Orders taken from high credit risk customers Orders cannot be honoured	To ensure that: • the order is recorded accurately • the customer is creditworthy • the order does not take customer over credit limit • the customer's order can be fulfilled	Confirm order in writing All new customers subject to credit check Credit limits imposed on customers Orders approved by sales and production managers.
Goods despatched	Goods not despatched Incorrect goods sent	To ensure that: • all orders are sent to warehouse • the right goods are in inventory • the goods are sent to the right customer	Sequentially numbered customer order pads. Copy of order sent to the warehouse for filing. Weekly order check to ensure sequence is complete (i.e. none missing) Order signed by inventory picker. Goods despatch note (GDN) matched to order (staple together and file) Customer signs a copy of the GDN and returns it to confirm receipt of goods. Use sequentially numbered GDNs and review frequently for incomplete sequence and unmatched items.

Stage	Risks	Control Objective	Control procedures
Invoice raised	Invoices may be missed, incorrectly raised or sent to the wrong customer	To ensure that: • invoices are raised for despatches	Copy of GDN sent to accounts and matched to copy of the invoice. Unmatched GDNs to be periodically reviewd.
	Credit notes may be raised incorrectly	• the invoice is raised for the correct amount	Copy invoice signed as agreed to original order, GDN, and customer price list
		• credit notes are raised accurately and are valid	Credit notes to be allocated to invoice it relates and authorised by manager.
Sale recorded	Invoiced may be inaccurately recorded, missed or recorded for the wrong customer	To ensure that: • all sales are recorded	Review receivables ledger for credit balances
			Receivables ledger reconciliation
		• the sale is recorded at the correct amount	Double check back to invoice
		• the sale is recorded in the right debtor's ledger	Customer statements sent out (customers let you know if error)
Cash received	Incorrect amounts received	To ensure that: • the customer pays the correct amount	Agree cash receipt back to the invoice
	Customer does not pay		Review receivables ledger for credit balances (customer overpaid)
		• the customer pays	Review aged debt listing and investigate old balances
			Debt chasing procedures/credit control

Stage	Risks	Control Objective	Control procedures
Cash recorded	Cash incorrectly recorded or recorded against the wrong account Cash stolen	To ensure that: • all cash receipts are recorded • cash is recorded at the correct amount • cash is recorded in the right debtor ledger • all money received is banked promptly	Monthly customer statements sent out Bank reconciliation Regular banking/physical security over cash (i.e. a safe) Reconciliation of banking to cash receipts records Segregation of duties

Sales controls tests

Tests of control should be designed to check that the control procedures are being applied and that objectives are being achieved. Example procedures include:

- Sequence checks on invoices, credit notes, despatch notes and orders. Ensure that all items are included and that there are no omissions or duplications.

- Review the existence of evidence for authorisation in respect of:
    - Orders - authorised by sales/production manager.
    - GDN's - signed by the foreman to confirm despatch of goods listed.
    - Credit notes signed by manager.

- Ensure invoices are signed to confirm that amounts have been posted and received in cash. This is often done by means of a "grid stamp" containing several signatures on the face of the document.

- Observe that control account reconciliations have been performed and reviewed.

Test your understanding 1

Rhapsody Co supplies a wide range of garden and agricultural products to trade and domestic customers. The company has 11 divisions, with each division specialising in the sale of specific products, for example, seeds, garden furniture, agricultural fertilizers. The company has an internal audit department which provides audit reports to the audit committee on each division on a rotational basis.

Products in the seed division are offered for sale to domestic customers via an Internet site. Customers review the product list on the Internet and place orders for packets of seeds using specific product codes, along with their credit card details, onto Rhapsody Co's secure server. Order quantities are normally between one and three packets for each type of seed. Order details are transferred manually onto the company's internal inventory control and sales system and a two part packing list is printed in the seed warehouse. Each order and packing list is given in a random alphabetical code based on the name of the employee inputting the order, the date and the products being ordered.

In the seed warehouse, the packets of seeds for each order are taken from specific bins and despatched to the customer with one copy of the packing list. The second copy of the packing list is sent to the accounts department where the inventory and sales computer is updated to show that the order has been despatched. The customer's credit card is then charged by the inventory control and sales computer. Bad debts in Rhapsody are currently 3% of the total sales.

Finally, the computer system checks that for each charge made to a customer's credit card account, the order details are on file to prove that the charge was made correctly. The order file is marked as completed confirming that the order has been despatched and payment obtained.

Required:

In respect of sales in the seeds division of Rhapsody Co:

(i)   identify and explain FOUR deficiencies in the sales system;

(ii) explain the possible effect of each deficiency; and

(iii) provide a recommendation to alleviate each deficiency.

(14 marks)

8 The purchases cycle

This is a summary of the purchases cycle, showing the possible problems and the related controls.

Stage	Risks	Control objective	Control procedures
Requisition raised	Unauthorised purchases made	To ensure that: • requisition is for a valid business reason • it is cost effective • items are actually needed	All requisitions authorised by manager Central purchasing dept Preferred suppliers/agreed price lists Check inventory levels first
Order placed	Invalid or incorrect orders made or recorded The most favourable terms not obtained	To ensure that: • order is raised for all requisitions • orders are accurately recorded by supplier • items are correctly costed	Sequentially numbered requisition pads, copies filed numerically with copy of order stapled to it. Periodically check that all are there Request order confirmation in writing Check quoted price against supplier price list
Goods received	Goods stolen Goods may be accepted that have not been ordered or are of wrong quantity or inferior quality	To ensure that: • goods received for all orders • goods received are as ordered + correct quality	One secure delivery area Inventory records updated on a timely basis Copy of purchase order sent to warehouse, sequentially numbered, filed, matched to GRN Raise GRN and grid stamp it, signed as goods checked to PO and checked for quality

Stage	Risks	Control objective	Control procedures
Invoice received	Invoices not recorded resulting in non-payment and loss of supplier goodwill	To ensure that: • an invoice is received for all goods received	Copy of sequentially numbered GRNs sent to invoicing department, filed and matched to copy of invoice (stapled)
	Invoices may be logged for goods not received	• invoices not processed for unordered goods	If no GRN ask supplier for proof of delivery + match to PO (authorised as mentioned above)
	Invoices may contain errors	• invoices are for right items, and price	Grid stamp invoice signed as checked items to PO, GRN, agree price to supplier's price list
			Check invoice calculations
Purchase recorded	Purchases missed or recorded incorrectly	To ensure that: • all purchases are recorded	Batch controls on input
		• all invoices are recorded at the correct amount	Stamp the invoice to indicate recorded, check all filed invoices are stamped
		• recorded in right supplier ledger	Suppliers send in monthly statements, reconcile these to suppliers ledger account

Cash paid	Invoices not paid or incorrect amount paid	To ensure that:	Stamp invoices when paid; check all invoices stamped
		• all invoices paid (and only once)	Keep paid invoices separately from unpaid ones
		• paid correct amount	
		• expenses are valid business costs	Cheque signatory to check to invoice when signing cheque/authorising BACS
			Have authorised cheque signatories
			Get invoices signed as authorised by relevant manager

Purchases control tests

Examples of control tests

As already noted, tests of control should be designed to check that the control procedures are being applied and that objectives are being achieved. One suggested way to design tests of control for a particular situation is to list the documents in a transaction cycle and generate appropriate tests of control for each document. This approach is illustrated here in connection with the purchases cycle – note that a similar technique could be applied to other transaction cycles.

- Obtain the ledger recording purchase orders; ensure each page has been signed by a responsible official to confirm all orders have been recorded and there are no gaps in the sequence of orders.

- Obtain a sample of purchase invoices; ensure each invoice has been signed by a responsible official to confirm checks on the invoice have been completed and the invoice is passed for payment.

- Obtain a sample of credit notes; ensure each credit note is signed by a responsible official to confirm credit note details (goods description and quantity) have been agreed to the relevant goods returned note.

- Review the purchase order for the relevant signature for approval.

- Review purchase invoice for evidence that the invoice has been reviewed and checked.

- Review purchase invoice for initialling of the grid stamp.

- Review/observe the supplier reconciliation note to ensure the control has been complied with.

Test your understanding 2

You are carrying out the audit of the purchases system of Spondon Furniture. The company has a turnover of about $10 million and all the shares are owned by Mr and Mrs Fisher, who are non-executive directors and are not involved in the day-to-day running of the company.

The bookkeeper maintains all the accounting records and prepares the annual financial statements.

The company uses a standard computerised accounting package.

You have determined that the purchases system operates as follows:

- When materials are required for production, the production manager sends a handwritten note to the buying manager. For orders of other items, the department manager or managing director sends handwritten notes to the buying manager. The buying manager finds a suitable supplier and raises a purchase order. The purchase order is signed by the managing director. Purchase orders are not issued for all goods and services received by the company.

- Materials for production are received by the goods received department, who issue a goods received note (GRN), and send a copy to the bookkeeper. There is no system for recording receipt of other goods and services.

- The bookkeeper receives the purchase invoice and matches it with the goods received note and purchase order (if available). The managing director authorises the invoice for posting to the purchase ledger.

- The bookkeeper analyses the invoice into relevant nominal ledger account codes and then posts it.

- At the end of each month, the bookkeeper prepares a list of payables to be paid. This is approved by the managing director.

- The bookkeeper prepares the cheques and remittances and posts the cheques to the purchase ledger and cashbook.

- The managing director signs the cheques and the bookkeeper sends the cheques and remittances to the payables.

Mr and Mrs Fisher are aware that there may be weaknesses in the above system and have asked for advice.

Identify the deficiencies in controls in Spondon's purchases system, explain what the impact is and suggest improvements.

(12 marks)

9 The payroll system

Objectives

The objectives of controls for the payroll cycle are to ensure that the company:

- pays the right people
- pays the right rate
- pays for valid work done
- deals correctly with taxes and other deductions.

This is a summary of the payrolls cycle, showing the possible problems and the related controls:

Stage	Risks	Control objectives	Control procedures
Timesheets submitted	Bogus employees paid or employees paid for hours not worked	To ensure that: • no bogus clock cards submitted • hours noted have actually been worked	Check number of cards to number of employees Keep all spare cards locked in cupboard Supervisor to authorise all timesheets Supervision of clocking in and out

Stage	Risks	Control objectives	Control procedures
Standing data input	Standing data could be compromised. Unprocessed updates may mean employees who have left are paid or joiners are missed	To ensure that: • leavers are not paid after they have left/joiners are paid when they start • standing data is accurate	Managers should complete a leavers/joiners form noting date of departure/arrival and send promptly to payroll dept Standing data files regularly printed out and sent to department managers for them to confirm Restriction to standing data files, e.g. passwords Monthly print of any changes to go to senior management for review and signature
Processing of data	Inaccurate processing of data could lead to wages and taxes being incorrectly calculated	To ensure that: • wagea are calculated correctly • tax is calculated correctly	Sample of wages recalculated manually Exception report produced automatically for anyone paid over $xxx, or paid under $yyy Sample of deductions (PAYE, NIC)recalculated Managerial review of weekly payment summaries
Recording of payroll	Recorded payroll may not match actual payroll	To ensure correct wages, NIC, PAYE recorded	Nominal ledger clerk signs payroll print out to confirm entries double-checked to print Senior management review wages expenses for reasonableness

Staff paid	Staff may not be paid	To ensure that:	Have two peopl[...] where cash wa[...] paid.
	Bogus staff could be paid	• all staff are paid	
		• no bogus employees are paid	Responsible individual should review any BACS payroll summary prior to paying staff – sign to confirm reviewed

Payroll control tests

A suggested programme of tests of control is set out below. This would, of course, be modified to suit the particular circumstances of the client.

- Test a sample of timesheets, clock cards or other records, for approval by a responsible official. Pay particular attention to the approval of overtime there relevant.

- Observe wages distribution for adherence to procedures ensuring employees sign for wages, that unclaimed wages are rebanked, etc.

- Test authorisation for payroll amendments by reference to personnel records.

- Test controls over payroll amendments by reviewing changes and seeing whether they have been authorised. You could print off an exception report highlighting changes and follow those through. You could also do a dummy transaction to see how the system handles change.

- Obtain the payment sheet for casual labour payments and ensure this has been signed by the chief accountant to authorise the payments made.

- Obtain the weekly payroll and ensure this have been signed by a responsible official to approval those payments.

- Examine evidence of independent checks of payrolls (e.g. by internal audit).

- Inspect payroll reconciliations done regularly, clearing wage control account, tying the PAYE liability up to the Inland Revenue records. Review the client working papers or observe the reconciliation process happening.

- Examine explanations for payroll expense variances.

- Test authorisation for payroll deductions by reviewing the employees records, looking at who is authorised to place through amendments, and observe the process.

- Test controls over unclaimed wages. You could do a dummy transaction to see how the system works, what happens to the wages unclaimed, are they place in a safe, if so tick the clients working to the amount in the safe.

Test your understanding 3

Bassoon Ltd runs a chain of shops selling electrical goods all of which are located within the same country.

It has a head office that deals with purchasing, distribution and administration. The payroll for the whole company is administered at head office.

There are 20 staff at head office and 200 staff in the company's 20 shops located in high streets and shopping malls all over the country.

Head office staff (including directors) are all salaried and paid by direct transfer to their bank accounts.

The majority of the staff at the company's shops are also paid through the central salary system, monthly in arrears. However, some students and part time staff are paid cash out of the till.

Recruitment of head office staff is initiated by the department needing the staff who generally conduct interviews and agree terms and conditions of employment. Bassoon has an HR manager who liaises with recruitment agencies, places job adverts and maintains staff files with contracts of employment, etc.

Shop managers recruit their own staff.

Shop staff receive a basic salary based on the hours worked and commission based on sales made.

The company has a fairly sophisticated EPOS (electronic point of sale) till system at all shops that communicates directly with the head office accounting system.

All staff when making a sale have to log on with a swipe card which identifies them to the system, and means that the sales for which they are responsible are analysed by the system and commissions calculated.

Store managers have a few 'guest cards' for temporary and part time staff, who generally do not receive commissions.

Store managers and regional supervisors are paid commissions based on the performance of their store or region. Directors and other head office staff usually receive a bonus at Christmas, depending on the company's performance. This is decided on by the board in consultation with departmental manages and put through the system by the payroll manager.

The payroll manager is responsible for adding joiners to the payroll and deleting leavers as well as for implementing changes in pay rates, tax coding and other deductions and for making sure that the list of monthly transfers is communicated to the bank.

The computerised payroll system is a standard proprietary system which is sophisticated enough to incorporate the commission calculations mentioned above which are fed in directly from the EPOS system.

The company employs an IT manager who is responsible for the maintenance of all IT systems and installing new hardware and software.

Comment on the strengths and deficiencies of the payroll system at Bassoon Ltd and recommend any changes which you think are appropriate.

(10 marks)

10 The inventory system

Objectives

The objectives of controls in the inventory cycle are to ensure that:

- inventory levels are in keeping with the needs of:
    - production (raw materials and bought in components)
    - customer demand (finished goods)
- inventory levels are not:
    - excessive
    - too low ('stockouts')
- value for money is achieved
- goods/services delivered are what was ordered
- quality of goods/services delivered is satisfactory

Process	Risks	Possible control procedures
Inventory received	Inventory stolen on arrival.	All goods inward received at set locations and signed for/logged in by stores manager.
	New purchases mixed up with returns.	
	Poor quality inventory accepted.	All returns sent to a returns department for checking.
	Inventory accepted that was never ordered.	Inventory matched to orders
	No record is made of its arrival.	
Inventory stored	Poor storage conditions lead to damaged inventory.	Storage areas fitted with sprinklers, fire alarms, temperature monitors.
	Inventory items not used before their useful life ends.	Inventory 'rotated' to ensure FIFO usage where relevant.
	Inventory stolen from storage areas.	Valuable inventories locked away and inventory areas limited to a single exit (security guard?).
Raw materials used in production	Materials over-ordered to enable theft.	All requisitions from stores to have signed authorisation from production manager.
		Use of standard quantity requirements.
Inventory despatched	Wrong goods sent.	See sales cycle.
	Goods being stolen (no real sale).	
	Poor quality sent.	
	Records not updated.	
Goods returned to suppliers	Returned goods actually being stolen.	See purchase returns.
Inventory count	Counting lacks accuracy.	All counted areas to be marked as completed.
	Staff lie about amounts counted to cover up their theft.	Managers to check by doing random second counts.

KAPLAN PUBLISHING

Inventory records lost during count.	Staff do not count areas that they are usually responsible for.
Inventory wrongly counted because it is moved during count.	Counting done in pairs.
	Inventory sheets sequenced and counters sign out (and in) the count sheets.
	All inventory movements during count authorised by management.
	Closure during inventory accounts to avoid problems.

Inventory control tests

- Observe physical security of inventories and environment in which they are held.

- Obtain inventory records. Where quantity of inventory has been changed without reference to GDN and GRN, ensure that amendment is signed by a responsible official to authorise that change.

- In the client's warehouse, observe client staff ensuring that where a movement in inventory occurs, that movement is recorded on the appropriate GDN or GRN.

- Test for evidence of authorisation to write off or scrapping of inventories (existence of signature).

- Observe controls over recording of movements of inventory belonging to third parties.

- Observe the procedures for authorisation for inventory movements i.e. the use made of authorised goods received and despatch notes.

- Inspect reconciliations of inventory counts to inventory records (this gives overall comfort on the adequacy of controls over the recording of inventory).

- Test for evidence of sequences checks of despatch and goods received notes for completeness.

- Assess adequacy of inventory counting procedures and attend the count to ensure that procedures are complied with.

11 Capital expenditure

Capital and revenue expenditure

This area looks at expenditure on items other than purchases. However, the controls are virtually identical to controls over purchases as seen above.

Some controls may vary, such as:

- Capital expenditure is often for substantial amounts. As such, most companies would require such items to be included in an annual budget and authorised by very senior level management.

- Regular revenue expense items may be monitored by simple variance analysis (i.e. actual versus budget) on a monthly basis.

- Capital items are likely to be stored on an asset register, which records details of supplier, price, insurance details, current location, responsible employee, etc.

- Just as inventories are counted, assets are likely to be checked against the register on a regular basis.

- When assets are sold second-hand, the items will be checked against similar items or price guides to ensure the company receives fair value.

- Ownership documents (title deeds, vehicle registration documents) will be safely stored.

12 Bank and cash system

Objectives

The objectives of controls over bank and cash are to ensure that:

- cash balances are safeguarded
- cash balances are kept to a minimum
- money can only be extracted from bank accounts for authorised purposes.

Possible controls

Objective	Possible control procedures
Cash balances are safeguarded.	Safes/strongroom/locked cashbox with restricted access. Security locks. Swipe card access. Key access to tills. Night safes. Imprest system. Use of security services for large cash movements. People making bankings vary routes and timings.
Cash balances are kept to a minimum.	Tills emptied regularly. Frequent bankings of cash and cheques received.
Money can only be extracted from bank accounts for authorised purposes.	Restricted list of cheque signatories. Dual signatures for large amounts. Similar controls over bank transfers and online banking, e.g. secure passwords and pin numbers. Cheque books and cheque stationery locked away. Regular bank reconciliations reviewed by person with suitable level of authority.

Bank and cash control tests

Cash receipts:

- observe that mail is opened by two staff to minimise the possibility of fraud (cash being stolen on receipt)
- test independent check of cash receipts to bank lodgements

- test for evidence of a sequence check on any pre-numbered receipts for cash

- test authorisation of cash receipts

- test for evidence of arithmetical check on cash received records.

Cash payments:

- inspect current cheque books for:
  - sequential use of cheques
  - controlled custody of unused cheques
  - any signatures on blank cheques

- test (to avoid double payment) to ensure that paid invoices are marked "paid"

- test for evidence of arithmetical checks on cash payments records, including cashbook

- obtain the file of direct debit payments – ensure each payment is authorised.

Bank reconciliations:

- examine evidence of regular bank reconciliations, at least once per month, but in larger organisations this should be done daily or weekly

- examine evidence of independent checks of bank reconciliations (e.g. a signature)

- examine evidence of follow up of outstanding items on the bank reconciliation. Pay particular attention to old outstanding reconciling items that should be written back such as old, unpresented cheques.

Petty cash:

- Test petty cash vouchers for appropriate authorisation.

- Test cancellation of paid petty cash vouchers.

- Test for evidence of arithmetical checks on petty cash records.

- Test for evidence of independent checks on the petty cash balance.

- Perform a surprise petty cash count and reconcile to petty cash records.

13 Reporting to those charged with governance

Auditors should communicate deficiencies in internal control to those charged with governance and management. In particular, significant deficiencies should be communicated in writing to those charged with governance. This is a requirement of **ISA 265** *Communicating Deficiencies in Internal Control to Those Charged with Governance and Management.*

The form, timing and addressees of this communication should be agreed at the start of the audit, as part of the terms of the engagement. This report, traditionally known as a **management letter** or **report to management**, is usually sent at the end of the audit process.

When the auditor reports deficiencies, it should be made clear that:

- the report is not a comprehensive list of deficiencies, but only those that have come to light during normal audit procedures
- the report is for the sole use of the company
- no disclosure should be made to a third party the without written agreement of the auditor
- no responsibility is assumed to any other parties.

The usual structure of the report is:

- covering letter (which will include the above list of points)
- appendix, noting the deficiencies, consequences, and recommendations (often with a space left for management to respond with their planned action).

In the exam, an internal control question may require you to analyse controls and report deficiencies in the form of a management letter. If so, it is the appendix (see below) that you need to produce. A covering letter would be specifically requested by your examiner.

The best structure is:

Weakness	Clear description of what is wrong.
Consequence	What could happen if the deficiency is not corrected. Focus on what matters to the client – the risk of lost profits, stolen assets, extra costs, errors in the accounts.
Recommendation	This must deal with the specific deficiency you have observed! It must also provide greater benefits than the cost of implementation.
	Try to suggest who should carry out the control procedures, and when.

Illustration

(A table format is the best format, it keeps you structured and the markers find it easier to mark.)

Weaknesses.

Consequence	Consequence	Recommendation
There appear to be purchase invoices missing from the sequentially numbered invoice file.	There is a possibility that purchases and liabilities are not completely recorded. Also, it would be difficult to provide proof of purchase where the invoice is missing. This may make it difficult to obtain refunds for faulty goods, leading to increased costs. As such, the accounts could be incomplete and items may have been purchased without control over quality, price, etc.	All invoices should be sequentially filed on receipt by the accounts department. Regular checks should be made to ensure a complete record, with any missing items investigated (and copies requested if necessary).

14 Chapter summary

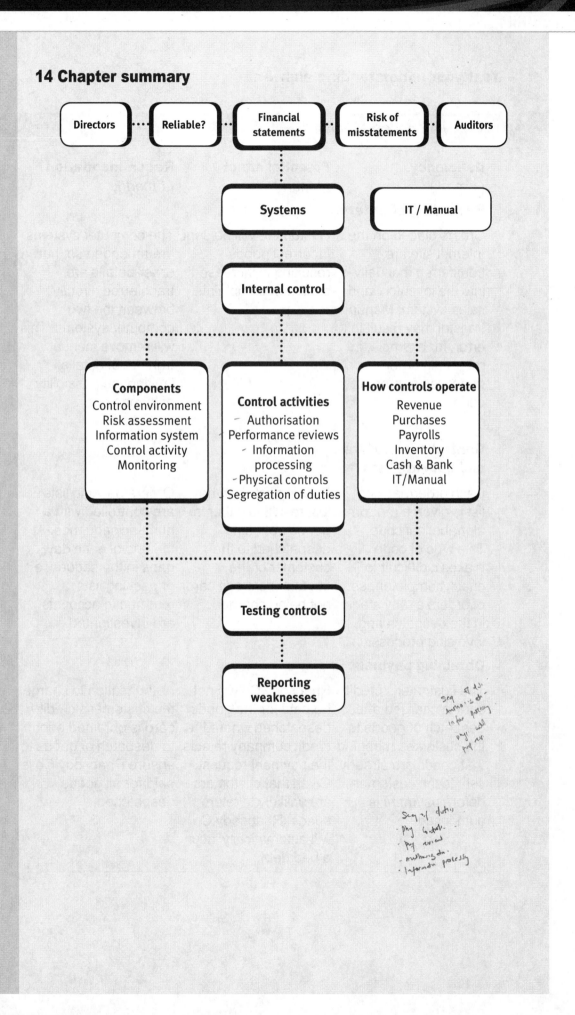

Test your understanding answers

Test your understanding 1

Deficiency (1 mark)	Potential effect (1 mark)	Recommendation (1 mark)
Recording of orders		
Orders placed on the Internet site are transferred manually into the inventory and sales system. Manual transfer may result in error, for example, in recording order quantities or product codes.	Customers will be sent incorrect goods resulting in increased customer complaints.	The computer systems are amended so that order details are transferred directly between the two computer systems. This will remove manual transfer of details limiting the possibility of human error.
Control over orders and packing lists		
Each order/packing list is given a random alphabetical code. This type of code makes it difficult to check completeness of orders at any stage in the despatch and invoicing process.	Packing lists can be lost resulting either in goods not being despatched to the customer or the customer's credit card not being charged.	Orders/packing lists are controlled with a numeric sequence. At the end of each day, gaps in the sequence of packing lists returned to accounts are investigated.
Obtaining payment		
The customer's credit card is charged after despatch of goods to the customer, meaning that goods are already sent to the customer before payment is authorised.	Rhapsody Co will not be paid for the goods despatched where the credit company rejects the payment request. Given that customers are unlikely to return seeds, Rhapsody Co will automatically incur a bad debt.	Authorisation to charge the customer's credit card is obtained prior to despatch of goods to ensure Rhapsody Co is paid for all goods despatched.

Completeness of orders

There is no overall check that all orders recorded on the inventory and sales system have actually been invoiced.	Entire orders may be overlooked and consequently sales and profit understated.	The computer is programmed to review the order file and orders where there is no corresponding invoice for an order, these should be flagged for subsequent investigation.

Test your understanding 2

Deficiency *(1 mark)*	Effect *(1 mark)*	Recommendation *(1 mark)*
(1) Hand written orders are done (with no numbering).	Orders for goods not required and a potential orders being missed for action. Therefore over spending or potential shock outs due to orders not being processed.	Have prenumber orders which are authorised by a manager.
(2) Purchase orders are not issued for all goods and services.	Goods/services being purchased that are not legitimate or required.	Purchase orders required for all goods, for services a budget should be set and quotes obtained.
(3) No system for recording receipt of other goods and services.	Goods received that are of poor quality or incorrect amounts.	Count goods in before they are signed.

(4)	It doesn't state that the GRN are checked to anything.	Goods received that are of poor quality or incorrect amounts.	Agree GRN back to the purchase order.
(5)	There is no review done of the bookkeeper posting the invoices into the nominal ledger.	Errors could go undetected, therefore pay suppliers the incorrect amount.	A review by a manager should be done on a regular basis.

Deficiency _(1 mark)_	Effect _(1 mark)_	Recommendation _(1 mark)_
(6) A list of payables is given to the managing director.	The managing director will not know if payables are valid or correct therefore could be paying incorrect amounts.	The managing director should also review source documents before signing the list.
(7) Lack of segregations		
The managing director authorises invoices, approves payment and signs cheques.	It is easy to place through a purchase invoice to pay himself and this would go undetected.	Segregate duties by sharing the responsibility with another manager.

Test your understanding 3

Strength	Deficiency	Recommendation
Salaries are paid by direct transfer to the employees bank accounts (less chance of mis-appropriation of cash).		
	Cash paid to part time staff (easier to misappropriate cash).	Apply the payroll system to all employees.
	No control over the appointment of head office staff the HR Manager deals with (may recruit unnecessary staff).	Head office staff should be approved by the board.

Strength	Deficiency	Recommendation
	No control over shop staff, the shop manager recruits own staff.	Should be approved by head office.
Having a sophisticated EPOS till system (unlikely for errors to occur).		
Individual swipe cards linked to commission (you know who is doing the transaction and because they receive a commission it encourages the staff to recognise the sale).		
	Guest cards, could be anybody and they could steal a card to access till at a later date to steal money.	A control system to monitor guest cards so management know who has a specific card.

Lack of segregation of duties, the payroll manager is responsible for all processing.	Split the responsibilities up, maybe get a manager to review the payroll managers work.
In the question it states the IT manager is responsible for systems, but doesn't state there is restricted access.	Place passwords on the system and change them on a regular basis.

Audit evidence

Chapter learning objectives

When you have completed this chapter you will be able to:

- explain the use of assertions in obtaining audit evidence
- discuss the sources and relative merits of the different types of evidence available
- define audit sampling and explain the need for sampling
- identify and discuss the differences between statistical and non-statistical sampling
- discuss the quality of evidence obtained
- explain the need for and the importance of audit documentation
- explain the procedures to ensure safe custody and retention of working papers.

1 Why does the auditor need evidence?

In order for the auditor's opinion to be considered trustworthy it must be based upon more than simple judgement and gut feeling. Auditors must come to their conclusions having completed a thorough examination of the books and records of their clients and they must have documentary evidence of these procedures necessary to support their conclusions in the future.

Imagine a court case where someone has been accused of theft: a judge could not simply say someone is or is not guilty based upon their appearance. They must consider evidence gathered by both the defense and the prosecution and then, based upon the evidence presented, the judge may then reach a conclusion.

2 Financial statements assertions

The objective of audit testing is basically to assist the auditor in coming to a conclusion as to whether the financial statements are free from material misstatement.

However, the auditor does not simply design tests with the broad objective to identify material misstatement. This is a difficult conclusion to reach and can only be based upon a series of detailed tests, each designed with a specific testing objective relating to certain areas of the financial statements.

For example: auditors have to assess whether inventory balances are free from material misstatement. Unfortunately, there are many ways inventory could be misstated:

- items could be missed out of inventory;
- items from the next accounting period could be accidentally included;
- it might not be valued at the lower of cost and net realisable value;
- damaged or obsolete stock might not be identified;
- purchase cost may not be recorded accurately; or
- the stock count may not be performed thoroughly.

Each of these concerns could result in misstatement, which ultimately could (alone or in aggregate) be material.

For this reason auditors have to perform a range of tests on the significant classes of transaction, account balances and disclosures to be reasonably sure that they are not misstated. These tests focus on what are known as financial statements assertions:

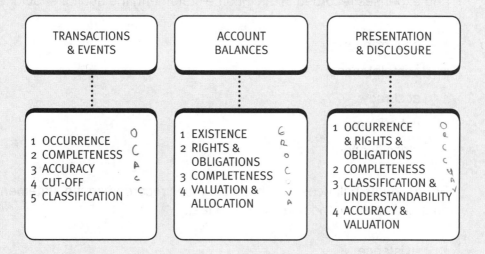

Occurrence – did the transactions and events recorded actual occur and pertain to the entity?

Completeness – have all transactions, assets, liabilities and equity interests that should have been recorded been recorded?

Accuracy – have amounts, data and other information been recorded and disclosed appropriately?

Cut-off – have transactions and events been recorded in the correct accounting period?

Classification and understandability – have transactions and events been: recorded in the proper accounts; and described and disclosed clearly?

Existence – do assets, liabilities and equity interests exist?

Rights and obligations – does the entity hold or control the rights to assets and are liabilities the obligations of the entity?

Valuation and allocation – are assets, liabilities and equity interests included in the financial statements at appropriate values?

Linking assertions to tests

When the auditor designs further audit procedures they must ensure that they test a range of the assertions listed. For transactions (i.e. incomes and expenses recorded in the income statement) the auditor should test:

- occurrence;
- completeness;
- accuracy;
- cut-off; and
- classification

For accounts balances (i.e. those balances recorded on the statement of financial position) the auditor should test:

- existence;
- rights and obligations;
- completeness; and
- valuation and allocation.

Whilst the testing of accounts balances and transactions will probably be the focus of the audit, the auditor must also design tests to ensure that transactions, balances and other relevant information/matters are appropriately disclosed in the financial statements. Assertions relevant to the disclosures are:

- occurrence;
- rights and obligations;
- completeness;
- classification and understandability; and
- accuracy and valuation.

To assist your studies and simplify this process consider the following four questions that an auditor needs to answer when approaching testing:

(1) Should items be in the accounts at all? (occurrence, existence, rights and obligations, cut-off).

(2) Are they included at the right value? (accuracy, valuation).

(3) Are there any more? (completeness).

(4) Are they disclosed properly? (classification, allocation, understandability).

Examples of typical procedures relevant to particular assertions include:

ASSERTION		ACTIVITY

E.G.

EXISTENCE		INSPECT THE ASSET
VALUATION		INSPECT EVIDENCE OF COST/VALUATION (INVOICES, ETC.)
RIGHTS & OBLIGATIONS		INSPECT EVIDENCE OF OWNERSHIP (TITLE DEEDS, INVOICES, ETC.)
CUT-OFF		INSPECT DOCUMENTS/ OBSERVE PROCESSES (DATES ON INVOICES, DESPATCH NOTES, ETC.)
COMPLETENESS		LOOK FOR EVIDENCE OF UNDISCLOSED ITEMS (PAYMENTS TO SUPPLIERS OMITTED FROM PAYABLES LIST, OMITTED DIVIDENDS FROM SHARES, ETC.)

3 Practical example

Auditing buildings

When designing a suite of tests to perform on a building, say a freehold property, the auditor may consider the following:

Assertion	Test
Existence	Inspect the property concerned.
Valuation	Agree the cost to the original contract of purchase. Inspect subsequent revaluation reports. Re-perform the depreciation calculation.
Rights and obligations	Inspect the title deeds.
Completeness	Review the repairs account to ensure that items of a capital nature have not been expensed. Inspect correspondence with lawyers and consultants for evidence that there are no additional properties or construction costs.

Test your understanding 1

(1) **List five assertions associated with transactions.**

- Occurance
- Completeness
- Cut-off
- Accuracy
- Classification

(2 marks)

(2) **List four assertions associated with account balances.**

- Existence
- Right ability etc
- Completeness
- Valuation

(2 marks)

(3) **List four assertions associated with disclosures in financial statements.**

- Occurran
- Rights & obligation
- Completness
- Accuracy
- Valued

(2 marks)

4 Audit procedures

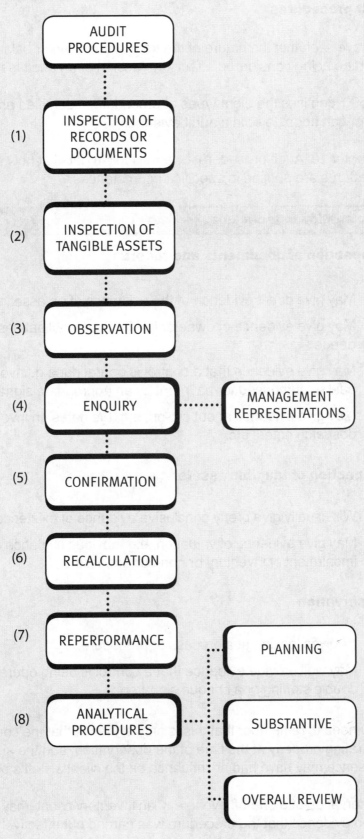

Audit procedures

We have seen that the nature of the transactions and/or balances and the assertion being considered affects the design of an audit test.

ISA 500 identifies the eight types of procedures, identified above, that the auditor can adopt to obtain audit evidence.

In chapter 10 'Audit procedures' we will look in detail at how these procedures are applied in specific circumstances.

Explanation of techniques

Inspection of documents and records

- May give direct evidence of the existence of an asset.

- May give evidence of ownership (rights and obligations), e.g. title deeds

- May give evidence that a control is operating, e.g. invoices stamped paid or authorised for payment by an appropriate signature.

- May give evidence about cut-off, e.g. the dates on invoices, despatch notes, etc.

Inspection of tangible assets

- Will usually give pretty conclusive evidence of existence!

- May give evidence of valuation, e.g. obvious evidence of impairment of inventory or non-current assets.

Observation

- Involves looking at a process or procedure.

- May well provide evidence that a control is being operated, e.g. double staffing or a cheque signatory.

You need to remember that this is only evidence that the control was operating properly at the time of the observation, and the auditor's presence may have had an influence on the client's staff's behaviour.

Observation of a one-off event, e.g. an inventory count, may well give good evidence that the procedure was carried out effectively.

Enquiry

Whilst a major source of evidence, the results of enquiries will usually need to be corroborated in some way through other audit procedures.

The answers to enquiries may themselves be corroborative evidence.

Management representations

Management representations are part of overall enquiries. These involve obtaining written repsonses from management to confirm oral enquiries. These are considered further in chapter 11.

Confirmation

- This refers to the auditor obtaining a direct response (usually written) from an external, third party.
- Examples include:
  - circularisation of receivables;
  - confirmation of bank balances in a bank letter;
  - confirmation of actual/potential penalties from legal advisers; and
  - confirmation of inventories held by third parties.
- May give good evidence of existence of balances, e.g. receivables confirmation.
- May not necessarily give reliable evidence of valuation, e.g. customers may confirm receivable amounts but, ultimately, be unable to pay in the future.

Recalculation

This involves checking the arithmetical accuracy of the client's calculations, e.g. depreciation amounts.

Reperformance

This involves reperforming client procedures, e.g. test checking inventory counts.

Analytical procedures

The consideration of the relationships between figures in the financial statements or between financial and non-financial information.

As well as using them at the planning and review phases of the audit, analytical procedures may also be used as substantive procedures. For example: considering changes in the gross margin as an indicator that either sales or cost of sales may be misstated or reviewing trends in receivables days to identify worsening credit control.

Test your understanding 2

(1) **List the eight types of audit procedure?**

(4 marks)

(2) **Why does the auditor need to obtain management representations?**

(2 marks)

(3) **List three examples where an auditor might use confirmations.**

(3 marks)

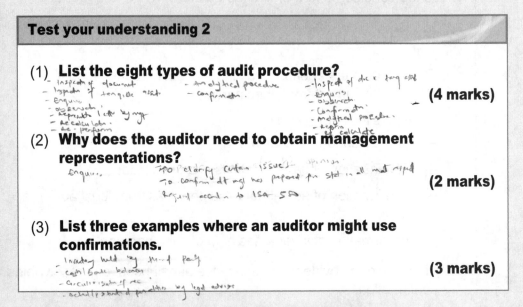

5 Sufficient appropriate evidence

Whilst the nature of an item under scrutiny (class of transaction, account balance, disclosure) and the assertion being tested affects the type of procedure performed, these issues do not necessarily affect considerations of how much evidence to gather. This is driven by three factors:

*   the risk assessment (of material misstatement);

*   the quality of the evidence available; and

*   the purpose of the procedure (test of control or substantive test?).

The overall objective of an auditor, in terms of gathering evidence, is described in audit standards, namely; **ISA 500** *Audit Evidence*.

"The objective of the auditor is to design and perform audit procedures in such a way to enable the auditor to obtain sufficient appropriate audit evidence to be able to draw reasonable conclusions on which to base the auditor's opinion.'

Sufficient evidence

There needs to be 'enough' evidence to support the auditor's conclusion. What is 'enough' at the end of the day is a matter of professional judgement. However, when determining whether they have enough evidence on file the auditor must consider:

- the risk of material misstatement;
- the results of controls tests;
- the size of a population being tested;
- the size of the sample selected to test; and
- the quality of the evidence obtained.

Consider, for example, the audit of a bank balance:

Auditors will confirm year-end bank balances directly with the bank. This is a good source of evidence but on its own is not sufficient to give assurance regarding the completeness and final valuation of bank and cash amounts. The key reason is timing differences. The client may have received cash amounts or cheques before the end of the year, or may have paid out cheques before the end of the year, that have not yet cleared the bank account. For this reason the auditor should also perform a bank reconciliation.

In combination these two pieces of evidence will be sufficient to give assurance over the bank balances.

Sufficiency is a key consideration when selecting the size of an audit sample. This is discussed later on in the chapter.

Appropriate evidence

Appropriateness of evidence breaks down into two important concepts:

- reliability; and
- relevance.

Reliability

Auditors should always attempt to obtain evidence from the most trustworthy and dependable source possible. Evidence is considered more reliable when it is:

- ✓ obtained from an independent external source;
- ✓ generated internally but subject to effective control;
- ✓ obtained directly by the auditor;

- ✓ in documentary form; and
- ✓ in original form.

Broadly speaking, the more reliable the evidence the less of it the auditor will need. However the converse is not necessarily true: if evidence is unreliable it will never be appropriate for the audit, no matter how much is gathered.

Relevance

To be relevant audit evidence has to address the objective/purpose of a procedure and the assertion being considered. For example:

- tests of control are designed to evaluate the operating effectiveness of controls in preventing or detecting and correcting material misstatement; and
- substantive procedures are designed to detect material misstatement.

Attendance at an inventory count provides us with a good example of the relevance of procedures. During counting the auditor considers the relationship between inventory records and physical inventories, as follows:

- identifying items of physical inventory and tracing them to inventory records to confirm the **completeness** of accounting records; and
- identifying items on the inventory record and tracing them to physical inventories to confirm the **existence** of inventory assets.

Whilst the procedures are perhaps similar in nature their purpose (and relevance) is to test different assertions regarding inventory balances.

Limitations of evidence

Auditors are only required to perform procedures to give **reasonable** assurance that the financial statements are free from material misstatement. They can never give absolute assurance. One of the reasons is that evidence can be persuasive in nature, rather than conclusive, for example:

- the auditor gathers evidence on a sample basis;
- mistakes will occur no matter how good controls are (human error);
- evidence can be manipulated (fraud); and
- the client may be 'economical with the truth' during enquiries (i.e. they may withhold vital information).

This is another reason that auditors need to gather evidence from a wide range of sources. This will inevitably increase the reliability of the evidence overall and lead to superior conclusions.

6 Sampling

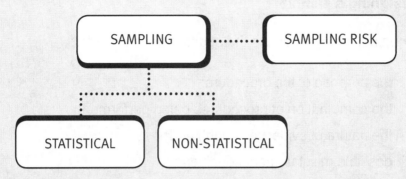

The need for sampling

It will usually be impossible to test every item in an accounting population because of the costs involved. Consider a manufacturer of fasteners (i.e. nuts, bolts, nails and screws); they will have many thousands, maybe millions, of items of inventory. It would simply be impossible to test the valuation of every single one.

It is also important to remember that auditors gives reasonable **not** absolute assurance and are therefore not certifying that the financial statements are 100% accurate.

Audit evidence is gathered on a test basis. Auditor therefore need to understand the implications and effective use of **sampling**.

Definition

The definition of sampling, as described in I**SA 530** *Audit Sampling* is:

"The application of audit procedures to less than 100% of items within a population of audit relevance such that all sampling units have a chance of selection in order to provide the auditor with a reasonable basis on which to draw conclusions about the entire population."

Statistical or non-statistical sampling

Statistical sampling means any approach to sampling that uses:

* random selection of samples; and

* probability theory to evaluate sample results.

Any approach that does not have both these characteristics is considered to be non-statistical sampling.

The approach taken is a matter of auditor judgement.

Designing a sample

When designing a sample the auditor has to consider:

- the purpose of the procedure;
- the combination of procedures being performed;
- the nature of evidence sought; and
- possible misstatement conditions.

The principle methods of sample selection are:

- **Random selection** - this can be achieved through the use of random number tables;
- **Systematic selection** - where a sampling interval is used (e.g. every 50th balance);
- **Monetary unit selection** - selecting items based upon monetary values (usually focussing on higher value items);
- **Haphazard selection** - auditor does not follow a structured technique but avoids bias or predictability; and
- **Block selection** - this involves selecting a block of contiguous (i.e. next to each other) items from the population. This technique is rarely appropriate.

When non-statistical methods are used the auditor uses judgement to select the items to be tested. Whilst this lends itself to auditor bias it does support the risk based approach, where the auditor focuses on those areas most susceptible to material misstatement. This usually leads to a focus on the higher value items within a population and is a common method in practice.

The sample size depends upon the level of sampling risk that the auditor is willing to accept. This is basically the risk that the auditor's conclusion based on a sample is different from the conclusion that would be reached if the whole population were tested.

In order to reduce sampling risk the auditor needs to increase the size of the sample selected.

Test your understanding 3

(1) **List three qualities audit evidence must have?**

— sufficient
— relevant
— reliable.

(3 marks)

(2) **List two reasons why audit evidence is likely to be persuasive rather than conclusive.**

— Truth may be economically hidden.
— Human error.
— Evidence may be manipulated (fraud)

(2 marks)

(3) **List two examples where it would be appropriate to use statistical sampling.**

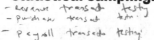

— Revenue transaction testing
— Purchase transaction testing.
— Payroll transaction testing.

(2 marks)

7 Audit documentation

Why do we need working papers?

The job of working papers is to:

*   provide a record of the basis for the auditor's report;

*   provide evidence that the audit was conducted in accordance with ISAs and legal and regulatory requirements;

*   assist with the planning, performance, supervision and review of the audit; and

*   aid the auditors' defence if subsequently sued for negligence.

Principles

There are two major principles

*   **If it's not recorded, it didn't happen.**

    If there is nothing on file, there is no evidence that the necessary procedures were completed, so there can be no basis for the audit opinion.

*   **If it can't be understood, it might as well not have happened.**

    Clarity is important for two reasons:

    —   If the working papers are easy to understand it will be more obvious if anything has been omitted.

– Working papers need to be reviewed for quality control purposes and to ensure that the audit opinion is justified. The reviewer may be at a senior level in the firm and therefore time will be charged at an expensive rate. Clear working papers will keep the time spent reviewing, and therefore costs, to a minimum.

Structure and layout of the file

There are two broad areas to an audit file:

- The control part, consisting of:
  - the planning section
  - the completion and review section.

- The main working papers, which are divided into the relevant sections of the financial statements, e.g. non-current assets, inventories, receivables, etc.

Presentation of a working paper

Working papers tend to follow the following structure:

- a lead schedule summarising the transactions, balances and disclosures under scrutiny;

- a summary of the key matters arising from the procedures performed (including identified misstatements);

- supporting work schedules for individual procedures; and

- copies of evidence obtained and referred to during testing.

The following is an illustrative example:

The lead schedule

Client: XYZ Ltd
Year ended: 31 December 2009
Subject: receivables

Prepared by: AB
Reviewed by

Reference J1
Date
Date

	Ref	This year Draft $	Adjustments $	Final $	Last Year Final $
Trade receivables					
Less irrecoverable debt					
Other receivables					
Prepayments					

Summary of work done	Ref
Circularisation of material receivables carried out	J10
Receivables ageing reviewed and discussed with xx	J20
Correspondence with disputed accounts reviewed	J21
Material other receivables agreed to confirmation or after date receipts	J30
Material invoices agreed to invoices and payment and calcualtions checked	J40

Conclusion
      Subject to satisfactory resolution of dispute with CDE Ltd (J2) receivables are fairly stated

This is an example of the lead schedule for the accounts receivable section.

Note

- The headings – client, year end, subject, preparer, reviewer.

- The account headings, which correspond to the analysis of accounts receivable in the note to the financial statements.

- Comparative figures.

- The suggested column headings, draft, adjustments and final, which allow the reviewer to see adjustments made to the client's original figures, while ensuring the final column agrees to the financial statements.

- Cross-references to supporting schedules.

- Brief summary of work done.

- Conclusion.

Section summary (matters arising)

- A schedule that summarises:
  - what you did
  - why you are confident in your conclusions
  - limportant issues for the partner and manager to consider.

Supporting schedules

These could be presented any number of ways. Examples include:

By sub-category, e.g. For non-current assets:

- land and buildings
- plant and machinery
- IT equipment
- motor vehicles.

Or:

Transaction testing schedules.

Client Year end Subject				Ref Initials Reviewed						
							Tests			
Item No	Details	£	£	A	B	C	D	E	F	G

Test your understanding 4

(1) **Why do auditors prepare working papers?**

serves: Defence document against litigation
- Ref point
- Evidence to back opinion

(1 mark)

(2) **List six things which appear usually at the top of every working paper.**

- client name   - Brief summary of work done.
- recon period   - cross ref
- Subject   - conclusion
- reference   - Figures

(3 marks)

(3) **What is the purpose of a lead schedule?**

(1 mark)

(4) **Why should all working papers be easy to review?**

- miss it obvious dd if anything has been omitted
- Quality of opinion

(1 mark)

Custody and retention of working papers

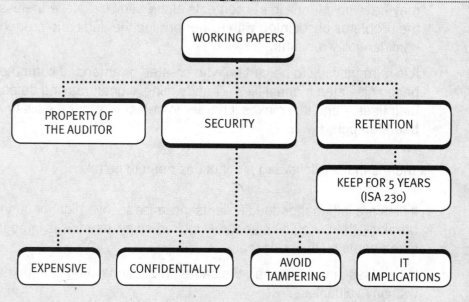

Who owns the working papers?

The auditor does. This is important because:

- Access to the working papers is controlled by the auditor, not the client, which is an element in preserving the auditor's independence.

- In some circumstances care may need to be taken when copies of client generated schedules are incorporated into the file.

Security

Working papers must be kept secure.

- Audits are expensive exercises. If the files are lost or stolen, the evidence they contain will need to be recreated, so the work will need to be done again. The auditors may be able to recover the costs from their insurers, but otherwise it will simply represent a loss to the firm. Either way, prevention is better than cure.

- By its nature, audit evidence will comprise much sensitive information that is confidential. If the files are lost or stolen, the auditor's duty of confidentiality will be compromised.

- There have been cases of unscrupulous clients altering auditors' working papers to conceal frauds.

The implications of IT based audit systems are also far reaching.

- By their nature, laptops are susceptible to theft, even though the thief may have no interest in the contents of the audit file. Nevertheless, all the problems associated with re-performing the audit and breaches of confidentiality remain.

- It is more difficult to be certain who created or amended computer based files than manual files – handwriting, signatures and dates have their uses – and this makes it harder to detect whether the files have been tampered with.

This means that the following precautions need to be taken.

- If files are left unattended at clients' premises – overnight or during lunch breaks – they should be securely locked away, or if this is impossible, taken home by the audit team.

- When files are left in a car, the same precautions should be taken as with any valuables.

- IT-based systems should be subject to passwords, encryption and backup procedures.

Retention

Audit files should be assembled in a timely fashion. This is, ordinarily, no longer than 60 days after the date of the auditor's report.

Once complete the files should be retained as long as required by national law. However, **ISA 230** *Audit Documentation,* states that this period is, ordinarily, no shorter than five years from the date of the auditor's report. This should therefore be considered the minimum retention period.

All of this means that firms need to make arrangements for:

- secure storage of recent files
- archiving older files
- archiving and backup of IT-based files.

8 Smaller entities

Smaller commercial entities will usually have the above attributes. This can lead to both advantages and disadvantages:

- **Lower risk**: Smaller entities may well be engaged in activity that is relatively simple and therefore lower risk. However, this will not be true for small – often one person businesses – where there is a high level of expertise in a particular field, e.g. consultancy businesses, creative businesses, the financial sector.

- **Direct control by owner managers** is a strength because they know what is going on and have the ability to exercise real control. They are also in a strong position to manipulate the figures or put private transactions 'through the books'.

- **Simpler systems**: Smaller entities are less likely to have sophisticated IT systems, but pure, manual systems are becoming increasingly rare. This is good news in that many of the bookkeeping errors associated with smaller entities may now be less prevalent. However, a system is only as good as the person operating it.

Evidence implications

- The normal rules concerning the relationship between risk and the quality and quantity of evidence apply irrespective of the size of the entity.

- The quantity of evidence may well be less than for a larger organisation.

- It may be more efficient to carry out 100% testing in a smaller organisation.

Small not-for-profit organisations

Small not for profit organisations have all the attributes of other small entities. Arguably, however, the position is more difficult for the auditor because small not-for-profit organisations tend to be staffed by volunteers and the culture is more likely to be one of trust rather than accountability.

Problems

- **Management override** – Smaller entities will have a key director or manager who will have significant power and authority. This could mean that controls are lacking in the first place or they are easy to override.

- **No segregation of duties** – Smaller entities tend to have few accounts clerks that processes information. To overcome this the directors should authorise and review the all work performed.

- **Less formal approach** – Smaller entities tend to have simple systems and very few controls due to the trust and the lack of complexity. It is therefore difficult to test the reliability of systems and substantive testing tends to be used more.

9 Chapter summary

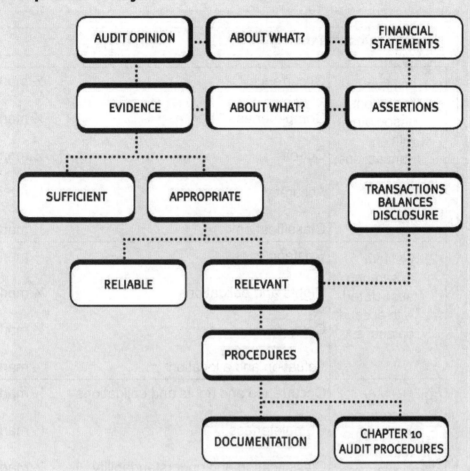

Test your understanding answers

Test your understanding 1

(1) List five assertions associated with transactions.	Occurrence	½ mark
	Completeness	½ mark
	Cut-off	½ mark
	Accuracy	½ mark
	Classification	½ mark
(2) List four assertions associated with account balances.	Existence	½ mark
	Rights and obligations	½ mark
	Completeness	½ mark
	Valuation and allocation	½ mark
(3) List four assertions associated with disclosures in financial statements.	Occurrence and rights and obligations	½ mark
	Completeness	½ mark
	Classification and understandability.	½ mark
	Accuracy and valuation	½ mark

Test your understanding 2

(1) List the eight types of audit procedure?	Inspection of records or documents.	½ mark
	Inspection of assets.	½ mark
	Observation.	½ mark
	Enquiry.	½ mark
	Confirmation.	½ mark
	Recalculation.	½ mark
	Reperformance.	½ mark
	Analytical procedures.	½ mark
(2) Why does the auditor need to obtain management representations?	Where the issue is material.	1 mark
	Where other sources of evidence cannot reasonably be expected to exist.	1 mark
	Where other evidence is of lower quality.	1 mark
	Where it is specifically required by an ISA.	1 mark
(3) List three examples where an auditor might use confirmations.	Circularisation of receivables.	1 mark
	Confirmation of bank balances.	1 mark
	Confirmation from legal advisers of actual or contingent liabilities arising from legal proceedings.	1 mark
	Confirmation of inventory held by third parties.	1 mark
	Confirmation of investment portfolios by investment managers.	1 mark

Test your understanding 3

(1) List three qualities audit evidence must have.	It must be:	
	• Sufficient. *& appropriate.* ^*Relevent* *reliable.*	1 mark
	• Relevant.	1 mark
	• Reliable.	1 mark
(2) List two reasons why audit evidence is likely to be persuasive rather than conclusive.	The auditor gathers evidence on a test basis (the sample may or may not be representative).	½ mark
	• People make mistakes (both client and auditor).	½ mark
	• Documents could be forged (increasingly easy with digital technology).	½ mark
	• The client's personnel may not always tell the truth.	½ mark
(3) List two examples where it would be appropriate to use statistical sampling.	Purchases transaction testing	1 mark
	Revenue transactions testing	1 mark
	Payroll transactions testing,	1 mark
	etc.	

↳ Statistical Sampling more appropriate

Test your understanding 4

Solution

(1)	Why do auditors prepare working papers?	To provide a record of work done and evidence that the work was performed in accordance with auditing standards, to assist in the planning, performance and review of the audit.	1 mark
(2)	List the six things which appear usually at the top of every working paper.	Client name / Year end / Subject / Prepared by / Reviewed by / Reference.	½ mark each
(3)	What is the purpose of a lead schedule?	To provide a summary of each area. *purpose of a lead schedule*	1 mark
(4)	Why should all working papers be easy to review?	To make it easier to spot anything that has been omitted, to ensure that the time spent by senior staff reviewing the audit file is minimised. *Rigid + working papers should be easy to review*	1 mark

Audit procedures

Chapter learning objectives

When you have completed this chapter you will be able to:

- explain the purpose of substantive procedures in relation to financial statements assertions

- explain the substantive procedures used in auditing accounting balances

- explain the use of computer assisted audit techniques in the context of an audit

- discuss and provide examples of how analytical procedures are used as substantive procedures

- discuss the problems associated with the audit of accounting estimates

- discuss the extent to which auditors are able to rely on the work of experts and internal audit

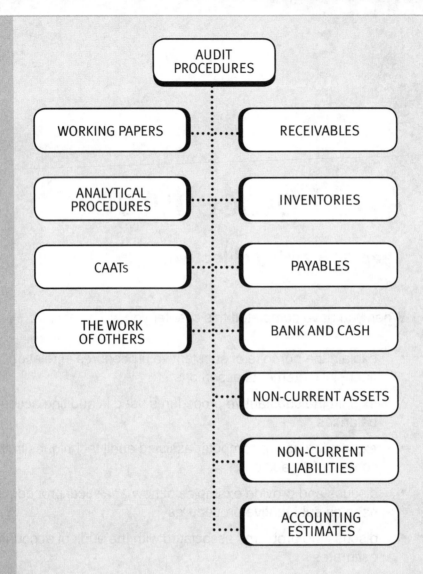

1 General principles

A word of warning: chapter 9 dealt with the **principles** of audit evidence. This chapter deals with the **application** of those principles.

A further warning: in the sections that follow, we will consider specific audit areas and suggest how these are usually tested. You may be tempted to learn these tests and repeat them 'parrot fashion' in the exam. This would be unwise. Audit procedures are designed to reflect the unique risks of an audit and the nature of items and assertions under scrutiny. You must always try and make your answers specific to any scenarios presented in the exam. This requires both knowledge and application skills.

Use this chapter as a starting point to familiarise you with the basic auditing techniques and then practice applying these skills to scenarios through question practice.

2 Analytical procedures

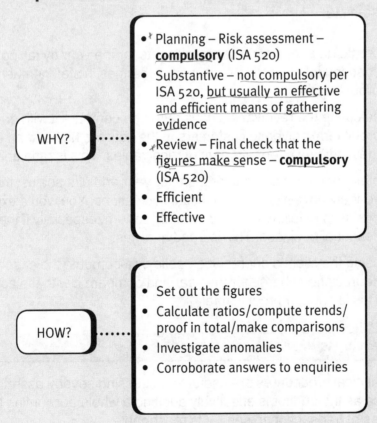

WHY?
- Planning – Risk assessment – **compulsory** (ISA 520)
- Substantive – not compulsory per ISA 520, but usually an effective and efficient means of gathering evidence
- Review – Final check that the figures make sense – **compulsory** (ISA 520)
- Efficient
- Effective

HOW?
- Set out the figures
- Calculate ratios/compute trends/ proof in total/make comparisons
- Investigate anomalies
- Corroborate answers to enquiries

Analytical procedures as substantive tests

We have already come across analytical procedures as a significant component of risk assessment at the planning phase of an audit. Later on in the text we will also see that they are a critical component of the completion of an audit.

However, here we consider their use as substantive procedures. Remember these are procedures designed to detect material misstatement. Analytical procedures are used to identify trends and understand relationships between sets of data. This in itself will not detect misstatement but will identify possible sources. As such, analytical procedures cannot be used in isolation and should be coupled with other, corroborative, forms of testing, such as enquiry of management.

In order to perform a thorough analytical review auditors do not simply look at current figures in comparison to last year. Auditors may consider other points of comparison, such as budgets and industry data. Other techniques are also available, including:

- ratio analysis;
- trend analysis; and
- proof in total.

For example:

- create an expectation of payroll costs for the year by taking last year's cost and inflating for pay rises and changes in staff numbers. This is a proof in total.

- calculate the receivables days ratio and compare it with prior year and credit terms given to customers. If the figure is higher than expected it may indicate overstatement of receivables. This is ratio analysis.

- plot monthly sales data for the prior year and plot against the current year and investigate any unusual fluctuations. You would expect the business to follow a similar monthly pattern, especially if they have a seasonal business. This is trend analysis.

- using the client's depreciation policy, re-compute the expected depreciation charge for the year and compare it with the actual charge. This is another proof in total.

Usefulness of analytical procedures

Analytical procedures are useful for assessing several assertions at once as the auditor is effectively auditing a whole accounting balance or class of transaction to see if it is reasonable.

They can be used to corroborate other audit evidence obtained, such as statements by management about changes in cost structures, such as energy savings.

By using analytical procedures the auditor may identify unusual items that can then be further investigated to ensure that a misstatement doesn't exist in the balance.

However, in order to use analytical procedures effectively the auditor needs to be able to create an expectation. It would be difficult to do this if operations changed significantly from the prior year. If the changes were planned, the auditor could use forecasts as a point of comparison. Although these are inherently unreliable due to the amount of estimates involved. In this circumstance it would be pointless comparing to prior years as the business would be too different to be able to conduct effective comparison.

It will also be difficult to use analytical procedures if a business had experienced a number of significant one-off events in the year as these would distort the year's figures making comparison to both prior years and budgets meaningless.

Key ratios

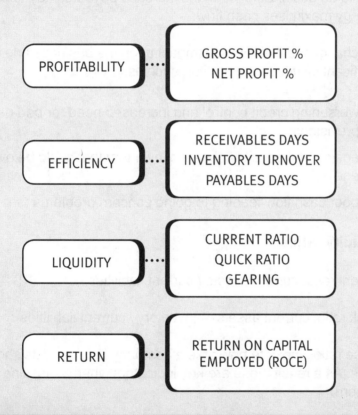

PROFITABILITY	GROSS PROFIT % NET PROFIT %
EFFICIENCY	RECEIVABLES DAYS INVENTORY TURNOVER PAYABLES DAYS
LIQUIDITY	CURRENT RATIO QUICK RATIO GEARING
RETURN	RETURN ON CAPITAL EMPLOYED (ROCE)

Expandable Text - Ratios

Profitability ratios:

Gross margin: gross profit / sales revenue × 100%

Net margin: profit before tax /sales revenue × 100%

Auditors would expect the relationships between costs and revenues to stay relatively stable. Things that can affect these ratios include: changes in sales prices, bulk purchase discounts, economies of scale, new marketing initiatives, changing energy costs, wage inflation.

Efficiency ratios

Receivables days: receivables / sales revenue × 365

Payables days: payables / purchases × 365

Inventory days: inventory / cost of sales × 365

These ratios show how long, on average, companies take to collect cash from customers and pay suppliers and how long they hold inventory for. Ultimately companies should strive to reduce receivables and inventory days to an acceptable level and increase payables days because this strategy maximises cash flow.

Any changes to this mix can impact upon the business and can indicate significant issues to the auditor, such as:

- worsening credit control and increased need for bad debt provisions;
- ageing and possibly obsolete inventory that could be overvalued; and
- poor cash flow leading to going concern problems (see later notes).

Liquidity ratios

Current ratio: current assets / current liabilities

Quick ratio: current assets – inventory / current liabilities

These ratios indicate how able a company is to meet its short term debts. As a result these are key indicators when assessing going concern.

Investor ratios

Gearing: borrowings/share capital + reserves.

Return on capital employed (ROCE): profit before interest and tax / share capital + reserves + borrowings.

Gearing is a measure of external debt finance to internal equity finance. ROCE indicates the returns those investments generate.

Any change in either the gearing or ROCE could indicate a change in the financing structure of the business or it could indicate changes in overall performance of the business. These ratios are important for identifying potentially material changes to the statement of financial position (new/repaid loans or share issues) and for obtaining an overall picture of the annual performance of the business.

The suitability of analytical procedures as substantive tests

The suitability of this approach depends on four factors:

- The assertion/s under scrutiny;
- The reliability of the data;
- The degree of precision possible; and
- The amount of variation which is acceptable.

Some examples.

(1) Suitability
   – Analytical procedures are clearly unsuitable for testing the existence of inventories.
   – They are, however, suitable for assessing the value of inventory in terms of the need for provisions against old inventories, identified using the inventory holding period ratio.

(2) Reliability
   – If controls over financial data are weak then it is likely to contain misstatement and is therefore not suitable as a basis for assessment. This may be true of manually prepared forecasts and industry data from unkown sources.

(3) Precision
   – There is likely to be greater consistency over time in information such as gross margins than in discretionary expenditure that is subject to change, like advertising or R&D.

(4) Acceptable variation
   – Variations that could have a minor impact on the results for the year (such as cleaning costs, utility accruals) will be regarded differently from variations in balances such as receivables, which could significantly affect the need for bad debt provisions.

3 The audit of receivables

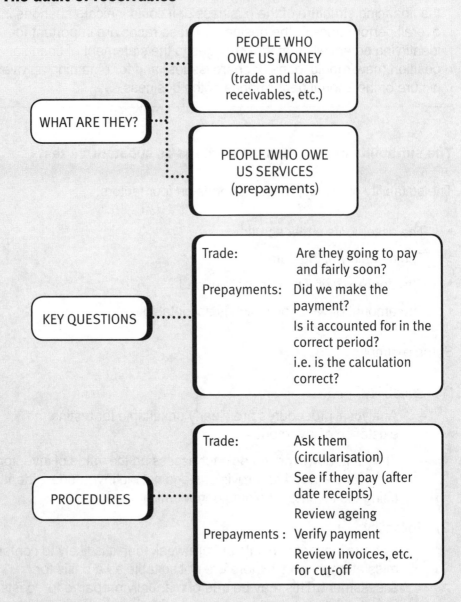

Key assertions

- **Existence** – the receivable actually exists;

- **Rights and obligations** – the company has rights to receive the benefit from receivables;

- **Valuation and allocation** – receivables are included in the financial statements at the correct amount, including provisions for bad and doubtful debt;

- **Completeness** – all receivables relating to the period have been accounted for; and

- **Classification and understandability** – receivables (Including provisions) are appropriately disclosed in the financial statements.

Audit procedures

Existence

- Perform a receivables circularisation (a direct confirmation from external sources - see below).
- Select a sample of receivables and trace amounts due to the original sales invoice to confirm that a transaction has taken place;

Rights and obligations

- Receivables circularisation;
- Select a sample of receivables and confirm the trade terms to original credit agreements and sales invoices.

Valuation and allocation

- Inspect the ageing profile of receivables to identify any significant, long outstanding balances that may require a provision.
- Analytically review the ageing profile in comparison to previous periods to identify any deterioration in credit control.
- Inspect post year-end cash book/bank statements and trace payments received to year-end receivables to confirm that amounts were indeed collectable.
- Discuss the results of the ageing and cash receipts analysis with management to identify if any further provisions are required for old, unpaid balances.
- Discuss the assumptions underlying any general provisions with management to ensure they are appropriate.
- Recalculate the provision based on management's assumptions and agree to the figure in the financial statements.
- Inspect invoices relating to prepaid balances, agree cost to calculations made.
- Inspect bank statements to confirm prepaid amounts have been paid.

Completeness

- Obtain a list of receivables balances, cast this and agree it to the receivables control account total at the end of the year. Differences should be reconciled.
- Perform a receivables circularisation.
- Inspect receivables ledger for credit balances and obtain explanations from management.

- Inspect a sample of the last five to ten goods despatched notes immediately prior to the year-end. Trace these through to year-end receivables to ensure they have been recorded.

Classification and understandability

- Inspect the draft financial statements and agree the receivables figures and disclosures to nominal ledger balances.

Receivables circularisations

If successful, circularisations provide evidence directly from the receivables themselves. These are considered to be reliable because they are external, third party confirmations. Circularisations are also written and original.

Procedure

- Select a sample of receivables to be circularised and notify client of those selected;
- Extract details of each receivable from the relevant ledger and prepare letters. This should state the balance outstanding at the year-end and include a reply slip for receivables to confirm the balance;
- Ask the chief accountant at the client (or other responsible official) to sign the letters;
- The auditor posts or faxes the letters to the individual receivables;
- Receivables complete the reply slips, confirming the amounts they owe the client at the year-end, and post them directly to the auditor; and
- Auditor investigates any disagreement by receivables.

Considerations

Whilst circularisations are undoubtedly a useful and efficient tool for providing good quality evidence, their success does depend on response rates. It must be remembered that the audit client's customers are under no obligation to reply and, for this reason, responses may be limited. If the response rate is poor then other forms of evidence must be sought. To maximise the response rate auditors should ensure:

- Letters are sent out as soon as possible after the year-end;
- That the outstanding balance is clearly displayed and all that receivables have to do is confirm whether this is correct or not;
- A reply slip is attached to minimise the work of the receivable; and
- Pre-paid return envelopes are supplied.

Confirmation letter example

Customer Ltd

Customer's address

Date of circularisation

Dear Sirs

As part of their normal audit procedures we have been requested by our auditors, Auditor & Co, to ask you to confirm the balance on your account with us at 31 December 2009, our year-end.

The balance on your account, as shown by our records, is shown below. After comparing this with your records will you please be kind enough to sign the confirmation and return a copy to the auditor in the prepaid envelope enclosed. If the balance is not in agreement with your records, will you please note the items making up the difference in the space provided.

Please note that this request is made for audit purposes only and has no further significance.

Your kind co-operation in this matter will be greatly appreciated.

Yours faithfully

Chief Accountant

Auditor & Co

Auditor's address

Dear Sirs

We confirm that, except as noted below[x], a balance of $10,000

was owing by us to Client Limited at 31 December 2009.

(*space for customer's signature*)

[x]Details of differences:

4 The audit of inventories

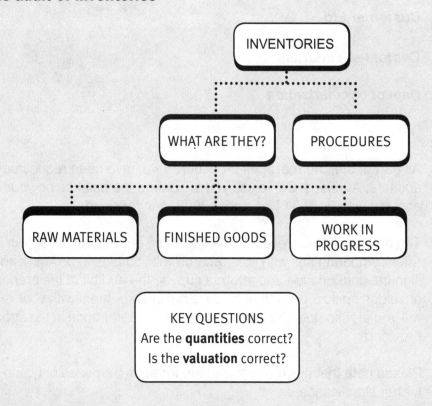

The audit of inventory is usually regarded as one of the higher risk areas of the audit:

- Inventories (opening and closing) are significant to the calculation of gross profits;

- Raw materials may be difficult to count accurately (e.g. weights of gold in a jewellers, oil reserves, scrap metal)

- Work in progress and finished goods cost calculations can be complex; and

- Calculations are subject to certain estimates (stage of completion, obsolescence etc).

chapter 1

Key assertions

- **Existence** – does the inventory recorded actually exist?

- **Completeness** – have all inventory balances been recorded?

- **Rights and obligations** – does the company have the rights to receive the benefits from inventories?

- **Valuation and allocation** – are inventories valued appropriately (i.e. at the lower of cost and net realisable value and net of any provisions for damaged and slow moving goods)?

- **Cut-off** – are inventory movements around the year-end recorded in the correct period?

- **Classification and understandability** – are inventories (including provisions) appropriately disclosed in the financial statements?

The inventory count

Principles

- A typical inventory count happens at the year-end, although continuous counting is possible throughout the year.

- The purpose of the count is to confirm that the **quantities** of inventory recorded on the client's system are accurate.

- Whilst the count is being performed items that are damaged and/or obsolete should be identified for either scrapping or sale at a discounted price.

- From an audit perspective, attendance at the count helps provide evidence regarding the **existence, completeness** and **valuation** of inventory balances.

- Inventory counting is the responsibility of the **client**. The auditor merely attends the count to help gather evidence to form an opinion regarding whether inventory is free from material misstatement or not.

Inventory counting procedures

Before the count:

- Obtain the client's counting instructions and review them for obvious flaws in the counting process. This may also help identify if there are any significant or risky elements of inventory that require special attention, or even precautions.

During the count

- Observe the count as it proceeds to ensure:
  - the counting instructions are being followed
  - all items are being counted and recorded
  - there is no risk of double counting
  - evidence of damaged or slow moving goods is being recorded
  - deliveries and despatches are not being made during the count
  - count recording sheets are being properly controlled (i.e. pre-numbered and filled in with ink).

- Conduct test counts, on a suitable sample selection basis, as follows:
  - select a sample of items from the inventory records and physically observe the items on the warehouse floor to prove the items **exist**.
  - select a sample of physical items from the warehouse floor and trace them to the inventory records to ensure that the latter is **complete**.

- Record cut-off information by obtaining details of the last deliveries and despatches prior to the year-end. These will then be traced to inventory records during final audit procedures.

Year-end counts and continuous inventory systems

The procedures suggested above apply to all inventory counts, whether as a one-off, year-end exercise or where inventory is counted on a rolling basis throughout the year. The objective is the same:

- To identify whether the client's inventory system reliably records, measures and reports inventory balances.

Where the client uses a continuous counting system, where lines of inventory are counted periodically (say monthly) throughout the year so that by the end of the year all lines have been reviewed, there are both advantages and disadvantages for the auditor.

Advantages

- The auditor is less time constrained and can pick and choose particular locations and inventory lines to count at any time to ensure the system is reliable.

- Slow moving and damaged inventory should be identified and adjusted for in the client's records on a continuous basis therefore, thus improving the valuation at the year-end.

Disadvantages

- The auditor will need to gain sufficient evidence that the system operates effectively at all times, not just at the time of the count.

- Additional procedures will need to be devised to ensure that the year-end inventory total is reliable, particularly with regard to cut-off and year-end provisions/estimates.

Inventory held at third parties

- Where the client has inventory at locations not visited by the auditor, the auditor normally obtains confirmation of the quantities, value and condition from the holder. The auditor needs to consider whether the holder is sufficiently independent to be able to provide relevant, reliable evidence.

- As with confirmations from receivables, the auditor requests details from the party holding the inventory on behalf of the client to confirm its existence.

- The confirmation request will be sent by the client to those parties identified by the auditor.

- The reply should be sent directly to the auditor to prevent it being tampered with by the client.

- Problems can occur if the third party uses a different description to that of the client and as always, a response is not guaranteed.

Final audit procedures

Completeness

- Obtain an inventory list showing each line of inventory categorised between finished goods, WIP and raw materials. Cast the list to ensure it is arithmetically correct. Make sure the totals agree to amounts disclosed in the financial statements.

- Trace the items counted during the inventory count to the final inventory list to ensure it is the same as the one used at the year-end and to ensure that any errors identified during counting procedures have been rectified.

Cut-off

- Trace the GRN's from immediately prior to the year-end (identified during the count) to year-end payables and inventory balances.

- Trace the GDN's from immediately prior to the year-end (identified during the count) to the nominal ledgers to ensure the items were removed from inventory prior to the year-end and have been recorded in receivables prior to the year-end.

Presentation and disclosure

- Inspect the financial statements and ensure that the figures disclosed agree to the audited nominal ledger balances and that inventories have been correctly analysed between finished goods, raw materials and work in progress.

Valuation

- Trace a sample of inventory items back to original purchase invoices to agree their cost.

- Trace a sample of inventory items to post-year-end sales invoices to determine if the appropriate cost or net realisable value has been used.

- Inspect the ageing of inventory items to identify any old/slow moving amounts that may require provision.

- Trace the above items to any inventory provisions and, if they have not been provided, discuss the reason with management.

- Recalculation of work in progress and finished goods using payroll records for labour costs and utility bills for overhead absorption.

- Calculate inventory turnover/days and compare to last year to assess whether inventory is being held longer and therefore requires greater provisions.

- Calculate gross profit percentage and compare to prior year to identify any significant fluctuations that may indicate either error or changes in inventory holding policies.

Test your understanding 1

(1) **List the audit procedures before the inventory count.**

(3 marks)

(2) **List the audit procedures to test for existence and completeness on inventory.**

(2 marks)

(3) **Saxophone Ltd runs a petrol filling station. List the audit procedures to test the quantities of petrol in inventory.**

(2 marks)

(4) **Flute Ltd makes large machines out of very heavy lumps of steel. List the audit procedures to test its inventory of sheet and bar steel.**

(2 marks)

(5) **Piccolo Ltd has a sheep farming business. List the audit procedures to verify the number of animals it owns at the year end.**

(2 marks)

5 The audit of payables and accruals

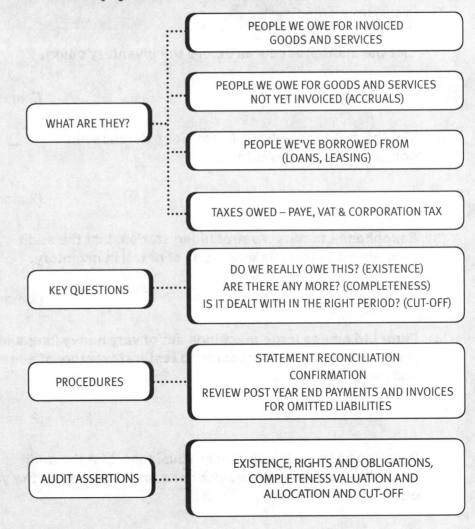

WHAT ARE THEY?

PEOPLE WE OWE FOR INVOICED GOODS AND SERVICES

PEOPLE WE OWE FOR GOODS AND SERVICES NOT YET INVOICED (ACCRUALS)

PEOPLE WE'VE BORROWED FROM (LOANS, LEASING)

TAXES OWED – PAYE, VAT & CORPORATION TAX

KEY QUESTIONS

DO WE REALLY OWE THIS? (EXISTENCE)
ARE THERE ANY MORE? (COMPLETENESS)
IS IT DEALT WITH IN THE RIGHT PERIOD? (CUT-OFF)

PROCEDURES

STATEMENT RECONCILIATION
CONFIRMATION
REVIEW POST YEAR END PAYMENTS AND INVOICES FOR OMITTED LIABILITIES

AUDIT ASSERTIONS

EXISTENCE, RIGHTS AND OBLIGATIONS, COMPLETENESS VALUATION AND ALLOCATION AND CUT-OFF

Key assertions

- **Existence** – the payables actually exist;

- **Rights and obligations** – the company has obligations to settle all payables;

- **Valuation and allocation** – payables are included in the financial statements at the correct amount;

- **Completeness** – all payables relating to the period have been accounted for.

- **Classification and understandability** – all payables are appropriately disclosed in the financial statements.

Completeness is usually the key consideration when testing payables due to the timing and nature of the items included. Provisions and accruals accounting do offer an opportunity for creative accounts to manipulate reported profits somewhat. Auditors therefore have to consider indicators that additional liabilities may exist, such as:

- payables not including known major suppliers;

- payables not including the significant suppliers from the equivalent list last year;

- traditionally recurring accruals not being made, e.g.: rent, utilities, telephone, etc.

- expected finance accruals not being made, e.g.: hire purchase, mortgages, loans etc.

- non-provision of tax balances, including: corporation tax, payroll taxes, sales taxes, etc.

- suppliers revealed only after a review of payments after the year-end; and

- suppliers revealed by a review of unpaid invoices at and after the year-end.

Classification and understandability

- Inspect financial statements to ensure that all liabilities from the nominal ledger have been adequately and accurately disclosed.

Existence

- Circularise a sample of trade payables to confirm the balance at the end of the year (this is uncommon and would only be performed in the absence of supplier statements).

- Inspect year-end statements of accounts sent by suppliers. Any differences between the statement and the nominal ledger should be reconciled.

- Trace a sample of payable/accruals balances to purchase invoices and/or contracts. In particular identify the date of receipt of the invoice and any evidence of payment (such as signatures).

Completeness

- Cast the payables ledger to ensure its accuracy.

- Inspect year-end statements of accounts sent by suppliers. Any differences between the statement and the nominal ledger should be reconciled.

- Investigate any major (by value of purchases in the year) or known regular suppliers that were shown on last year's payables listing but do not have a balance showing in this year's list of balances.

- Enquire of management why the above suppliers do not feature in this year's payables list.

- Inspect after date payments in the cash book and bank statements and ensure they have been provided for at the year-end, as appropriate.

- Perform analytical procedures on the list of payables, such as: payables days, payables as a percentage of purchases, monthly payables levels. Investigate any unusual variances.

- Compare the purchase ledger control account to the list of payables. Reconcile any variations.

- Inspect the list of balances for debit balances. Discuss results with management.

Cut-off

- Select a sample of GRN's raised immediately prior to the year-end and trace them through to year-end payables.

- Likewise, select a sample of GRN's raised immediately after the year-end and trace them to the nominal ledger to ensure they have been recorded in the next accounting period.

Supplier Statements

Companies may send out monthly statements of account as part of their credit control procedures. Therefore it is likely that audit clients will receive a number of these statements from suppliers at the year-end. These can be reconciled to their own payables control account to ensure that their records are correct. This is known as a supplier statement reconciliation and are an important source of audit evidence. Like most statements sent through the post there are a number of reasons why there may be variances:

(1) **Timing differences:**

  − Invoices sent by the supplier but not yet received by the client.

  − Payments sent by the client but not yet received by the supplier.

  − Returns and credit notes not yet appearing on the supplier's statement.

(2) **Errors**

  − Supplier errors that will remain as part of the reconciliation until the supplier corrects them.

  − Client errors, which the client needs to adjust.

Auditors can inspect or reperform the supplier statement reconciliations to ensure the completeness, existence and valuation of payable balances. They are a reliable source of evidence because they are produced by the suppliers, who are (usually - intergroup trading and related parties!!) independent, external sources.

Expandable Text - Supplier reconciliation example

Tuba Ltd

You are auditing the payables of Tuba Ltd and have found that the balance according to Tuba's purchase ledger does not agree to the statement from its supplier Trombone Ltd.

Solution

Trombone Ltd statement reconciliation

	$	$
Balance per supplier statement		1,500
Less:		
Returns/credit notes not yet credited	200	
Payments not yet received by supplier	750	
Agreed balance		950
		550
Balance per purchase ledger		350
Invoices not yet posted		150
Goods received not invoiced		50
Reconciled balance		550

The following is relevant:

	$
Balance per Tuba Ltd's purchase ledger	350
Balance per Trombone Ltd's statement	1,500
Invoices in file on purchase ledger clerks' desk awaiting posting	150
Goods returned by Tuba to Trombone in last week of the year, not yet reflected on Trombone's statement	200
Value of goods from Trombone received by Tuba's goods inwards department and invoiced by Trombone on the very last day of the year (invoices are sent by mail)	50
Payment by cheque sent by mail by Tuba to Trombone on the very last day of the year	750

> **What is the correct figure for the balance between Tuba and Trombone that should form part of Tuba's payables figure in its financial statements?**

Accruals

- Inspect invoices received after the year-end that relate to services provided before the year-end. Trace them to any accruals made to ensure completeness and accuracy of the amounts.

- Obtain the list of accruals from the client, cast it to confirm arithmetical accuracy.

- Agree the figure per the schedule to the general/nominal ledger and financial statements

- Recalculate a sample of accrued costs by reference to contracts and payment schedules (e.g. loan interest).

- Analytically review in comparison to previous period to try and identify if any balances are perhaps missing.

Tax balances

- Corporation/Profits taxes – agree to tax computations.

- Payroll taxes – agree to payroll records.

Overdrafts, loans, etc.

- Agree to bank letter confirmation of outstanding amounts.

Leases, hire purchase

- Agree details to underlying agreement/contracts and recalculate interest amounts and the split between current and non-current.

6 The audit of bank and cash

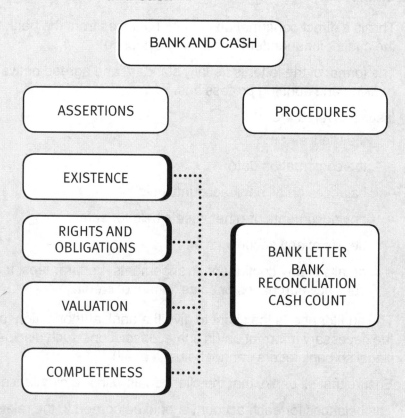

Key assertions

- **Existence** – cash and bank balances actually exist;
- **Rights and obligations** – the company has rights to receive the benefit from those balances;
- **Valuation and allocation** – balances are included in the financial statements at the correct amount;
- **Completeness** – all balances have been accounted for.
- **Classification and understandability** – balances are appropriately disclosed in the financial statements?

The bank letter

- This is a direct confirmation of bank balances from the bank that gives the auditor independent, third-party evidence.

- The format of the letter is usually standard and agreed between the banking and auditing professions.

- Issues covered are:
  - the client's name
  - the confirmation date
  - balances on all bank accounts held
  - any documents or other assets held for safekeeping
  - details of any security given
  - details of any contingent arrangements – guarantees, forward currency purchases or sales, letters of credit.

- The auditor needs the client to give the bank authorisation to disclose the necessary information (in some jurisdictions such disclosures are illegal so bank letters cannot be used at all).

- Ensure that all banks that the client deals with are circularised.

- The balances for each account should be agreed to the relevant bank reconciliation at the year end;

- Details of loans should be agreed to the disclosure in the statement of financial position as either current or non-current.

Bank and cash – other evidence

- Obtain a list of all bank accounts, cash balances and bank loans and overdrafts and agree to totals to figures included in current assets and current liabilities in the financial statements

- Obtain a copy of the client's bank reconciliation, cast and agree the balances to the cash book and bank letter

- Trace all outstanding lodgements and unpresented cheques to pre-year-end cash book and post-year-end bank statements

- Ensure all accounts in the bank letter are included in the financial statements

- Ensure bank loans and overdrafts are not offset against positive bank balances in the financial statements

- Count the petty cash in the cash tin at the end of the year and agree the total to the balance included in the financial statements

Presentation and disclosure

- Inspect the draft financial statements and ensure that amounts are disclosed correctly as either assets (positive balances) or liabilities (overdrafts) and that the amounts recorded agree to the nominal ledger.

7 The audit of tangible non-current assets

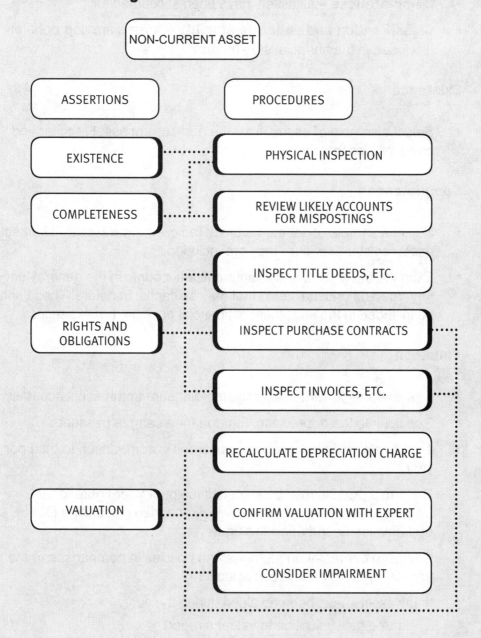

Key assertions

- **Existence** – assets actually exist;
- **Rights and obligations** – the company has rights to receive the benefit from those assets;
- **Valuation and allocation** – assets are included in the financial statements at the correct amount;
- **Completeness** – all assets have been accounted for.
- **Classification and understandability** – assets are appropriately disclosed in the financial statements?

Existence

- Select a sample of assets from the non-current asset register and physically inspect them.

Completeness

- Select a sample of assets visible at the client premises and inspect the asset register to ensure they are included.
- Examine the repairs and maintenance accounts in the general ledger for large and unusual items that may be capital in nature. These should be included in the statement of financial position, not expenses.

Valuation

- Cast the non-current asset register to ensure arithmetical accuracy.
- Recalculate the depreciation charge for a sample of assets.
- Analytically review depreciation charges in comparison to the prior year.
- Perform a proof in total by adjusting the prior year figure for all additions, disposals and revaluations and then calculating total depreciation based upon this figure.
- Compare depreciation methods and policies in comparison to the previous year to ensure consistency.
- If any assets have been revalued during the year:
  - agree new valuation to valuer's report
  - verify that all assets in the same class have been revalued
  - reperform depreciation calculation to verify that charge is based on new carrying value.
- When physically inspecting assets, take note of their condition and usage in case of impairment.

- For a sample of asset additions, agree the cost to purchase invoices (or other relevant documentation).

- If any assets have been constructed by the company, obtain analysis of costs incurred and agree to supporting documentation (timesheets, materials invoices, etc.).

Rights and Obligations

- For a sample of recorded assets, obtain and inspect ownership documentation:
  - title deeds for properties
  - registration documents for vehicles
  - insurance documents may also help to verify ownership (and asset values).

- Where assets are leased, inspect the lease document to assess whether the lease is operating or finance (if the latter, the asset should be included on the company's statement of financial position).

Disclosure

- Agree opening balances with prior year financial statements.

- Compare depreciation rates in use with those disclosed.

- For revalued assets, ensure appropriate disclosures made (e.g. name of valuer, revaluation policy).

- Agree breakdown of assets between classes with the general ledger account totals.

8 The audit of non-current liabilities

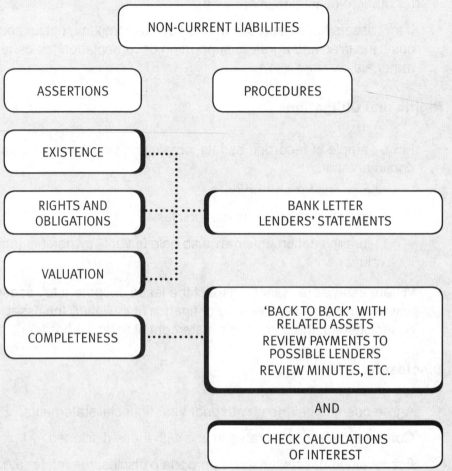

Key assertions

- **Existence** – liabilities actually exist;
- **Rights and obligations** – the company has obligations to pay the liabilities;
- **Valuation and allocation** – liabilities are included in the financial statements at the correct amount;
- **Completeness** – all liabilities have been accounted for.
- **Classification and understandability** – liabilities are appropriately disclosed in the financial statements?

Loan payables

- Agree the year-end loan balance to any available loan statements to confirm obligations, existence and valuation.
- Agree interest payments to the loan agreement and the bank statements.
- Analyse relevant disclosures of interest rates, amounts due (e.g. between current and non-current payables) to ensure complete and accurate.

- Recalculate the interest accrual to ensure arithmetical accuracy.

Provisions and contingencies

Provisions are a form of payable where the amount or timing of payment is uncertain. As such they are harder to audit.

Where the likelihood of payment is only **possible**, rather than **probable**, no amounts will be entered in the accounts. However, the matter (**contingent liability**) must be adequately disclosed.

- Discuss the matter giving rise to the provision with the client to verify whether an obligation exists.

- Obtain confirmation from the clients lawyers as to the possible outcome and probability of having to make a payment.

- Review subsequent events. By the time the final audit is taking place the matter may have been settled.

- Obtain a letter of representation from the client as the matter is one of judgement and uncertainty. (see chapter 11 for further discussion).

- Recalculate the provision if possible, e.g. warranty provisions for repairs.

Test your understanding 2

(1) **Describe the audit procedures to confirm unpresented cheques are included on a client's bank reconciliation.**

(1 mark)

(2) **List 4 things that might be included on a bank letter besides the balances on a client's accounts.**

(2 marks)

(3) **Describe an audit procedure to test the rights and obligations assertion for a freehold property.**

(1 mark)

(4) **Describe an audit procedure to test the completeness of a client's hire purchase and leasing liabilities.**

(1 mark)

9 Relying on the work of others

```
┌─────────────────────────────────────┐
│      RELYING ON THE WORK OF OTHERS   │
└─────────────────────────────────────┘
```

WHO DO WE MEAN?	....	**EXPERTS** – E.G. SURVEYORS, VALUERS, SPECIALISED STOCK CHECKERS **INTERNAL AUDIT** **SERVICE ORGANISATIONS**
NO DELEGATION OF RESPONSIBILITY	....	WE NEED: • SUFFICIENT • APPROPRIATE AUDIT EVIDENCE
CONSIDERATIONS	....	COMPETENCE INDEPENDENCE OBJECTIVITY
REFERENCE IN AUDIT REPORT?	....	**NO!**

Why rely on the work of other people?

*   In certain circumstances auditors may need to rely on the work of, or consult parties not involved in the audit process.

*   Auditors may also choose to rely on the work of others because they find it effective and efficient to do so.

The need to consult others

Auditors do not need to be experts in all aspects of their clients' businesses. Where they lack the technical knowledge and skills to gather evidence about transactions, balances and disclosures they should seek the assistance of an expert. For example:

*   property valuation;
*   construction work in progress.

KAPLAN PUBLISHING

- assessment of oil reserves;
- specialist inventory – livestock, food and drink in the restaurant trade, jewellery; oil reserves; and
- actuarial valuations for pension schemes.

Using an Auditor's Expert

ISA 620 *Using the Work of an Auditor's Expert* states that the auditor should obtain sufficient and appropriate evidence that the work of the expert is adequate for the purpose of the audit.

In making this assessment the external auditor must assess the expert's:

- independence and objectivity; and
- competence (i.e. qualifications, memberships of professional bodies and experience)

Before any work is performed by the expert the auditor should agree in writing:

- The nature, scope and objectives of the expert's work;
- The roles and responsibilities of the auditor and the expert;
- The nature, timing and extent of communication between the two parties; and
- The need for the expert to observe confidentiality.

Once the work has been completed the auditor must than assess it to ensure it is appropriate for the purposes of the audit. This involves consideration of:

- the consistency of the findings with other evidence;
- the significant assumptions made;
- and the use and accuracy of source data.

Relying on Internal Audit

An internal audit department forms part of the client's system of internal control. If this is an effective element of the control system it may well reduce control risk, and therefore reduce the need for the auditor to perform detailed substantive testing. This will obviously be taken into account during the planning phase of the audit.

Additionally, auditors may be able to co-operate with a client's internal audit department and place reliance on their procedures in place of performing their own.

ISA 610 *Using the Work of Internal Auditors* states that before relying on the work of internal auditors, the external auditor must determine whether it is likely to be adequate for the purposes of the audit. This involves an evaluation of:

- the objectivity of the internal audit function;
- the technical competence of the internal audit function;
- whether the internal audit function is carried out with due professional care; and
- whether there is likely to be effective communication between the internal and external auditor.

If the auditor considers it appropriate to use the work of the internal audit function they then have to incorporate this into their planning to assess the impact on the nature, timing and extent of further audit procedures. They also have to plan adequate time to review the work of the internal audit function to evaluate whether:

- the work was performed by people with adequate technical training and proficiency;
- the work was properly supervised, reviewed and documented;
- sufficient and appropriate evidence has been obtained to be able to draw reasonable conclusions;
- the conclusions reached are appropriate in the circumstances; and
- any unusual matters are properly resolved.

Service Organisations

The client may outsource certain functions to another company – a service organisation, e.g.

- payroll
- receivables collection
- the entire finance function
- internal audit.

Advantages from the auditor's point of view

- The independence of the service organisation may give increased reliability to the evidence obtained;
- Their specialist skills tend to make them more reliable at processing information; and
- The auditor may be able to place a high degree of reliance on the reports they produce as a result (reduced control risk).

Disadvantages

- The auditor may not be able to obtain information from the service provider;
- The auditor may not be allowed to test controls at the service provider;
- This would lead to difficulties in assessing the accuracy and reliability of the information produced by the service provider; and
- Ultimately this could lead to a lack of sufficient appropriate evidence and a modified audit report.

References to the work of others in the audit report

It is the auditors' responsibility to obtain sufficient and appropriate audit evidence in order to arrive at their audit opinion. Therefore, no reference should be made in the audit report regarding the use of others during the audit. This might be considered as some form of modifying statement, deflecting responsibility from the auditor to a third party.

10 Accounting estimates

```
                    ┌──────────────────────────┐
                    │  ACCOUNTING ESTIMATES    │
                    └──────────────────────────┘
```

┌──────────────────────────────────┐
│ E.G.   │
│ • INVENTORY PROVISIONS   │
│ • DEPRECIATION RATES   │
│ • ACCRUED REVENUE   │
┌─────────────────┐·········│ • DEFERRED TAX   │
│ WHAT ARE THEY? │   │ • LOSSES FROM LAWSUITS   │
└─────────────────┘   │ • LOSSES ON CONSTRUCTION   │
│   CONTRACTS   │
│ • WARRANTY CLAIMS   │
└──────────────────────────────────┘

┌──────────────────────────────────┐
│ POTENTIAL FOR MATERIAL   │
│ MISSTATEMENT?   │
┌─────────────────┐·········│ SIGNIFICANT RISK?   │
│ KEY QUESTIONS   │   │ SUFFICIENT?   │
└─────────────────┘   │ EXCESSIVE?   │
└──────────────────────────────────┘

┌──────────────────────────────────┐
│ POTENTIAL FOR MATERIAL   │
│ MISSTATEMENT?   │
┌─────────────────┐·········│ SIGNIFICANT RISK?   │
│ PROCEDURES   │   │ SUFFICIENT?   │
└─────────────────┘   │ EXCESSIVE?   │
└──────────────────────────────────┘

Accounting estimates are of particular concern to the auditor as, by their nature, there may not be any physical evidence to support them and they are prone to inaccuracy. They are also subjective and therefore prone to management bias. If the directors wished to manipulate the accounts in any way, accounting estimates are an easy way for them to do this. The auditor must take care when auditing estimates to ensure this has not been the case.

Auditors need to obtain an understanding of:

- how management identifies those transactions, events and conditions that give rise to the need for estimates; and

- how management actually makes the estimates, including the control procedures in place to minimise the risk of misstatement.

In response to this assessment auditors should perform the following further procedures:

- Review of the outcome of the estimates made in the prior period;

- Consider events after the reporting date that provide additional evidence about estimates made at the year-end;

- Test the basis and data upon which management made the estimate (e.g. review mathematical methods);

- Test the operating effectiveness of controls over how estimates are made;

- Develop an independent estimate to use as a point of comparison; and

- Consider whether specialist skills/knowledge are required (e.g. lawyer).

11 Computer assisted audit techniques (CAATs)

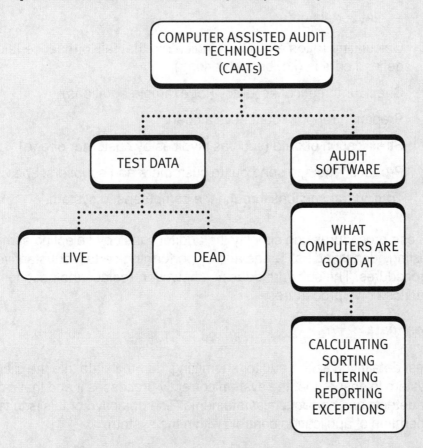

The use of computers as a tool to perform audit procedures is often referred to as a 'computer aided auditing technique' or CAAT for short.

There are two broad categories of CAAT:

(1) Audit software; and

(2) Test data.

Audit software

Audit software is used to interrogate a client's system. It can be either packaged, off-the-shelf software or it can be purpose written to work on a client's system. The main advantage of these programs is that they can be used to scrutinise large volumes of data, which it would be inefficient to do manually. The programs can then present the results so that they can be investigated further.

Specific procedures they can perform include:

- Extracting samples according to specified criteria, such as:
    - Random;
    - Over a certain amount;
    - Below a certain amount;
    - At certain dates.
- Calculating ratios and select indicators that fail to meet certain pre-defined criteria (i.e. benchmarking);
- Check arithmetical accuracy (for example additions);
- Preparing reports (budget vs actual);
- Stratification of data (such as invoices by customer or age);
- Produce letters to send out to customers and suppliers; and
- Tracing transactions through the computerised system.

These procedures can simplify the auditor's task by selecting samples for testing, identifying risk areas and by performing certain substantive procedures. The software does not, however, replace the need for the auditor's own procedures.

Test data

Test data involves the auditor submitting 'dummy' data into the client's system to ensure that the system correctly processes it and that it prevents or detects and corrects misstatements. The objective of this is to test the operation of application controls within the system.

To be successful test data should include both data with errors built into it and data without errors. Examples of errors include:

- codes that do not exist, e.g. customer, supplier and employee;
- transactions above pre-determined limits, e.g. salaries above contracted amounts, credit above limits agreed with customer;

- invoices with arithmetical errors; and

- submitting data with incorrect batch control totals.

Data maybe processed during a normal operational cycle ('live' test data) or during a special run at a point in time outside the normal operational cycle ('dead' test data). Both has their advantages and disadvantages:

- Live tests could interfere with the operation of the system or corrupt master files/standing data;

- Dead testing avoids this scenario but only gives assurance that the system works when not operating live. This may not be reflective of the strains the system is put under in normal conditions.

Other Techniques

There are other forms of CAAT that are becoming increasingly common as computer technology develops, although the cost and sophistication involved current limits their use to the larger accountancy firms with greater resources. These include:

Integrated test facilities - this involves the creation of dummy ledgers and records to which test data can be sent. This enables more frequent and efficient test data procedures to be performed live and the information can simply be ignored by the client when printing out their internal records; and

Embedded audit software - this requires a purpose written audit program to be embedded into the client's accounting system. The program will be designed to perform certain tasks (similar to audit software) with the advantage that it can be turned on and off at the auditor's wish throughout the accounting year. This will allow the auditor to gather information on certain transactions (perhaps material ones) for later testing and will also identify peculiarities that require attention during the final audit.

Auditing Around the Computer

> This term means that the 'internal' software of the computer is not documented or audited by the auditor, but the inputs to the computer are agreed to the expected outputs to the computer.

Audit outcome

Increase the AUDIT RISK Why?

> The actual computer files and programs are NOT TESTED.
>
> Therefore no DIRECT evidence that the programs are working as documented

> Where errors are found it maybe difficult or even impossible to determine why those errors have occurred.
>
> If amendments cannot be made, there is an increased likelihood of audit qualifications.
>
> Since controls are being tested, all discrepancies between predicted and actual results must be fully resolved and documented, irrespective of financial amounts involved.

The Practical Implications of CAAT's

Planning and Risk Assessment

Of course, the most obvious point to note is that CAAT's, whilst efficient, are limited in terms of their cost and the availability of resources. The software itself either has to be purchased or designed and then the accountancy firm would need individuals with IT expertise to perform the tests. This may render them inefficient for many audit procedures. The client's permission (and cooperation when designing bespoke software) must also be sought before programs are loaded onto the client's system. Their use must therefore be considered at the planning phase of the audit.

If they are considered appropriate then they will have many uses when performing risk assessment procedures. One of their primary functions is to test IT application controls. The results of this will then be used to assess control risk and design further audit procedures.

Further Audit Procedures

As previously mentioned CAAT's will be extremely useful for assisting with sample selections through stratification and other techniques. For example, identification of:

- receivable, payable or inventory balances over a certain age;
- individually material assets and liabilities;
- transactions over agreed limits (e.g. customer's credit limits);
- changes to standing data, e.g. authorised supplier lists;
- credit balances within receivables and debit balances in payables;
- non-current asset purchases over a certain amount;

CAAT's can also be used to perform certain substantive procedures, such as:

- ratio calculations;
- recalculation of non-current asset depreciation;
- recalculation of employee taxes, state pension schemes and employment pension scheme balances;
- confirmation of batch totals to individual records, e.g. wages and salary payments to payroll records;
- casting of all ledger balances.

Computers and audit admin

When planning an audit partners need to make sure they have sufficient resources available. This can be done using unsophisticated software to identify who is free at that time, such as an Excel based staff timetable.

Audit reports and letters are predominantly produced using common software packages (again Excel and Word are examples). They look professional and can aid client understanding.

Software packages may also be used to prepare working papers/documentation and are very useful for the aggregation, disaggregation and stratification of data and calculation of complex arithmetical formulas.

12 Not for profit organisations

A not for profit organisation is an organisation whose primary objective is not making a profit. For example:

- charities;
- clubs;
- public institutions; and
- public schools.

Differences to private institutions

Not for profit organisations tend to have weaker systems due to:

- lack of segregation of duties, as the organisation will be restricted with the amount of staff; and
- the use of volunteers, who are likely to be unqualified and have little awareness of the importance of controls.

In not for profit organisations the transactions tend to be less formal, so there may not be physical documentation of transactions. For example: a lot of income received by charities is by way of donation. These transactions will not be accompanied by invoices, orders or despatch notes.

Assessing the going concern of a not for profit organisation may also be more difficult, particularly for charities who are reliant on voluntary donations. Many issues, such as the state of the economy, could impact on their ability to generate revenue in the short term.

Not for profit organisations do not have shareholders to report to. They are more likely to have trustees or governors, who are interested in performance criteria other than profits.

Audit implications

Auditors of not for profit organisations will be required to assess whether the aims of the organisation are being met in an economic, efficient and effective manner.

Testing tends to concentrate on substantive procedures where control systems are lacking. In the absence of documentary evidence procedures rely heavily on analytical review, enquiry and management representation.

The volumes of transactions in not for profit organisations may be lower than a private one, therefore auditors may be able to test a larger % of transactions.

Ultimately, if sufficient appropriate evidence is not available the auditor will have to modify their audit report.

13 Chapter summary

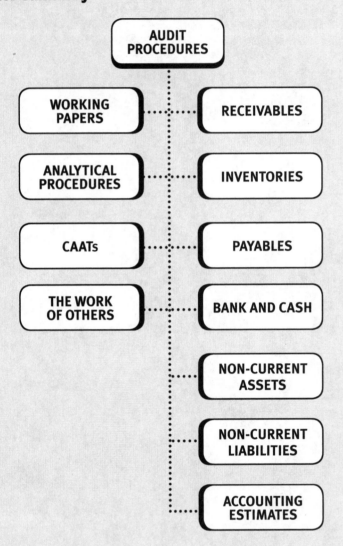

Test your understanding answers

(1) List the audit procedures before the inventory count.	Review the instructions to ensure valid and appropriate.	1
	Confirm the date of inventory count.	1
	Discuss any potential issues with management which may need addressing prior to count.	1
(2) List the audit procedures to test for existence and completeness on inventory.	Select items from the client's final inventory listing and compare with the results of the auditor's test counts	1
	Trace the items counted by the auditor into the client's final inventory listing.	1
(3) Saxophone Ltd runs a petrol filling station. List the audit procedures to test the quantities of petrol in inventory.	If the tank has a gauge – read the results. The accuracy of the gauge can be tested by noting the reading just before and after a new delivery of fuel is made and comparing with the quantity delivered.	1
	If there is no gauge, it will be necessary to 'dip the tank' using a measuring stick.	1
(4) Flute Ltd makes large machines out of very heavy lumps of steel. List the audit procedures to test its inventory of sheet and bar steel.	Test count bars sheets of steel.	1
	Assess average weights of bars and sheets from delivery/ weighbridge records	1
(5) Piccolo Ltd has a sheep farming business. List the audit procedures to verify the number of animals it owns at the year end.	Count them at dipping time or when they are herded together for some purpose.	1
	Or (preferably) use the report of a relevant expert.	1

Test your understanding 2		
(1) Describe the audit procedures to confirm unpresented cheques are included on a client's bank reconciliation.	Review post-year-end bank statements to test that all cheques drawn before year end but clearing after the statement of financial position date are included on the reconciliation.	1
(2) List 4 things that might be included on a bank letter besides the balances on a client's accounts.	Deeds and other documents or assets held.	½
	Guarantees.	½
	Forward currency contracts	½
	Bills of exchange and letters of credit.	½
(3) Describe an audit procedure to test the rights and obligations assertion for a freehold property.	Review title deeds and register of charges, for owners details and ensure they agree.	1
(4) Describe an audit procedure to test the completeness of a client's hire purchase and leasing liabilities.	For all assets acquired in the year review correspondence to ensure there are no hire purchase or leasing liabilities in relation to the asset.	1

KAPLAN PUBLISHING

11

Completion and review

Chapter learning objectives

Upon completion of this chapter you will be able to:

- explain the purpose of and the procedures involved in a subsequent events review

- define and discuss the significance of going concern

- explain the responsibilities of auditors and management regarding going concern

- discuss the procedures to be applied in performing going concern reviews

- discuss the reporting implications of going concern reviews

- explain the purpose of and procedures for obtaining management representations

- discuss the overall review of evidence obtained

- explain the significance of unadjusted differences.

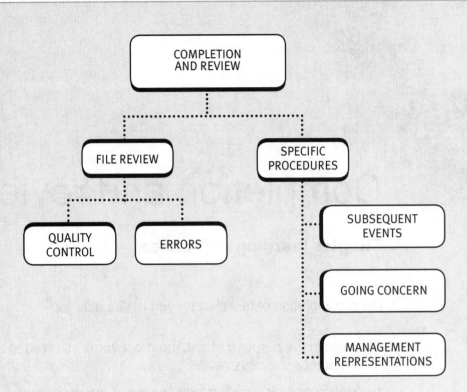

1 Introduction

After an auditor has gathered their evidence there are still many procedures that need to be completed before they can actually sign the audit report. These include:

- the subsequent events review;

- the going concern review;

- obtaining written management representations;

- consideration of misstatements; and

- the audit file review.

2 Subsequent Events Review

Subsequent events

Definition: Subsequent events are events occurring and facts discovered between the period end and the date the financial statements are authorised for issue.

✓ Auditors must take steps to ensure that any such events are properly reflected in the financial statements.

✓ This is done by **events after the reporting period review**.

Auditors responsisibltiy

Year end 31/12/09	Auditors sign	Authorised issue	Annual General meeting
ACTIVE DUTY	**PASSIVE DUTY**	**PASSIVE DUTY**	

• Auditors have an active duty to search for all material events between the statement of financial positon date and the date the audit report is signed.	Between signing the audit report and issuing the financial statements. • Auditors have a passive duty. • Auditors only have to act if they are made aware of something – but once they are aware, they have a duty to take the necessary action.	

ACTIONS	**ACTIONS**	**ACTIONS**

✓ Discuss with management ask them to revise Financial Statements
✓ If client updates the financial statements the auditor would give a clean audit report
✓ If the client refuses to change the financial statements the audit report will need to be qualified
	✓ Discuss with management
	✓ Review the financial statements to ensure revised and redraft audit report
	✓ If client refuses
	  – seek legal advice
	  – attend Annual General Meeting
	  – resign
		✓ Discuss with management but the directors will have to recall the financial statements
		✓ Review the financial statements to ensure revised and redraft audit report
		✓ If client refuses
		  – seek legal advice
		  – attend Annual General Meeting
		  – resign

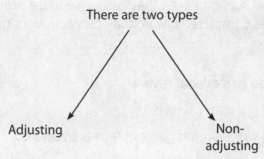

The auditor has done the subsequent event review and has found a material event

There are two types

Adjusting

Non-adjusting

- **Adjusting** – events providing additional evidence relating to conditions existing at the balance sheet date; they require **adjustments** in the financial statements.

- **Non-adjusting** – events concerning conditions which arose after the statement of financial position date, but which may be of such materiality that their **disclosure** is required to ensure that the financial statements are not misleading.

Examples

✓ Trade receivables going bad
✓ Credit notes relating to sale invoices in the year end
✓ Inventory at the year end sold lower than cost

Examples

✓ Take over
✓ Legal issues after the year end
✓ A fire happening after the B/S date which had to impact on the inventory because it was sold prior to the fire

ISA 560 *Subsequent Events* details the responsibilities of the auditors with respect to subsequent events and the procedures they can use. As can be seen above auditors are responsible for performing these procedures right up until the day that they sign the audit report. After this date they can relax a little but whilst they no longer have to perform procedures they must act if they are made aware of any significant subsequent events.

Audit procedures

The nature of procedures performed in a subsequent events review depends on many variables, such as the nature of transactions and events and the availability of data and reports. However the following procedures are typical of a subsequent events review:

- Enquiring into management's procedures/systems for the identification of subsequent events;

- Inspection of minutes of members' and directors' meetings;

- Reviewing accounting records including budgets, forecasts and interim information.

- Enquiring of directors if they are aware of any subsequent events that require reflection in the year-end account;

- Obtaining, from management, a letter of representation that all subsequent events have been considered in the preparation of the financial statements;

- Inspection of correspondence with legal advisors;

- Enquiring of the progress with regards to reported provisions and contingencies; and

- 'Normal' post reporting period work performed in order to verify year-end balances:

    - checking after date receipts from receivables;

    - inspecting the cash book for payments/receipts that were not accrued for at the year-end; and

    - checking the sales price of inventories.

Test your understanding 1

The date is 3 September 2008. The audit of Brand Co is nearly complete and the financial statements and the audit report are due to be signed next week. However, the following additional information on two material events has just been presented to the auditor. The company's year end was 30 June 2008.

Event 1 – Occurred on 6 July 2008

The filaments in a new type of light bulb have been found to be defective making the light bulb unsafe for use. There have been no sales of this light bulb; it was due to be marketed in the next few weeks. The company's insurers estimate that inventory to the value of $600,000 has been affected. The insurers also estimate that the light bulbs are now only worth $125,000. No claim can be made against the supplier of filaments as this company is in liquidation with no prospect of any amounts being paid to third parties. The insurers will not pay Brand for the fall in value of the inventory as the company was underinsured. All of this inventory was in the finished goods store at the end of the year and no movements of inventory have been recorded post year-end.

Event 2 – Occurred 3 August 2008

Production at the Bask factory was halted for one day when an oil truck reversed into a metal pylon, puncturing the vehicle allowing oil to spread across the factory premises and into a local reservoir. The Environmental Agency is currently considering whether the release of oil was in breach of environmental legislation. The company's insurers have not yet commented on the event.

Required:

(a) **For each of the two events above:**

   (i) **Explain whether the events are adjusting or non-adjusting according to IAS 10** *Events After the Reporting Period.*

   (4 marks)

   (ii) **Explain the auditors' responsibility and the audit procedures and actions that should be carried out according to ISA 560** *(Redrafted) Subsequent Events.*

   (12 marks)

(b) Assume that the date is now 15 September 2008, the financial statements and the audit report have just been signed, and the annual general meeting is to take place on 10 October 2009. The Environmental Agency has issued a report stating that Brand Co is in breach of environmental legislation and a fine of $800,000 will now be levied on the company. The amount is material to the financial statements.

   Required:

   Explain the additional audit work the auditor should carry out in respect of this fine.

   (4 marks)
   (20 marks)

3 Going concern

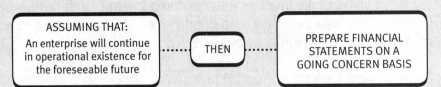

The going concern concept – definition

According to IAS1 financial statements should be prepared on the basis that the company is a going concern unless it is inappropriate to do so.

- The **going concern concept** is defined in IAS1 as the assumption that the enterprise will continue in operational existence for the foreseeable future.

- Any consideration involving the 'foreseeable future' involves making a judgement about future events, which are inherently uncertain.

- Uncertainty increases with time and judgements can only be made on the basis of information available at any point – subsequent events can overturn that judgement.

- The period that management (and therefore the auditor) is required to consider is usually defined by financial reporting standards. Generally (but not exclusively) the period is a minimum of twelve months from the year-end, with twelve months from the date the financial statements are published being preferred.

- There may be circumstances in which it is appropriate to look further ahead. This depends on the nature of the business and their associated risks.

The going concern concept – significance

Whether or not a company can be classed as a going concern affects how its financial statements are prepared.

- Financial statements are usually prepared on the basis that the reporting entity is a going concern.

- IAS1 states that 'an entity should prepare its financial statements on a going concern basis, unless
    - the entity is being liquidated or has ceased trading, or
    - the directors have no realistic alternative but to liquidate the entity or to cease trading.'

- Where the assumption is made that the company will cease trading, the financial statements are prepared using the **break-up basis** under which:
    - assets are recorded at likely sale values
    - inventory and receivables are likely to require more provisions, and
    - additional liabilities may arise (severance costs for staff, the costs of closing down facilities, etc.).

Going concern – responsibilities

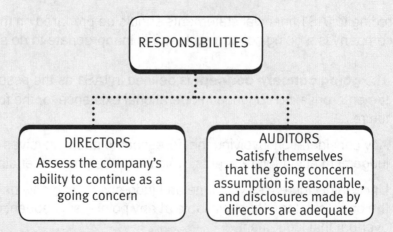

RESPONSIBILITIES

DIRECTORS	AUDITORS
Assess the company's ability to continue as a going concern	Satisfy themselves that the going concern assumption is reasonable, and disclosures made by directors are adequate

Directors and Auditors Responsibilities

Both directors and auditors of an entity have responsibilities regarding going concern.

Directors

- It is the directors' responsibility to assess the company's ability to continue as a going concern when they are preparing the financial statements.

- If they are aware of any material uncertainties which may affect this assessment, then IAS 1 requires them to disclose such uncertainties in the financial statements.

- When the directors are performing their assessment they should take into account a number of relevant factors such as:
    - current and expected profitability
    - debt repayment
    - sources (and potential sources) of financing.

Auditors

- ISA 570 Going Concern states that the auditor needs to consider the appropriateness of management's use of the going concern assumption. The auditors need to assess the risk that the company may not be a going concern.

- Where there are going concern issues, the auditor needs to ensure that the directors have made sufficient disclosure of such matters in the notes to the financial statements.

Going concern – what the auditor has to do (Audit procedures)

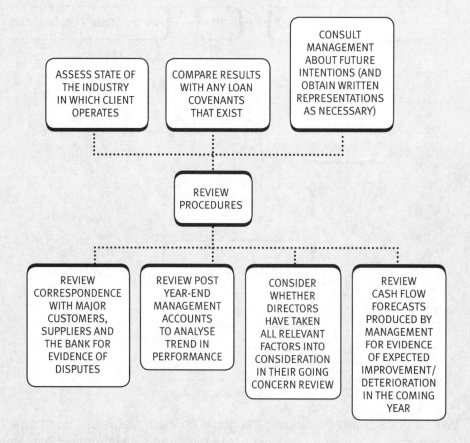

Indicators of going concern problems

Typical indicators of going concern problems include the following:

- Net current liabilities (or net liabilities overall!).
- Borrowing facilities not agreed or close to expiry of current agreement;
- Defaulted loan agreements;
- Unplanned sales of non-current assets;
- Missing tax payments;
- Failure to pay staff;
- Negative cash flow;
- Inability to obtain credit from suppliers;
- Major technology changes;
- Legal claims;
- Loss of key staff; and
- Over-reliance on a small number of products, staff or customers.

Going concern – disclosure requirements

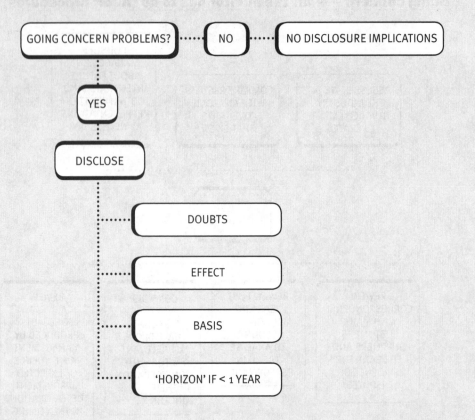

Where there is any doubt over the going concern status of a company, the directors should include disclosures in the financial statements explaining:

- the doubts
- the possible effect on the company.

Where the directors have been unable to assess going concern in the usual way (e.g. for less than one year beyond the date on which they sign the financial statements), this fact should be disclosed.

Where the financial statements are prepared on a basis other than the going concern basis, the basis used should be disclosed.

Going concern reviews – reporting implications

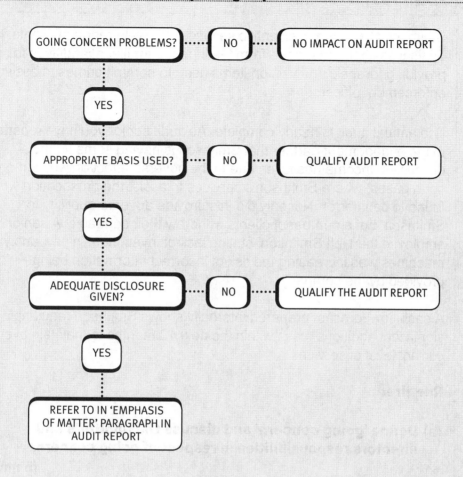

We will look at the detail of the contents of the auditor's report in Chapter 12.

In relation to going concern it is important to understand the following:

- Financial statements are normally prepared on the going concern basis;

- Where the going concern basis is used and is appropriate, the auditors **do not** need to mention the fact in their report;

- If the auditor believes that the going concern basis used in the financial statements is inappropriate they may have to modify the audit report;

- If the directors appropriately disclose an uncertainty with regard to going concern the auditor (without modifying their opinion) will refer to this in the audit report in an 'emphasis of matter' paragraph; and

- If the directors prepare the financial statements on another basis (i.e. not going concern) and this is appropriate the auditor will also refer to this in an emphasis of matter paragraph.

FIXED TEST 3 - Smithson

Smithson Co provides scientific services to a wide range of clients. Typical assignments range from testing food for illegal additives to providing forensic analysis on items used to commit crimes to assist law enforcement officers.

The annual audit is nearly complete. As audit senior you have reported to the engagement partner that Smithson is having some financial difficulties. Income has fallen due to the adverse effect of two high-profile court cases, where Smithson's services to assist the prosecution were found to be in error. Not only did this provide adverse publicity for Smithson, but a number of clients withdrew their contracts. A senior employee then left Smithson, stating lack of investment in new analysis machines was increasing the risk of incorrect information being provided by the company.

A cash flow forecast prepared internally shows Smithson requiring significant additional cash within the next 12 months to maintain even the current level of services.

Required:

(a) **Define 'going concern' and discuss the auditor's and directors responsibilities in respect of going concern.**

(5 marks)

(b) **State the audit procedures that may be carried out to try to determine whether or not Smithson Co is a going concern.**

(10 marks)

(c) **Explain the audit procedures the auditor may take where the auditor has decided that Smithson Co is unlikely to be a going concern.**

(5 marks)

4 Written (management) representations

What are written representations?

A written representation is a (written) statement by management provided to the auditor to confirm certain matters or to support other audit evidence (**ISA 580** *Written Representations*). The purpose of obtaining this form of evidence is twofold:

- to obtain representations that management, and those charged with governance, have fulfilled their responsibility for the preparation of the financial statements, including;
    - preparing the financial statements in accordance with an applicable financial reporting framework;
    - providing the auditor with all relevant information and access to records;
    - recording all transactions and reflecting them in the financial statements.
- to support other audit evidence relevant to the financial statements if determined necessary by the auditor or required by ISA's.

The latter point may be relevant where the auditor deems that other, more reliable forms of evidence are not available to them. Examples include:

- plans or intentions that may affect the carrying value of assets or liabilities;
- confirmation of values where there is a significant degree of estimation or judgement involved, e.g. provisions and contingent liabilities;
- formal confirmation of the directors' judgement on contentious issues, e.g. the value of assets where there is a risk of impairment; and
- aspects of laws and regulations that may affect the financial statements, including compliance.

How are written representations obtained?

As the audit progresses, the audit team will assemble a list of those items about which it is appropriate to seek management representations. During completion the auditors will write to the client confirming the issues about which they are seeking representations. The client must formally document, and sign, a response and send it to the auditor.

The representations themselves may take any of the following forms.

- A letter from the client to the auditors responding to the necessary points. (It is common for the auditor to draft the letter for the client, who simply reproduces it on their own letter-headed paper, approves it and signs it).

- A letter from the auditors to management setting out the necessary points, which management signs in acknowledgement and returns to the auditors.

- Minutes of a meeting where representations were made orally, which can be signed by management.

The quality and reliability of written representations

Unfortunately, written representations are internal sources of evidence, and are therefore subject to bias, and tend to focus on contentious areas of the financial statements. They are therefore potentially unreliable forms of audit evidence. **They do not, on their own, constitute appropriate evidence.**

ISA 580 also clearly states that written representations should only be sought to support other audit evidence. **They do not, on their own, constitute sufficient evidence.**

It is clear that the quality of written representations is somewhat dubious. However, there are instances where no other, better quality forms of evidence are available to the auditor, particularly where disclosures in the financial statements are restricted to matters of management judgement. Before they can be used the auditor must consider their reliability in terms of:

Reliability must be considered in terms of diff

- inconsistencies with other forms of evidence; and

- concerns about the competence, integrity, ethical values or diligence of management;

With inconsistency the auditor will be required to reconsider their initial risk assessment and, perhaps, perform further procedures. If the latter is true (about competence, integrity etc) then the audit must consider whether the engagement can be conducted effectively. If they conclude that it cannot then they should withdraw, where permitted by laws and regulations. If they are not permitted to withdraw they should consider the impact on the audit report. It is likely that this would lead to them disclaiming their opinion.

The last point is also relevant if management refuses to provide written representations.

Additional matters requiring written representation

In addition to the matters identified in the passages above, the following issues may also be documented in a written representation:

directors have assessed the risk of fraud and consider it to be low;

directors are not aware of any actual, or suspected, instances of fraud;

all related parties have been identified and transactions with them disclosed in the financial statements;

directors consider the aggregate of all uncorrected misstatements to be immaterial;

the directors have considered all subsequent events in preparing the financial statements; and

the directors have considered all possible events, matters and contingencies in performing their going concern review.

Test your understanding 2

(1) **List three reasons why auditors obtain written representations.** _To confirm ds thoyd with governor hv carried_ _where no oche be the quelly of_ _out thur responsibility in prepary fin statemt_ _evidance is available._ **(3 marks)** _- Required by ISA SBA ad ode_ _- To confirm certain issues · access to related info v_ _ISA_ _records_ _- To support audit evidue·_

(2) **List six items that could be in a written representation letter.**

(3 marks)

- Fin Statemat bn prepard accord. to fin regulatory framework·
- Risk of fraud idehfied to be minimal.
- Related party trasach disclosed·
- Unaware of any suspected or related fraud issue·
- Subsequent events hv bn considered by director in prepary fin statemets
Aggregoh of all uncorrdd misstatemats consedard immatrial

5 Overall review of evidence

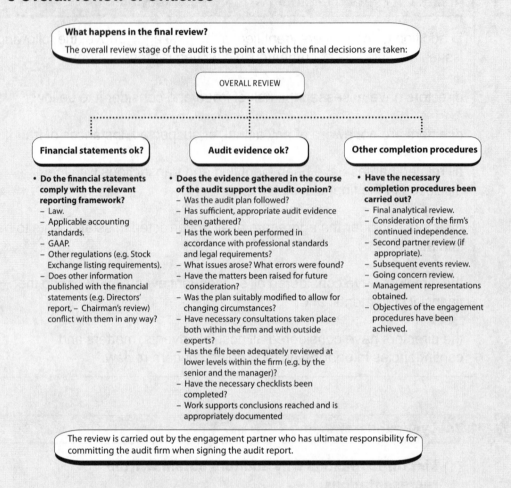

What happens in the final review?

The overall review stage of the audit is the point at which the final decisions are taken:

OVERALL REVIEW

Financial statements ok?

Audit evidence ok?

Other completion procedures

- **Do the financial statements comply with the relevant reporting framework?**
  - Law.
  - Applicable accounting standards.
  - GAAP.
  - Other regulations (e.g. Stock Exchange listing requirements).
  - Does other information published with the financial statements (e.g. Directors' report, – Chairman's review) conflict with them in any way?

- **Does the evidence gathered in the course of the audit support the audit opinion?**
  - Was the audit plan followed?
  - Has sufficient, appropriate audit evidence been gathered?
  - Has the work been performed in accordance with professional standards and legal requirements?
  - What issues arose? What errors were found?
  - Have the matters been raised for future consideration?
  - Was the plan suitably modified to allow for changing circumstances?
  - Have necessary consultations taken place both within the firm and with outside experts?
  - Has the file been adequately reviewed at lower levels within the firm (e.g. by the senior and the manager)?
  - Have the necessary checklists been completed?
  - Work supports conclusions reached and is appropriately documented

- **Have the necessary completion procedures been carried out?**
  - Final analytical review.
  - Consideration of the firm's continued independence.
  - Second partner review (if appropriate).
  - Subsequent events review.
  - Going concern review.
  - Management representations obtained.
  - Objectives of the engagement procedures have been achieved.

The review is carried out by the engagement partner who has ultimate responsibility for committing the audit firm when signing the audit report.

What is the purpose of a final review?

It is the responsibility of the engagement partner to perform a review of audit documentation (including a discussion with the engagement team) in order to satisfy themselves that sufficient appropriate evidence has been obtained to support any conclusions reached and, ultimately, the audit opinion.

Considerations include, for example:

- has work been performed in accordance with professional standards?

- have the significant risks identified during planning been addressed?

- are there any critical areas of judgement relating to difficult or contentious matters?

- are then any significant matters for further consideration?

- have appropriate consultations taken place or are more needed?

- have the objectives of the engagement procedures been achieved?

- does the work documented support the conclusions made?

- is there a need to revise the nature, timing and extent of procedures?

- is the evidence sufficient to support an opinion?

Reviews are also significant for a firm's appraisal system and development of staff. Additionally they are an important element of any monitoring system, implemented to identify and rectify deficiencies in a firm's practices that could lead to poor quality work.

Appropriate review procedures are an integral part of an audit and are a requirement of **ISA 220** *Quality Control for an Audit of Financial Statements.*

6 Evaluation of misstatements

All misstatements should be communicated to management on a timely basis, unless they are clearly trivial. Management should be asked to correct **all** misstatements identified during the audit. Auditors should try and obtain an understanding of management's reasons for refusing to adjust any of the misstatements.

Prior to evaluating the significance of uncorrected misstatements the auditor should reassess materiality to confirm whether it remains appropriate to the financial statements. Then the auditor must assess whether uncorrected misstatements are, individually or in aggregate, material. To do this they should consider the size and nature of the misstatements, both in relation to the financial statements as a whole and to particular classes of transaction, account balances and disclosures.

Finally, the auditor should obtain a written representation from management and those charged with governance that they believe the effect of the uncorrected misstatements is immaterial, individually and in aggregate.

Once these procedures have been completed the auditor should then consider the impact of uncorrected misstatements on their reporting. The impact on the audit report is considered in chapter 12. Other reports are considered below.

ISA 260 *Communication with Those Charged with Governance* requires the auditor to make additional communications to managers, directors and those charged with governance at the conclusion of the audit of matters significant to the oversight of the financial reporting process.

One of the matters requiring communication is 'significant findings from the audit.' The existence of errors may indicate that a client's accounting practices or policies contravene financial reporting requirements or that the internal control systems are deficient. Either way these matters should be communicated to the client.

Test your understanding 3

List three examples of findings that could result in unadjusted differences (material or immaterial).

(3 marks)

7 Chapter summary

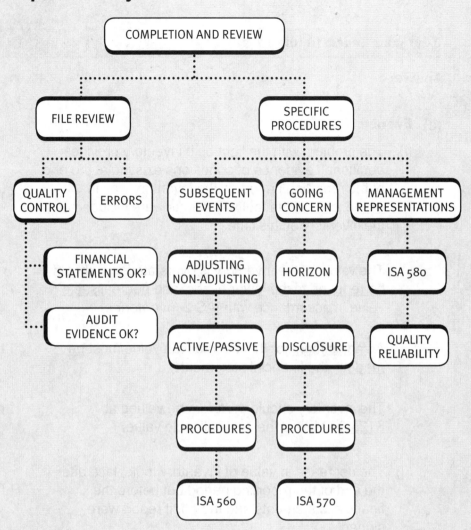

Test your understanding answers

Test your understanding 1

Answer

(a) **Event 1**

(i) The problem with the light bulb inventory provides additional evidence of conditions existing at the end of the reporting period as the inventory was in <u>existence</u> and the faulty filaments were included in the inventory at this time.

        1 mark

The value of the inventory is overstated and should <u>be reduced</u> to the <u>lower of cost</u> and <u>net realisable</u> value in accordance with IAS 2 *Inventories*.

        1 mark

An <u>adjustment</u> for this decrease in value must <u>be made</u> in the financial statements.

        1 mark

The inventory should therefore be valued at <u>$125,000</u> being the net realisable value.

        1 mark

(ii) The decrease in value of inventory took place after the end of the reporting period but before the financial statements and the audit report were signed.

        1 mark

The auditor is therefore <u>still responsible</u> for identifying material events that affect the financial statements.

        1 mark

Audit procedures are therefore required to determine the net book value of the inventory and check that the $125,000 is the sales value of the light bulbs.

        1 mark

Audit procedures will include:

– Obtain <u>documentation</u> from the <u>insurers</u> confirming their estimate of the value of the light bulbs and that no further <u>insurance claim</u> can be made for the loss in value.

        1 mark

–	Obtain the amended financial statements and ensure that the directors have included $125,000 as at the end of the reporting period.	1 mark
–	Ensure that the year-end value of inventory has been decreased to $125,000 on the statement of financial position, statement of financial position note and the income statement.	1 mark
–	Review inventory lists to ensure that the defective filaments were not used in any other light bulbs and that further adjustments are not required to any other inventory.	1 mark
–	Obtain an additional management representation point confirming the accuracy of the amounts written-off and confirming that no other items of inventory are affected.	1 mark

Event 2

(i)	The release of oil occurred after the end of the reporting period, so this is indicative of conditions existing after the end of the reporting period – the event could not be foreseen at the end of the reporting period.	1 mark
	In this case, no adjustment to the financial statements appears to be necessary.	1 mark
	However, the investigation by the Environmental Agency could result in legal claim against the company for illegal pollution so as a material event it will need disclosure in the financial statements.	1 mark
(ii)	As with event 1, the event takes place before the signing of the audit report, therefore the auditors have a duty to identify material events affecting the financial statements.	1 mark
	Audit procedures will include:	
–	Obtain any documentation on the event, for example board minutes, copies of environmental legislation and possibly interim reports from the Environmental Agency to determine the extent of the damage.	1 mark

– Inquire of the directors whether they will disclose the event in the financial statements.

1 mark

– If the directors plan to make disclosure of the event, ensure that disclosure appears appropriate.

1 mark

– If the directors do not plan to make any disclosure, consider whether disclosure is necessary and inform the directors accordingly.

1 mark

– Where disclosure is not made and the auditor considers disclosure is necessary, modify the audit opinion on the grounds of material misstatement and explain the reason for the qualification in the report. This will be for lack of disclosure (not provision) even though the amount cannot yet be determined.

1 mark

– Alternatively, if the auditor considers that the release of oil and subsequent fine will affect Brand's ability to continue as a going concern, draw the members' attention to this in an emphasis of matter paragraph.

1 mark

(b) The notification of a fine has taken place after the audit report has been signed.

Audit procedures will include:

– Discuss the matter with the directors to determine their course of action.

1 mark

– Where the directors decide to amend the disclosure financial statements, audit the amendment and then re-draft and re-date the audit report as appropriate.

1 mark

– Where the directors decide not to amend the financial statements as the disclosure the auditor can consider other methods of contacting the members. For example the auditor can speak in the upcoming general meeting to inform the members of the event.

1 mark

– Other options such as resignation seem inappropriate due to the proximity of the annual general meeting (AGM). Resignation would allow the auditor to ask the directors to convene an extraordinary general meeting, but this could not take place before the AGM so the auditor should speak at the AGM instead.

1 mark

FIXED TEST 3 - Smithson

THIS IS A FIXED TEST – Please answer the question in full (long form written). Then log on to en-gage at the following address: www.en-gage.co.uk. Follow the link to 'Fixed Test 3' and answer the questions based on your homework answer.

Once you have answered the questions on en-gage a model answer will be available for your reference.

Test your understanding 2

(1) Formal confirmation by management of their responsibilities. **1 mark**

Contentious matter where no other, better quality, evidence is available. **1 mark**

Required by ISA 580 and other ISAs. **1 mark**

(2) No irregularities involving management or employees that could have a material effect on the financial statements **½ mark**

All books of account and supporting documentation have been made available to the auditors **½ mark**

Information and disclosures with reference to related parties is complete **½ mark**

Financial statements are free from material misstatements including omissions **½ mark**

No non-compliance with any statute or regulatory authority **½ mark**

No plans that will materially alter the carrying value or classification of assets or liabilities in the financial statements **½ mark**

No plans to abandon any product lines that will result in any excess or obsolete inventory **½ mark**

No events, unless already disclosed, after the end of the reporting period that need disclosure in the financial statements **½ mark**

Test your understanding 3

| List three examples of findings which could result in unadjusted differences (material or immaterial). | Lots of possibilities – some suggestions:

 • year-end inventory counted incorrectly

 • trade receivables unrecoverable

 • over-provisions

 • under-provisions

 • depreciation incorrectly calculated

 • cash book/payables ledger/ receivables ledger closed too early/ late

 • sales revenue cut-off incorrectly applied

 • accruals and prepayments calculated incorrectly

 • interest charge/income not recognised. | 1 mark each |

Reporting

Chapter learning objectives

Upon completion of this chapter you will be able to:

- describe and analyse the format and content of unmodified and modified audit reports

- discuss the type of opinion provided in statutory audits.

1 The audit report

The objectives of an auditor, in accordance with **ISA 700** *Forming an Opinion and Reporting on Financial Statements,* are:

- to form an opinion on the financial statements based upon an evaluation of their conclusions drawn from audit evidence; and
- to express clearly that opinion through a written report.

2 Forming an Opinion

The auditor forms an opinion on whether the financial statements are prepared, in all **material** respects, in accordance with the applicable financial reporting framework. In order to do that they must conclude whether they have obtained **reasonable assurance** about whether the financial statements as a whole are free from material misstatement (whether due to fraud or error).

In particular the auditor should evaluate whether:

- the financial statements adequately disclose the significant accounting policies;
- the accounting policies selected are consistently applied and appropriate;
- accounting estimates are reasonable;
- information is relevant, reliable, comparable and understandable;
- the financial statements provide adequate disclosures to enable the users to understand the effects of material transactions and events; and
- the terminology used is appropriate.

When the auditor concludes that the financial statements are prepared, in all material respects, in accordance with the applicable financial reporting framework they issue an **unmodified** opinion.

If they conclude that either:

- the financial statements as a whole are not free from material misstatement; or
- they have been unable to obtain sufficient appropriate evidence;

then they have to issue a **modified** opinion.

3 Contents of the Audit Report

ISA 700 provides guidance as to the nature and wording of the audit report. Most importantly the report must be in writing.

In addition it recommends that the audit report be broken into distinct sections that explain the purpose, nature and scope of an audit. The main reason for this is to ensure that the users of the audit report understand the nature of audit procedures and that only reasonable assurance is being offered. One of the primary purposes of this is to reduce the 'expectations gap.'

The recommended elements of the report are as follows:

Title

- The title should be 'appropriate'. The use of 'Independent Auditor's Report' distinguishes this report from any other report produced internally or by other non-statutory auditors.

Addressee

- The report should be addressed to the intended user of the report which is usually the shareholders, or other parties as required by the circumstances of the engagement.

Introductory paragraph

- Identifies the entity whose financial statements have been audited;
- States that the financial statements have been audited;
- Identifies the components of the financial statements (by name and even page reference);
- Refers to the accounting policies applied to the financial statements; and
- Specifies the date or period covered by the financial statements.

Statement of responsibilities of management

- Preparation of the financial statements in accordance with the applicable financial reporting framework; and
- Designing and implementing an effective internal control system to enable the preparation of financial statements that are free of material misstatement;

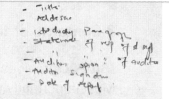

Statement of responsibilities of the auditors

- Express an opinion.
- The audit was conducted in accordance with ISA's;
- Requirement to comply with ethical standards;
- The fact that the audit was planned and performed to obtain reasonable assurance about whether the financial statements are free from material misstatement.
- Audit involves procedures designed to obtain evidence about amounts and disclosures in the financial statements;
- The procedures are based upon auditor judgement, including a risk assessment and consideration of internal controls;
- Obtain sufficient, appropriate audit evidence on which to base the opinion.

Auditor's opinion (headed 'Opinion')

- When expressing an unmodified opinion the auditor (unless otherwise required by relevant laws or regulations) uses one of the following phrases:
  - "the financial statements present fairly, in all material respects........"; or
  - "the financial statements show a true and fair view of ....".

Auditor's signature

- The report may be signed in the name of the firm, or the personal name of the auditor, as appropriate for the particular jurisdiction.
- There may also be a requirement to state the auditor's professional accountancy designation or that the firm is recognised by the appropriate licensing authority (i.e. that the firm/partner is a member of a body such as ACCA and is registered to audit).

Date of report

- The audit report should be dated no earlier than the date on which the auditor has obtained sufficient appropriate evidence upon which to base their opinion.
- This requires that all the statements and notes/disclosure that comprise the financial statements are finalised and that those with responsibility for preparation of the financial statements have acknowledged their role.

- Practically this means that <u>the auditor should sign their report **after** the directors</u> have approved the financial statements.

Auditor's address

- The audit report should name a specific location, which is normally the city where the auditor maintains the office that has responsibility for the audit.

Example of an audit report

Example of an unmodified audit report

INDEPENDENT AUDITOR'S REPORT — *Title*

(Appropriate Addressee) — *Address*

Report on the Financial Statements — *Introductory para*

We have audited the accompanying financial statements of the ABC Company, which comprise the balance sheet as at 31 December, 20X1, and the income statement, statement of changes in equity and cash flow statement for the year then ended, and a summary of significant accounting policies and other explanatory information.

Management's Responsibility for the Financial Statements *mgt resp*

Management is responsible for the preparation and fair presentation of these financial statements in accordance with International Financial Reporting Standards, and for such internal control as management determines necessary to enable the preparation of financial statements that are free from material misstatement, whether due to fraud or error.

Auditor's Responsibility — *audit resp*

Our responsibility is to express an opinion on these financial statements based on our audit. We conducted our audit in accordance with International Standards on Auditing. Those Standards require that we comply with ethical requirements and plan and perform the audit to obtain reasonable assurance about whether the financial statements are free from material misstatement.

An audit involves performing procedures to obtain audit evidence about the amounts and disclosures in the financial statements. The procedures selected depend on the auditor's judgement, including the assessment of the risks of material misstatement of the financial statements, whether due to fraud or error. In making those risk assessments, the auditor considers internal control relevant to the entity's preparation and fair presentation of the financial statements in order to design audit procedures that are appropriate in the circumstances, but not for the purpose of expressing an opinion on the effectiveness of the entity's internal control. An audit also includes evaluating the appropriateness of accounting policies used and the reasonableness of accounting estimates made by management, as well as evaluating the presentation of the financial statements.

We believe that the audit evidence we have obtained is sufficient and appropriate to provide a basis for our audit opinion.

Opinion   — audit opinion

In our opinion, the financial statements present fairly, in all material respects (or *give a true and fair view of*) the financial position of ABC Company as at December 31 20X1, and (*of*) its financial performance and its cash flows for the year then ended in accordance with International Financial Reporting Standards.

Auditor's signature   — Auditors Signatur

[Date of auditor's report]   — Date of report

[Auditor's address]   Auditor eddy

(**ISA 700,** appendix 1)

Test your understanding 1 (All Q2 types)

(1) **List the main contents of an unmodified audit report?**
  - Title
  - Address
  - Introductory para
  - Statement of mgt responsibility
  - " " auditors
  - Auditors opinion
  - Auditor signature
  - Date of report
  - Auditors address

(3 marks)

(2) **What opinion does the auditor give in an unmodified audit report?**
  An opinion that of fin statements hv bn audited, prepared in accordance with regulatory framework and free from all material misstatement

(2 marks)

(3) **When should the audit report be signed?**
  After the director hv approved fin statements

(1 mark)

(4) **Who should sign the audit report and what further information about the signatory should be provided?**
  The audit firm delegated by the audit senior or the name of the firm

(1 mark)

4 Modifications to the Audit Report

So far we have explored the nature and wording of an unmodified audit report. There are two ways that the audit report can be modified:

(a) • by modifying the audit opinion; or

(b) • through inclusion of additional paragraphs

Modifying the audit opinion

There are two reasons why an auditor would be unable to give an unmodified audit opinion:

(i) • they conclude that the financial statements as a whole are not free from material misstatements; or

(ii) • they have been unable to obtain sufficient appropriate evidence to conclude that the financial statements as a whole are free from material misstatement.

If the auditor comes to either of the above conclusions they must then consider how significant the matter is. If the matter is considered immaterial then it should not affect the wording of the opinion and a 'present fairly' or 'true and fair' wording may be used.

However, if the auditor concludes that the matter is material they must modify the wording of their opinion. If, in addition to being material, the auditor considers the matter to be pervasive to the financial statements, then this must also be incorporated into the audit opinion (as shown below). Pervasive means that the matter is:

- not confined to specific elements of the financial statements;
- if confined represents a substantial proportion of the financial statements; or
- is fundamental to users understanding of the financial statements.

The affects on the wording of the opinion can be summarised as follows:

Nature of Matter	Auditor's Judgement Regarding the Pervasiveness of the Matter	
	Material but Not Pervasive	Material and Pervasive
Financial statements are materially misstated	Qualified opinion	Adverse opinion
Inability to obtain sufficient appropriate evidence	Qualified opinion	Disclaimer of opinion

When the auditor modifies their opinion they have to include a 'Basis for Modification Paragraph' in the audit report that describes the matter giving rise to the modification. This paragraph should be placed before the opinion paragraph.

With a qualified opinion the auditor is basically stating that whilst there are, or may be, material misstatements, they are confined to a specific element of the financial statements but the remainder may be relied upon. Accordingly the opinion usually states that "except for the matters described in the basis for modification paragraph, the financial statements present fairly (or *give a true and fair view of*) ...."

If the auditor concludes that the matter is pervasive, they are claiming that the financial statements may not be relied upon in any part. Accordingly:

- if they give an adverse opinion they will state that the financial statements "do not present fairly (or *give a true and fair view of*).........."
- if they give a disclaimer they will state that they "do not express an opinion on the financial statements."

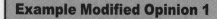

Example Modified Opinion 1

Example of wording where the auditor concludes that the financial statements contain a material, but not pervasive, misstatement:

Basis for Qualified Opinion

As discussed in Note X to the financial statements, no depreciation has been provided in the financial statements which practice, in our opinion, is not in accordance with International Financial Reporting Standards. The provision for the year ended 31 December, 20X9, should be XXX based on the straight-line method of depreciation using annual rates of 5% for the building and 20% for the equipment. Accordingly, the non-current assets should be reduced by accumulated depreciation of XXX and the loss for the year and accumulated deficit should be increased by XXX and XXX, respectively.

Opinion

In our opinion, **except for** the effect on the financial statements of the matter referred to in the Basis for Qualified Opinion paragraph, the financial statements present fairly in all material respects (or *give a true and fair view of*) the financial position ....(remainder of wording as per an unmodified report).

Example Modified Opinion 2

Example where the auditor concludes that the financial statements are materially and pervasively misstated:

Basis for Adverse Opinion

As explained in Note X, the company has not consolidated the financial statements of subsidiary XYZ Company. Under International Financial Reporting Standards the subsidiary should have been consolidated because it is controlled by the company. Had XYZ been consolidated many elements in the accompanying financial statements would have been materially affected.

Adverse Opinion

In our opinion, because of the significance of the matter discussed in the Basis for Adverse Opinion paragraph , the financial statements **do not** present fairly (or *give a true and fair view of*) the financial position**.......**

Example Modified Opinion 3

Example where the auditor concludes that they have been unable to gather sufficient appropriate evidence and the possible effects are deemed to be material but not pervasive.

Basis for Qualified Opinion

We did not observe the counting of the physical inventories as at 31 December 20X9, since that date was prior to our appointment as auditor to the company. Owing to the nature of the company's records, we were unable to satisfy ourselves as to inventory quantities by other audit procedures.

Qualified Opinion

In our opinion, **except for** the possible effects of the matter described in the Basis for Qualified Opinion paragraph, the financial statements present fairly (or *give a true and fair view* of) the financial position............

Example Modified Opinion 4

Example where the auditor concludes that they have been unable to gather sufficient appropriate evidence and the possible effects are deemed to be both material and pervasive.

Basis for Disclaimer of Opinion

The company's investment in its joint venture XYZ Company is carried at $xxx on the statement of financial position, which represents over 90% of the company's net assets at 31 December 20X9. We were not allowed access to the management and auditors of XYZ and, as a result, we were unable to determine whether any adjustments were necessary in respect of the company's proportional share of the assets, liabilities, income and expenses for the year and the elements making up the changes in equity and statement of cash flows.

Disclaimer of Opinion

Because of the significance of the matter described in the Basis of Disclaimer of Opinion paragraph, we have not been able to obtain sufficient appropriate evidence to provide a basis for an audit opinion. Accordingly, we **do not express and opinion** on the financial statements.

5 Additional Paragraphs

Having formed their opinion there are circumstances where the auditor must also draw the users attention to additional matters that are significant to their understanding of the financial statements. These circumstances are categorised as follows:

- matters already presented/disclosed in the financial statements that are fundamental to understanding the financial statements. These are presented in "Emphasis of Matter" paragraphs; and

- other matters relevant to either understanding the audit, the auditor's responsibilities or the audit report. These are presented in "Other Matter" paragraphs.

emphasis of matter par

other matter par.

Emphasis of Matter Paragraphs

These are presented immediately after the opinion paragraph. It is important to note that they have **do not affect the audit opinion**, nor are they a substitute for one.

These paragraphs simply draw the readers attention to a note already disclosed in the financial statements. The matters referred to have to be fundamental to the readers' understanding of the financial statements. Widespread use of them would diminish their effectiveness.

Examples of where it may be necessary to add an Emphasis of Matter paragraph include:

- an uncertainty relating to the future outcome of exceptional litigation or regulatory action;

- early application of a new accounting standards that has a pervasive effect on the financial statements;

- a major catastrophe that has had, or continues to have, a significant effect on the entity's financial position.

Other Matter Paragraphs

Circumstances where these may be necessary include:

- when a pervasive inability to obtain sufficient appropriate evidence is imposed by management but the auditor is unable to withdraw from the engagement;

- when national laws/regulations require, or permit, the auditor to elaborate on their responsibilities;

- when the client issues another set of financial statements (e.g. one according to IFRS and one according to UK GAAP) and the auditor has also issued a report on those financial statements;

- when a set of financial statements is prepared for a specific purpose and user group and the users have determined that a general purpose framework meets their financial information needs; and

- if there is a material inconsistency between the audited financial statements and the 'other information' contained in the annual report (such as the Chairman's Report).

Example Additional Paragraph

The following is an example of an Emphasis of Matter Paragraph:

Emphasis of Matter

We draw attention to Note X to the financial statements. The Company is the defendant in a lawsuit alleging infringement of certain patent rights and claiming royalties and punitive damages. The Company has filed a counter action, and preliminary hearings and discovery proceedings on both actions are in progress. The ultimate outcome of the matter cannot presently be determined, and no provision for any liability that may result has been made in the financial statements. **Our opinion is not qualified in respect of this matter**.

Test your understanding 2

(1) **List four types of modified audit report?**

    (2 marks)

(2) **Give an example of when each type of report would be appropriate.**

    (4 marks)

(3) **What is an 'emphasis of matter' paragraph?**

    (3 marks)

6 Chapter summary

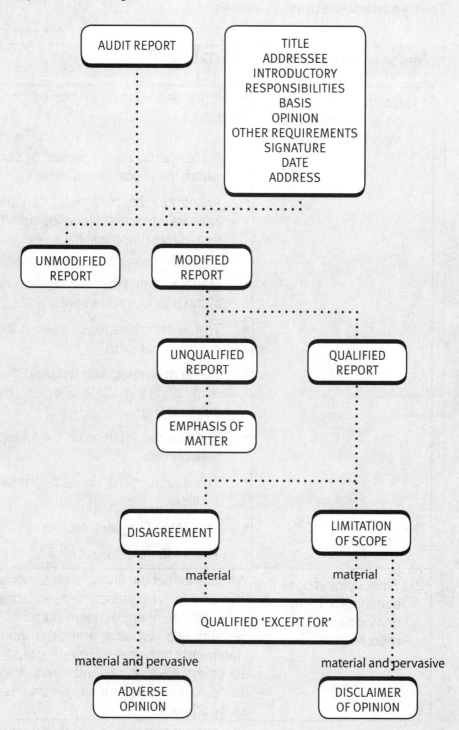

Test your understanding answers

Test your understanding 1 (All Q2 types)

(1)	List the contents of in an unmodified audit report?	An unmodified audit report should include the following. • A title identifying the person or persons to whom the report is addressed. • An introductory paragraph identifying the financial statements audited and the respective responsibilities of directors and auditors. • Management's responsibilities in respect of the financial statements. • The auditors' responsibilities in forming their audit opinion. • The scope paragraph detailing the nature of the audit e.g. ISA's followed, limitation of audit testing. • The auditors' opinion on the financial statements. • The manuscript or printed signature of the auditors. • The date of the auditors' report. • The auditors' address.
(2)	What opinion does the auditor give in an unmodified audit report?	Whether or not the financial statements are 'true and fair', or 'present fairly in all material respects' the financial position and performance. Whether or not the financial statements have been properly prepared in accordance with the financial reporting framework and statutory requirements where appropriate.
(3)	When should the audit report be signed?	The audit report should be signed after the directors have signed the financial statements
(4)	Who should sign the audit report and what further information about the signatory should be provided?	The auditor's signature should refer to Registered Auditor status and be signed either by the firm or the auditor individually.

Test your understanding 2	
List four types of modified audit report?	**Inability to gather sufficient appropriate evidence:** • Qualified opinion ("except for"). • Disclaimer of opinion. **Financial statements are materially misstated:** • Qualified opinion ("except for"). • Adverse opinion.
Give an example of when each type of report would be appropriate?	Examples of the above could be: **Inability to gather sufficient appropriate evidence – material** No inventory count carried out at a branch. **Inability to gather sufficient appropriate evidence – pervasive** Destruction of accounting records. **Financial statements are materially misstated – material** Failure to provide for a doubtful debt. **Financial statements are materially misstated– pervasive** Inappropriate basis of preparation used e.g. if the going concern basis has been used when the break up basis should have been used.
What is an emphasis of matter paragraph?	An 'emphasis of matter' highlights a matter affecting the financial statements and draws the reader's attention to a note that more fully explains the position. An emphasis of matter does not constitute a modified opinion. It is situated after the opinion paragraph.

Index

Index

KAPLAN PUBLISHING